THE SCIENTIFIC EXAMINATION OF DOCUMENTS:
Methods and Techniques

THE SCIENTIFIC EXAMINATION OF DOCUMENTS:
Methods and Techniques

DAVID ELLEN
Metropolitan Police Forensic Science Laboratory
London

ELLIS HORWOOD LIMITED
Publishers · Chichester

Halsted Press: a division of
JOHN WILEY & SONS
New York · Chichester · Brisbane · Toronto

First published in 1989
Reprinted in 1993 by
ELLIS HORWOOD LIMITED
Market Cross House, Cooper Street,
Chichester, West Sussex, PO19 1EB, England
The publisher's colophon is reproduced from James Gillison's drawing of the ancient Market Cross, Chichester.

Distributors:

Australia and New Zealand:
JACARANDA WILEY LIMITED
GPO Box 859, Brisbane, Queensland 4001, Australia

Canada:
JOHN WILEY & SONS CANADA LIMITED
22 Worcester Road, Rexdale, Ontario, Canada

Europe and Africa:
JOHN WILEY & SONS LIMITED
Baffins Lane, Chichester, West Sussex, England

North and South America and the rest of the world:
Halsted Press: a division of
JOHN WILEY & SONS
605 Third Avenue, New York, NY 10158, USA

South-East Asia
JOHN WILEY & SONS (SEA) PTE LIMITED
37 Jalan Pemimpin # 05–04
Block B, Union Industrial Building, Singapore 2057

Indian Subcontinent
WILEY EASTERN LIMITED
4835/24 Ansari Road
Daryaganj, New Delhi 110002, India

© **1989 D. Ellen/Ellis Horwood Limited**

British Library Cataloguing in Publication Data
Ellen, David
The scientific examination of forensic documents: methods and techniques. —
(Ellis Horwood series in forensic science).
1. Forensic science
I. Title
363.2'5

Library of Congress CIP data available

ISBN 0–7458–0551–5 (Ellis Horwood Limited)
ISBN 0–470–21347–7 (Halsted Press)

Typeset by Ellis Horwood Limited
Printed and bound in Great Britain
by Bookcraft (Bath) Limited, Midsomer Norton, Avon

Table of contents

1

Introduction

Within the wide field of forensic science the scientific examination of documents has one purpose, to provide information about the history of a document for the benefit of a court of law, or before that, to an investigating police officer or other agent seeking what evidence is present in the document. The same philosophy which pervades forensic science applies to document examination — the application of scientific method and techniques to the problems relevant to the situation.

SCIENTIFIC METHOD

Scientific method is a way of thinking. It is about the study of observed phenomena and the seeking of a correlation between them based on the philosophy that there is order and consistency in the Universe. Observations about the heavens, animals, or chemical changes can be and have been made for many centuries, but it is the essentially scientific process of discovering a pattern behind these observations which has led to the technological progress of the last century or so.

   The scientific method of correlating the observations is to construct a hypothesis and test it by other observations and measurements and specially devised experiments. If these confirm the hypothesis, it stands; but if not, a new hypothesis must be sought and tested. Thus a corpus of knowledge is built up which can be relied upon to provide a basics for extending the process further.

   Science, however, is more than philosophy; it has a purpose. The exploitation of scientifically based discoveries, mostly for the good of mankind, has been the hallmark of the nineteenth and twentieth centuries, but another benefit has been in the development of methods of analysis to determine, for instance, the presence or proportion of components or impurities in many substances.

ANALYTICAL METHODS

Analytical methods are based on the testing of the material in question against the background of knowledge of the subject. To show, for instance, that the sulphate ion is present in a solution, barium chloride can be added. The resulting precipitate indicates that it is there, because barium sulphate, which is insoluble, is always produced in these circumstances. The corpus of knowledge of the chemistry of barium and its compounds is the basis for confidence in the results. Similar dependence on totally consistent and reproducible results is the basis of other analytical techniques of far greater complexity. By these methods qualitative and quantitative analyses of many materials is carried out.

Such scientific analyses are of value in many fields, one of which is the investigation of crime and other matters which are the concern of courts of law. Forensic science employs many analytical techniques to identify, measure, and compare. The identification and measurement of drugs and alcohol employ relatively conventional methods similar to those used in other fields of qualitative and quantitative chemical analysis. Comparison is important in many fields of crime investigation. Traces of blood, glass, paint, and fibres are left at scenes of crime or are transferred from the scene to the culprit. Similarly, marks made by tools, fingers, or shoes of the attacker can be found at a scene. It is of importance to show whether or not the traces or marks match their possible origin, and if they do, how likely it is that they could have come from a different source. Similarly, identification and comparison are essential in the forensic examination of documents.

DOCUMENTS

A convenient definition of a document is something that contains information. Although information can now be held on wax or tapes, or stored electronically, documents considered in this book are those normally made of paper, but other materials including boards, walls, or even bodies can bear written messages.

The information contained in a document can be considered as occurring at two levels, the superficial where what is conveyed by the document is expressed in writing, typewriting, or printing, or a combination of any of these, and at a deeper level where other less obvious evidence can be found. It is in the latter field, which is the province of the document examiner, where information about the identity of the writer, the source of the typewriting or printing, the presence of traces of erased entries, and many other factors can be discovered. The significance of such discoveries can be of interest to many people in different occupations, but it is when documents contain incriminating information that their origins are the concern of investigating police officers and, later, of courts. If a document is not what it seems but once bore different information now removed or altered, the deceit it carries in itself will be of vital interest to a civil or criminal court. It is for these reasons that most scientific examinations of documents are carried out by forensic document examiners whose conclusions are put before the court as written statements or given orally as expert evidence.

Material properly deduced from a document by comparing it with one or more other documents can provide invaluable evidence on which a magistrate, judge, or jury may reach a decision. A connection between a crime and an individual, or the exclusion of that individual from the investigation, can be established. The principle involved in all these comparisons is the same as that already referred to in other branches of forensic science: the testing of various parameters and reference to the background knowledge of the subject in order to reach a conclusion. Similarly, information can be adduced from a document by methods other than comparison. By exploiting methods which detect more than the eye can see, facts of value to an investigator or to a court of law can be obtained.

Thus scientific method is now established as the correct and proper way of evaluating such evidence provided by documents. It is not the only way; there are still practitioners all over the world who use methods which cannot be so described. Conclusions are reached and stated with great certainty on insufficient evidence, and the value of proper deduction is underestimated. This is particularly true in the case of handwriting comparison where 'experts' practise without the benefit of proper training or method, working on instinct and in their own unconventional ways. Most document examiners, however, follow the standard methods outlined here, and provide an invaluable service to investigators and courts.

In any science there are areas of uncertainty; the complete knowledge of a subject is never obtainable. But in others, especially those allowing accurate measurements to be made, an analysis based on these provides precise results. Much of the work of the document examiner falls in the former category. Handwriting comparison does not permit exactly reproducible measurements, therefore precise calculations of the probability that two writings came from one source cannot be made. This means that some degree of subjectivity must be present; without a technique which automatically produces the exact result any analytical method must depend on the experience and ability of the analyst.

In every analytical method the limitations must be appreciated. It is erroneous to express any conclusion with a certainty which does not recognise the limitations of the method and of the accuracy of the observations on which it is based. However, although these limitations exist, conclusions can be properly drawn if they are recognised; the danger of wrong results occurs when they are not.

In handwriting comparisons, proper account must be taken of the difficulties such as the variations found in the writing of one person which at first seem to indicate another writer, or, conversely, the possibility of accidental coincidence of a number of similarities in the writings of two people. If these factors are not taken into account, false attributions can be made.

DOCUMENT EXAMINERS

The work of the forensic examiner of questioned documents, the term 'questioned' indicating that not everything about the document is accepted for what it appears to be, is described in this book. The man or woman practising the profession may do so as a full time or part time occupation, he or she may be referred to as a forensic scientist, forensic document examiner, document examiner, document expert, handwriting expert, or by a combination of these and other descriptions. He (and from this point this should be taken to include she; there being nearly as many women as men in the field) may work in private practice or be part of a university or a national or local authority laboratory. He will normally be trained in a science or in another subject to degree or doctorate level, the discipline often being decided by the tradition of the country. There is often a division in the types of examination carried out, handwriting and perhaps typewriting being examined by people different from those who examine alterations and ink comparisons.

Although there are a number of techniques used in the examination of documents it is not beyond the ability of a properly trained scientist to be able to tackle all to an adequate degree. However, as developments of sophisticated methods such as scanning electron microscopy play an increasing part in document examination, some assistance from specialists in these fields is required; a wide knowledge of all the available techniques is a great advantage in document examination. In any examination there is likely to be a considerable overlap of the techniques required. For instance, an entry written by another person in a different ink may not be considered separately from the bulk of writing on a page, and therefore, if the inks are not compared, may cause confusion. If a signature written across a passport photograph needs to be authenticated, both its writing and its ink must be examined. Although handwriting comparisons and other examinations can be made separately, much is gained by a comprehensive study of the document.

Qualifications and training
The wide range of disciplines involved in document examination do not lend themselves to one single academic qualification. Chemists, physicists, and biologists can all claim that they have a function. In West Germany, psychologists are widely employed for handwriting comparisons, not because they study the psychology of the writer but because handwriting is regarded as an aspect of human behaviour.

Whatever the discipline, scientific training is the most suitable basic qualification for those entering the profession of document examination. Because few, if any, of the techniques employed are taught in academic study, further 'on the job' training is required. This is virtually the only way available to acquire sufficient expertise; courses in document examination at educational establishments have been attempted, but the demand has so far proved too small for these to be viable. Document examination laboratories or sections of forensic science laboratories continually train new examiners, and, less frequently, those in private practice may take an apprentice assistant.

There are few diplomas which certify that forensic scientists are qualified to practise, but in document examination moves have been made to remedy this. In the United States of America, the American Board of Forensic Document Examiners, Inc., issues certificates of qualification, and in the United Kingdom the Forensic Science Society has introduced a similar scheme. In Australia, membership of the Australian Society of Forensic Document Examiners is regarded as a qualification because the society restricts its membership to those considered by their peers to be suitable.

Generally, however, the establishment at which a document examiner in the public service is employed will allow him to practise only when he has reached the required standard. Those examiners not so employed do not have to be tested in this way, but have to build up their own reputation. Many examiners in private practice have been previously employed in the public service and have received their training in established laboratories.

Not every practitioner in document examination has been properly trained or has acquired an adequate knowledge or ability to perform the work to the required standard. Without available qualifications which ensure that proper training has been given and examinations have been passed, any person may set up in business and claim to be a document examiner. It is a regrettable fact that the client may not be able to distinguish the competent from the charlatan. Courts, when considering the quality of an expert before them, tend to put great store on experience. This is often a poor guide to ability; some of those who claim long experience show little competence to do the work properly.

There is, therefore, a problem for those who require a comparison of handwriting and need to choose an expert to assist them. There is also some confusion between those practising graphology, which aims to assess the personality of the writer, and those who work in forensic handwriting examination. The confusion is not helped by some graphologists who erroneously appear to see no difference between the two disciplines. Perhaps the term 'handwriting expert' is one cause of the confusion in that it can be applied to both areas. The term in its legal sense is a definition of those who give expert evidence in court. The expertise is that which the court requires, and does not include a variety of other studies which might be deduced from the examination of handwriting. Because the description can be applied to other aspects of the subject, care has to be taken to distinguish between the different expertises when looking for the right person for the job.

OBJECTS OF THIS BOOK

This book describes in outline the principles, methods, and techniques employed in forensic document examination. It is aimed at lawyers, police officers, and other investigators to enable them to understand the basis of the science. It is not intended as a text book for document examiners — the detail is sufficient only to provide an introduction to the subject; but as it deals with the essential requirements of the discipline it should serve as a guide to those entering the profession. It may also be of some assistance to those already in practice.

The description of document examination is divided into chapters according to the subject of examination. Handwriting comparison is given a coverage greater than any other subject because of its complexity and importance. The features found in handwriting and their variation occupy two chapters. The third chapter on handwriting discusses how expert conclusions on handwriting are reached and a fourth describes what is required from the investigator to enable a handwriting comparison to be carried out. These are followed by chapters on typewriting, printing, writing materials and their alteration and comparison, accidental marks and other examinations, and special techniques. The final chapter discusses some of the aspects of presentation of findings to a court.

LITERATURE ON DOCUMENT EXAMINATION

Books

A number of books on document examination have been produced, some more detailed than this; they have been of variable quality and therefore importance. Document examination has also been referred to in more general books covering forensic science. Many of these are now out of print, but some have been reprinted by other publishers.

The first book of note in document examination to be written in English was A. S. Osborn's *Questioned Documents* published in the USA by Boyd in 1910 and 1929. The most significant publication in the United Kingdom was W. R. Harrison's *Suspect Documents* (Sweet & Maxwell, London 1958 and 1966). The works of both Osborn and Harrison have been reprinted by Nelson-Hall Inc. of Chicago. Other books, *Scientific Examination of Questioned Documents* by Ordway Hilton and *Evidential Documents* by James V. P. Conway, are also highly regarded. The standard text book in German is *Gerichtliche Schriftvergleichung* by Lothar Michel (de Gruyter, Berlin, 1982).

Journals
Like any other profession, forensic science has organisations dedicated to its advancement which publish journals and organise meetings. Many papers are written for these publications or are read at meetings and, through these, advances in the subject are made known. Document examination, as a branch of forensic science, is well represented in these areas.

Journals which publish papers on document examination include, in the United Kingdom, the *Journal of the Forensic Science Society* and *Medicine, Science and the Law*; in the United States, the *Journal of Forensic Sciences* and *Forensic Science International*; in Canada, the *Journal of the Canadian Forensic Science Society*; and in Germany, *Kriminalistik* and *Archiv für Kriminologie*. Also, the Mannheimer *Hefte für Schriftvergleichung* specialises in the subject. The *International Criminal Police Review* published by the International Criminal Police Organisation also prints articles on document examination, but these are for limited circulation.

Meetings in forensic science are arranged every three years by the International Association of Forensic Sciences and by the Asian Pacific Congress on Legal Medicine and Forensic Sciences, and annually by the American Academy of Forensic Sciences. These include sections on document examination, as do meetings of the Forensic Science Society in the United Kingdom. This latter body also arranges meetings specially in document examination, usually twice a year. In Germany, a symposium is held on document examination. The American Society of Questioned Document Examiners holds a meeting every year for its members and invited guests. Other national organisations in Canada, Australia, India, and other parts of the world hold regular gatherings.

In this book, references to papers published in the above mentioned or other journals and publications are listed at the end of each chapter, and some are also cross-referenced in the text. These are relevant to what has been discussed in the chapter, and cover parts of the subject in greater detail. It is impossible to refer to every paper, but emphasis has been given to the more recent publications.

RESEARCH AND DEVELOPMENT

Document examination makes progress by the development of new techniques, some of which are invented by document examiners, while others are adaptations of advances made elsewhere in science. In recent years, for instance, the electrostatic detection of indented impressions, the use of the laser, visible light spectroscopy of inks, liquid chromatography of ink, and pattern recognition techniques for the examination of handwriting have been introduced, and these are not the only examples of progress in the field.

It follows, therefore, that this book will be in some ways out of date before it appears and will become increasingly so. This is inevitable in any book covering a scientific subject. Further changes have been, and will be, brought about by changes in office technology. Different problems are caused by new methods of producing type on paper and by modern ways of printing and photocopying. However, most of the general principles and methods described here are likely to remain unchanged or modified only to a small extent. The employment of scientific method through whatever technique is used will remain the most important factor.

ACKNOWLEDGEMENTS

Not every source of material on which this book has been based has been published; papers read at meetings and personal communications have been of value. In this context, acknowledgements are due to colleagues of the author at the Metropolitan Police Forensic Science Laboratory in London, expecially to Mr K. E. Creer (photography), Mr R. H. Keeley (scanning electron microscopy), and Dr F. R. Lewington (paper). Thanks are also due to Drs Angela Morrissey and James Robertson for editorial assistance and to Mr Tony Olivari for invaluable suggestions.

2

Handwriting — the variations between normal writings

INTRODUCTION

In courts of law, expert evidence is frequently given on handwriting, and the giver of that evidence is not unnaturally described as a handwriting expert. This epithet can be misleading. It seems to imply that here is a man or woman who knows all about handwriting. He or she knows how many different scripts there are now and in the past, how they have developed, how they are taught, how they are affected by difficult circumstances, why one person writes the way he does, and so on. In fact this is not the case. It is true that there are people who study the development of scripts used by different peoples, others who study handwriting to discover the personality of the writer, and others who specialise in the teaching of handwriting. All of these can be described as experts in handwriting, but that description when used in courts of law applies to those who perform a task within clear limitations. They are concerned with identification of the writer of a piece of questioned writing, the recognition of simulated signatures and other related matters.

To do this on a scientific basis it is necessary to build up a background knowledge by study of what is found in handwriting in many different circumstances. Thus, to identify the handwriting of an individual person it is necessary to know how the writing of one person differs from that of another, and how the writing of one individual varies within itself. It is not necessary to know why one person writes the way he does, nor to know how he was taught to write or what teaching methods are available, but some knowledge of these basic facts can be of assistance.

More important is the study of what is found in writings on documents, how they can be examined to determine whether or not they have a common writer. This and the following two chapters describe the way this is achieved.

In this chapter, natural handwriting is considered, how it varies within the output of one person and between different people. In Chapter 3, differences caused by accidental events or deliberate actions are described. Chapter 4 discusses how the background knowledge referred to in Chapters 2 and 3 is used to reach conclusions on the examination of handwriting. Chapter 5 considers a peripheral but important aspect of forensic handwriting comparison. Because of the relationship between the content of the four chapters on handwriting, some repetition of certain points occurs between chapters; this is necessary to avoid too much cross-referencing.

VARIATIONS IN WRITING

Writings made in England in the second half of the twentieth century have much in common with each other; they differ from writings from the nineteenth century or earlier. Similarly, they are different from contemporaneous French writings. The beautiful copper plate style of the Victorian period is rarely found today; a figure 1 with a long stroke at the left is common in France, a letter s ending with a tail is common in the USA, while both are rare in England.

But even within a single country at a particular time there are other variations in style caused by different teaching methods. The teaching of these styles will obviously influence the writing of those who learn from them, but no teacher has ever succeeded in making all his or her pupils write in precisely the same way. In fact, most school teachers find that they can recognise each child's writing at an early stage of the acquisition of the ability to write.

Although it is true to say that having learned to write in a particular style and diverged from it in an individual way, one therefore has a unique method of writing, clearly distinguishable from that of any other person, more is required. It is necessary to find out more about this individual method, how it varies within itself, and how it differs from that of others.

A complicated action such as the manipulation of a pen into universally recognisable shapes, using a combination of the muscles of the arm, hand, and fingers controlled by the brain both consciously and unconsciously, is clearly likely to give rise to wide variations in method and effect.

Whatever their cause, the examiner of questioned documents must build up a background knowledge of these variations, systematise them if possible, and discover whether any order prevails.

BLOCK CAPITAL WRITING

The Roman script used in Western European languages can be written in three forms: capital writing, cursive writing, and disconnected script, which is usually written like cursive writing but not connected. Block capital writing will be considered first.

Methods of construction

It is sometimes thought that block capital writings do not differ much from person to person, but this is not correct. Consider first the capital letter E. This can be shaped in two ways, one as a vertical semicircle with a horizontal line in the middle and the second as the more common rectilinear shape. This consists of four specially arranged lines which together are recognisable as a letter E. To construct this letter with a pen each stroke has to be made separately, but, provided that they are all present, the order in which they are made is immaterial. Any one of the strokes can be executed first, and any of them can be made in either direction. There are therefore many different ways in which this letter can be constructed simply by varying the order and direction of the production of the strokes. This number could be increased if certain of the strokes are joined to others without lifting the pen. In theory, then, many writers could be found each of whom writes the letter in a way which differs from that of each of the others.

In practice this is not found. Only a few of the theoretically possible methods are used, presumably because some are easier to execute than others. Each writer chooses subconsciously to employ the way which is easiest for him. Some methods are frequently found, and others less so or rarely. The methods usually employed to write a block capital E are shown diagrammatically in Fig. 1.

Similarly, all other block capital letters can be executed with different pen movements. Some, such as C and S, are written with a single stroke, rarely made other than from top to bottom, so little variation can be found in this aspect. Other letters, being more complicated, afford greater possible variation. In some letters a different pen movement will result in a slightly different shape. Thus a G can be made with the bottom right-hand straight stroke either horizontal, vertical, or vertical with an additional horizontal added above it. In the last alternative the complicated shape at the bottom right of the letter can be made in at least three different ways.

Other letters which provide alternative shapes are I and U. Letter I is sometimes written with a dot and U with an extra downstroke on the right, both forms not strictly correct in the block capital forms of the letters but not infrequently found. Letter I can also be written with horizontal strokes at the top and bottom. H and K are two letters which are sufficiently complicated to afford different methods of construction. In the making of a block capital letter H the first stroke to be made is usually the left-hand upright, but after that either the right-hand upright or the horizontal stroke can be made next. The downstroke of the K is also usually the first made, but the two diagonals can be made in several different ways (see Fig. 1). In making the letter T, either stroke can be made first.

A number of letters such as B and D consist of a downstroke and a curved remainder. As in most block letters, the first part to be written is the left-hand downstroke, but the rest can either be made by retracing this line and finishing the letter all in one stroke or by lifting the pen and making the rest as a separate entity. However, this difference is not always clear-cut. Sometimes the pen is only partly lifted, and the resulting thin line gives rise to doubt as to whether any distinction can be made between the two forms of the letters.

There are, then, various ways of making different block capital writings (Fig. 1). Generally speaking, each individual writer will adopt one method of construction for each letter without knowing why he or she chooses it, or even, without the fact being pointed out, being aware that these different methods of construction are available. Some forms are found only in writings made with the left hand because the natural movement away from the body tends to predominate. It is rare for one person to use more than one method of construction of any letter, although two distinct types of letter, such as a 'semi-circular' and a normal rectangular form of E, might be used in conjunction. There are exceptions to this. It is not uncommon for two forms of block capital letter N to be found in the writing of one person. One form ends with the right-hand vertical stroke moving upwards and the other with the letter ending

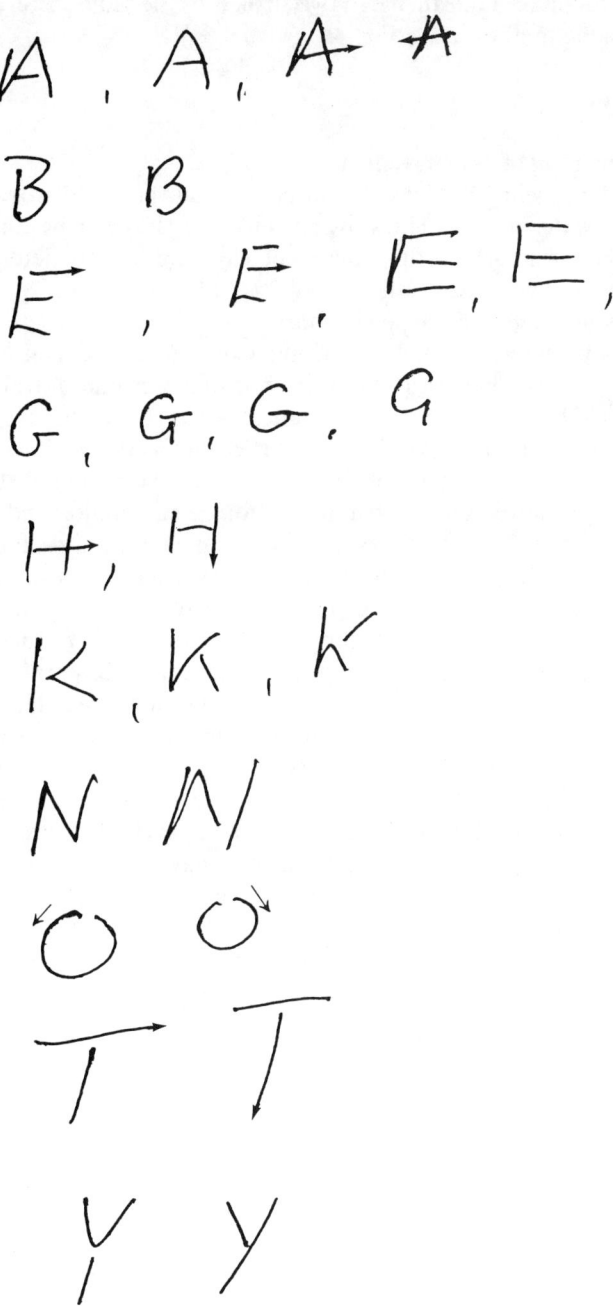

Fig. 1 — Different methods of construction of block capital letters.

downwards. Also, letters made with a vertical stroke and a curved remainder, such as B or D, might be made in one or two strokes by the same writer, each being variations of the same method.

Determination of pen movement
The order in which strokes of a letter are made can be discovered in two ways. The first is to watch or record how the pen moves in the act of writing; and the second, the only one available to the document examiner, is to determine the method of construction from the written letter.

The movement of the pen in constructing the letters is determined by study of the continuous, unbroken lines of writing. Continuous lines can sometimes be confused with two lines which join but were not made in one movement. Similarly, what appears to be one stroke can be a retrace where the pen moves back along the same path on which it just travelled. The vertical line at the beginning of letters such as A, R, and N is likely to be a retrace if it continues to form the next part of the letter; it is rare for such strokes to begin at the bottom. Examination under a microscope giving approximately 20 to 40 times magnification can usually establish whether a break occurs between two touching lines or whether the pen has changed its direction without being lifted from the page. Similarly, a retrace can be discovered by the finding of the beginning or ending of a line not exactly retraced.

The movement of the pen to form a letter can be determined even when it is lifted in the act of writing. The pen leaves the paper not like a helicopter rising vertically from the point at which it is resting, but gradually, like a fixed-wing aircraft taking off. In doing so the line becomes thinner, tailing off to nothing. This is sometimes called 'feathering'. However, unlike an aeroplane, the pen will often change direction to move towards its next landing place before it has finally left the paper. When the pen touches the paper again it may be still travelling from its departure point and will alter its direction to form the letter after it has 'landed'. As the landing is also at an angle and not vertical, gradually thickening lines are produced. These beginnings and endings of strokes enable the pen movement to be determined. In some cases the pen will not entirely leave the paper, and very thin connecting lines between the strokes will remain. Such evidence of pen movement can be found both within a letter and between letters.

Ink lines
The line of writing itself can provide evidence of the direction in which it was made. The point of a ball-point pen will be nearly devoid of ink when it begins to write a new line, so there may be a thinning of the deposited ink where the stroke begins. On some surfaces the ink direction can be ascertained from the appearance of the crossing point between two lines. This is apparent when a pen using liquid ink writes on shiny paper. On close examination 'tram lines' can be seen at the edges of the line. These are formed where the ink has concentrated before drying. A line crossing another will remove the 'tram lines' of the first line and leave its own across the width

BIN TRAVELER FORM

Cut By: Giorgina C.   #22   **Qty** 30   **Date** 06/16

Scanned By: _____ **Qty** _____ **Date** _____

Scanned Batch ID's _____

Notes / Exceptions

of that line. Another method which, in the right conditions, can demonstrate the direction of the line depends on the build-up of ball-point ink in the 'V' between two crossing fibres of the paper. This can be seen if the ink is fairly thinly applied. Magnification of around 100× is required [13].

Striations

Another method depends on striations being present in the line made by a ball-point pen. These are thin lines found within the line made by a pen and are caused by damage or dirt on the ball housing which prevents an even flow of ink. When such striations appear to run off the outside of the curve of a line the line has been made in the direction in which the striation seems to be travelling (see Fig. 2) [24]. None of

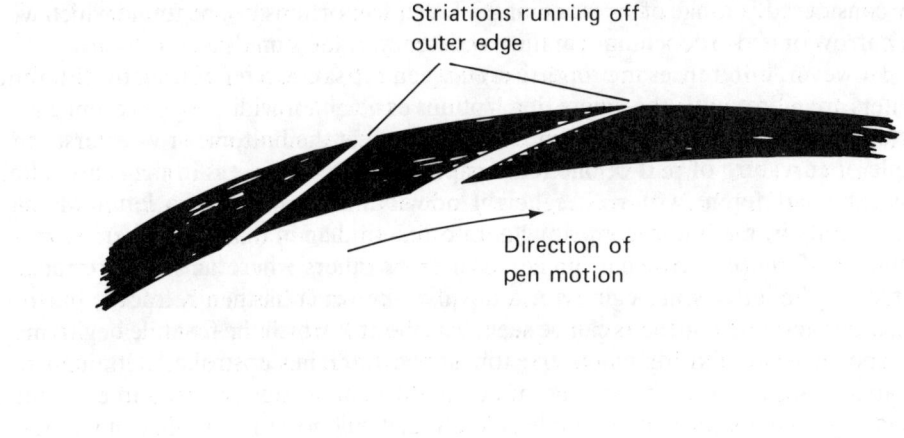

Striations running off outer edge

Direction of pen motion

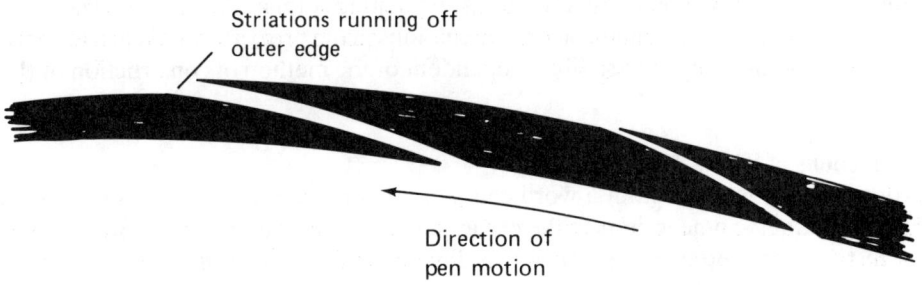

Striations running off outer edge

Direction of pen motion

Fig. 2 — Determination of direction of stroke of ball-point pen lines.

these methods will be certain to give a clear indication of line direction, but they will not give the wrong answer if properly applied. Normally, with several examples of each letter and employment of a combination of the methods described above the pen movement can be established.

Proportion of letters
In block capital writings the method of construction of individual letters is not the only means of distinguishing between the writing of one person and that of another. Another way is in the proportions of each individual letter. When method of construction was considered, the forms referred to were for the most part discrete. They could be easily defined and did not gradually merge into each other. The exceptions mentioned were letters like B and D. With proportions within a letter the parameters are not so easily distinguished. To say, for instance, that one writer's letter O is tall and thin and that of another is short and fat may be generally true, but not easily demonstrated for every such letter. The human being is not a machine producing an identical product over and over again. As in every other activity, variations occur, and these variations are greater for some people than for others. Thus, when all the examples of a particular block capital letter in a sample of writing are considered, a range of variation of the letter proportions will be found which will be narrow or wide, depending on the consistency of the sample.

However, differences in proportion between the same letter written by different writers are more subtle than mere descriptions of height or width. More complicated letters such as B or S may be wider at the top than at the bottom, or vice versa; the angle of curvature of part of one letter may be greater than it is in the same letter made by a different writer. The height or width of one half of a letter M may consistently be greater in the writing of one person than in that of another. A more minute difference may occur in the letter A or others where an initial retrace is present. The letter will begin with a downstroke which is then retraced, but not usually exactly, so both lines can be seen. The point at which the first line begins may be above, level with, or below the top of the retracing upstroke. Although the relative positions of the beginnings of the lines will not be exactly the same for each example of that letter in one sample of writing, it will be within a range of variation which will be different from that found in the writings of many other persons.

There are, therefore, many possible variations in the proportions of each letter of the alphabet, and they are usually independent of the method of construction of the letter.

Proportions of letters within words
Proportions of letters within a word can be another discriminatory factor in block capital writings. Some writers make certain letters smaller than others. Sometimes, for instance, the letters O or I or both will be shorter than the other letters, or the letters P, R, or T might be taller, the cross bar of the latter overhanging the adjacent letters. A letter Y might be written with its tail below the line or above it.

Another feature of some writers is to introduce lower case script into writing which is intended to be in block capitals. Sometimes all examples of one or more letters are written in detached lower case script because the writer seems incapable of writing the appropriate block capital form.

This does not exhaust the ways in which block capital writings can vary from person to person. The actual pressure used to write indicated by the depth of the impression made into the paper, the quality of line, that is whether curves are smooth or shaky, whether or not some letters are joined to the next, the position of the writing on the page, whether margins are left, the spacing between words — all can produce variation between the writing of one person and that of another.

NUMERALS

The numerals 0–9 can be regarded in the same way as block capital writings. They, too, show the same sort of variation in method of construction and proportion. Figures 8 and 0 are variable in both the point at which the writing line starts and ends, as well as in the direction of the pen movement which can, as can letter O, be related to the left or right-handedness of the writer. Although they are sometimes the only questioned materials, numerals usually occur in conjunction with other writings. Other characters such as signs for the pound or dollar also give scope for a wide variation between writers.

CURSIVE WRITING

Cursive writing is so called because it is running writing (Latin *currere,* to run). Unlike block capital writing, which is usually preferred if the main consideration is legibility, cursive writing has the advantage of rapid execution and speed of production. Other considerations apply as well. Some people are proud of the beauty of their handwriting and take great care over it; italic styles of writing are an example of this. More care is taken in teaching cursive than block capital writing and there is a choice of styles available; the style taught is the choice of the teacher, school, or education authority. This choice is dictated by fashion, invention of new methods, and other factors. Once the basic methods are learned, the pupil will modify them either to express individuality, or because he cannot achieve the standard of the copy book, or for reasons too obscure to determine. Whatever the reason, it is clear from observation that, far from a teacher producing identical results like a printing press turning out copy, each person will produce something different both from that taught and from that produced by other pupils.

Development of cursive writing
The individuality of his or her own writing is often regarded by a child or adolescent as a form of self-expression, so experiments are made, methods are changed, and factors such as slope and size are altered according to the dictates of taste as well as to increasing skill. Eventually, usually around the late teens, a method is arrived at which is much more consistent and is likely to remain much the same throughout the life of the individual. Some people will develop more than one method, changing perhaps from italic to more conventional style at will. Others can write in two very different ways, one when writing carefully and one when writing rapidly. Some people are ambidextrous and write somewhat differently with one hand than with the other.

Although many people can write by more than one method of cursive writing, most cannot. This may sound surprising, as it is commonly believed that one's own writing can be considerably altered. In fact what usually occurs is that the same basic method is used, but only size of writing, evenness and control vary. The tendency to modify writing is not even. Some writers are very consistent, and they allow little to distract them from turning out their very uniform products. Other writers are inconsistent for no apparent reason, and, even within a single piece of writing, size, slope, and neatness may vary.

Inter-personal differences
Despite these personal variations, it is common knowledge that the writings of different people vary to a much greater extent. Most people on receiving a handwritten letter can recognise the writing of the sender. We all have a memory store of a number of familiar writings, and can refer to these immediately. Normally, the comparison of the writing, on the basis of overall appearance, with those stored in the memory is successful, and the writer is recognised. This works because relatively few writings are involved, the memory store is small, and therefore the task is not difficult. It is less easy when two writings are somewhat similar; mistakes are then made.

Although there seems to be scope for very many writings which are recognisably different at a quick glance, there are far more writers than can be accommodated by the number of such variants. It follows, therefore, that the writings of many people must share a common overall appearance. This means that as an indication of two similar writings being by one person, the quick glance at overall appearance is as unreliable as it is when apparently different writings are taken to indicate two different writers.

There is far more scope within the detail of writings to separate different writers than there is in overall appearance. As discussed earlier in relation to block capitals, the method of construction and proportion of each individual letter can show enormous variation even within one general style of writing. The same consider-ations apply to cursive writing. Some letters can be constructed in several ways, although there are fewer variants than for block capitals, and all can be made by employing a wide range of proportions within and between the letters.

Methods of construction and proportion of individual letters
As an example of this the letter a can be considered. A common way to construct the letter is to begin with the top of the curve and to draw a circle in an anticlockwise direction, following this with a downstroke on the right-hand side. Another way is to begin the anticlockwise circle beginning from the bottom and finishing as before; a third is to write a circle and a right-hand vertical line separately as two strokes or joined by a bar at the top. Similar letters such as d and g afford the same variation in construction, also without basically altering the final shape of the letter. However, most different methods of construction or movement of the pen produce different shapes to the letter. In the case of letters b and r two or more methods of construction are taught. A letter b can be written either with its lower part made as a near-circle drawn in a clockwise direction after the downstroke or by including a bowl shaped curve with an opening at the top. A letter r can be written with a loop at

the top or as a retraced downstroke angled at the top towards the next letter. Other differences in pen movement which produce smaller differences in final shape occur in the direction in which lower loops of letters like f and y are made. Having moved down, the pen can either turn to the left or to the right to produce a loop, or sharply change direction making an angled tail rather than a loop.

A greater potential variation between writers is found in the proportions within individual letters. These will to some extent be dependent on how the letter has been made, but within any one method of construction great differences can be found. Further differentiation can be caused by the connections between letters. In the letter 'a' considered earlier the first method of construction was an anticlockwise circle joined to a downstroke on the right. This can be complicated by a connecting stroke from the previous letter, or, if the letter begins the word or is the indefinite article, it can begin with a similar stroke called a 'lead-in' stroke.

From this apparently simple shaped pattern many variations can arise. Firstly the circular part of the letter can be oval, angled upwards, lengthways or at approximately 45° to the vertical. It can be a narrow oval or nearly circular. The connecting or lead-in stroke can be present or absent, it can join at an acute angle or with a small loop or it can penetrate deeply down the right-hand side of the circle before retracing to begin the circle. The downstroke on the right of the letter can be relatively tall or short, it can be separate from the beginning of the circle or touching it, and it can end in a curve or angled tail on the way to the next letter or it can end straight downwards without either.

The letter a is a relatively simple letter, and others such as h and k provide greater scope for variation between writers. The letter h is usually made in one movement, writing the loop first and then the lower part of the letter, all in one stroke; there is little room for different pen motion here. The proportions, however, can be very different without any danger of the letter being unrecognisable as such. The loop can be non-existent (merely a straight line), tall and thin, short and fat, or anything in between. It can be pear-shaped, or straight on one side and more curved on the other. The height of the loop in relation to the height of the arch can be very different when made by different writers; the position of the bottom of the loop in relation to the beginning of the arch affords another means of variation, as does the shape of the arch. The arch can begin as an exact retrace of the downstroke extending some way up the line, or it can separate at an early stage, producing an angle which may be narrow or wide. In this, as in all the alternatives indicated, there are intermediate possibilities.

All the other letters of the alphabet, both cursive capitals and lower case letters, can be similarly analysed. Other examples worth brief mention include the letter i where the most simple feature anywhere in handwriting, the dot, can be surprisingly variable. Apart from its position which can be high, low, to the left or to the right, it may be written as a line, a small v, as a circle or not at all. Letter t has a cross bar which can be variable in length, angle, height, and position relative to the upright part of the letter; sometimes it is written well away from the upright.

The ratio between the length of the loops and tails, sometimes called the upper and lower zones of the writing and that of the main body of the letters (the middle zone), although often similar between different letters in the writing, shows wide variation between writers.

Variations within words

In addition to the variations found within different examples of a single letter, short, frequently used words such as 'of', 'to' and 'the' are sometimes written in a way different from that expected by comparison with their component letters found elsewhere in the text. There is room for variation between writers within words as well as within letters. The connections between letters can be short or long, so that the individual letters are close to each other or separated.

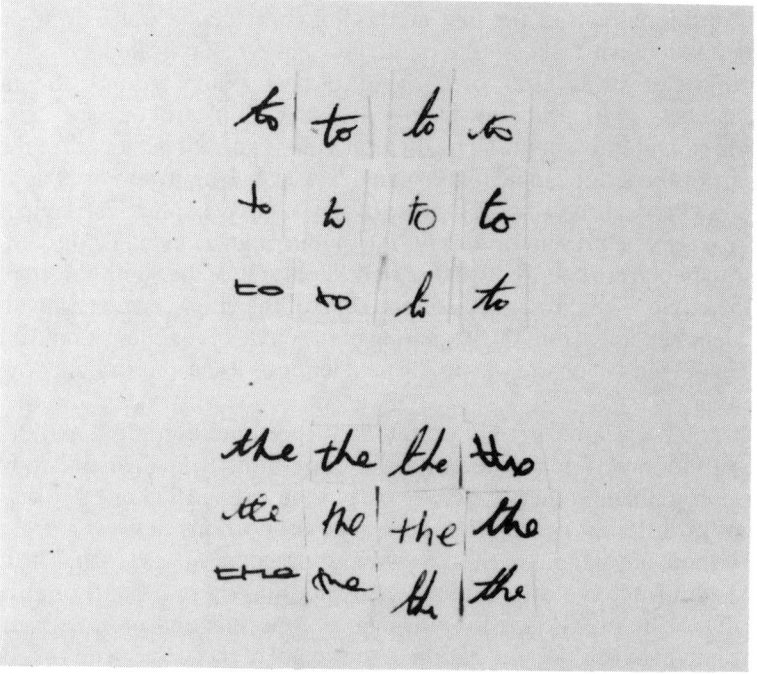

Fig. 3 — Some examples of the words 'to' and 'the' written by different writers. Note the wide variation in the proportions of the letters.

Not every letter in every word is necessarily connected to the next; some writers will connect only a few, say, no more than three letters, while others will write long words without any break. Some writers seem reluctant to join a certain letter of the alphabet to the next in the word, as if they had not learned to make a connection from that letter.

DISCONNECTED SCRIPT

Another form of writing occasionally found is known as disconnected script. This can be regarded as occupying a position between block capital and cursive writings. Instead of writing letters of a cursive style joined together, the same forms can be written separately, a method which has the effect of slowing the writing but making it clear to read. The forms of the capital letters used are usually the same as that of the writer's block capital letters, and the small or lower case letters match those of his cursive writing. There will be differences caused by the lack of connecting strokes, and sometimes a completely different form will be used for a particular letter, but often a considerable resemblance will be found between the lower case letters of one person's detached script and those of his cursive writing.

SIGNATURES

Signatures are usually another form of cursive writing, but need to be considered separately. A few people use their name written in block capitals as their signatures but normally cursive writing is used. Generally, signatures can be divided into two types, those that closely resemble the normal cursive writing of the person and are really no more than the name written in his or her normal writing, and others where a distinctive mark is made, often barely readable or completely illegible.

Whatever the normal forms of the letters in the cursive writing of the subject may be, the signature must be considered separately. What is written is consciously chosen, whether it is the whole name, the first name and other initials, or just initials and the surname. The initials can be joined to each other or to the surname or separated, and the whole may have an underlining of varying complexity.

When people are not used to writing much it is quite possible that their signature is the piece of writing they most commonly perform, and so it may be of a higher standard of fluency than their other writings. This may sometimes give the impression that a piece of writing and the signature following it are by different hands. Sometimes, of course, this is the case; one person will write out a receipt or agreement or any other document and a second will sign it. If it is necessary to compare a signature with writing above it, care is needed because the writer may have adopted a special method of writing his signature, or may be more skilful at writing it.

Like other writings a signature is subject to variation. No one can reproduce a signature exactly, like a printing process, and there are commonly wide variations found in the output of one person. As with other writings, some people are quite consistent and others extremely variable. Signatures can be made in a variety of different places; some are comfortable and therefore conducive of the most natural results. In others where there is difficulty in writing, the results may be somewhat different. The significance of these differences are discussed in the next chapter.

LAYOUT

Apart from the writing itself there are other factors on a written page which vary from person to person but tend to remain constant in the output of one person. The way the writing is arranged on the page, the size of gaps between words and lines, the use of punctuation marks, the employment of margins either side of the text, the separation of paragraphs and where they begin, all give scope for variation between writers. Special documents, for instance envelopes and cheques, provide further areas of diversity between writers. The address written on an envelope can begin near the top or further down; the lines of writing can be well spaced or not and can be staggered. Commas or full stops may be present at the ends of lines or after a house number. Parts of cheques can be written in many different combinations of methods. The ways chosen to write the date and the money amount in writing and figures, the position of the payee's name and other features, can vary greatly.

Such layout factors tend to remain consistent even when deliberate changes are made in writing style, and can add evidence to that gained from the study of the writing itself.

Variations within the writings of one person

Reference has been briefly made to the variations found within the writings of one person, especially differences in overall appearance due to speed of writing and other factors. In these conditions, much of the detail described above will remain unchanged, and characteristic or unusual features will still be found. However, no writer is so consistent that each example of a particular letter of the alphabet is so similar to the same letter written elsewhere that it could be exactly superimposed on it as could two printed letters. For instance, to say that the letter h when it occurs several times has a tall thin pear-shaped loop and an arch which is narrow is to give a verbal description to a number of letters h which are not in themselves identical. Nevertheless, they all differ from one described as without a loop and with a wide arch. This is typical of most letters in a sample of handwriting. Although not identical to each other, they fall within a range which is relatively small and excludes many other variants for this letter.

Often, samples of writing from two people will include a number of letters which are indistinguishable. To put it another way, the variations of two samples of a particular letter can occupy the same range partly or completely. In some writings, more than a few letters can show this similarity, but there are always some letters which are consistently different.

Although the variations found in the writings of one person can be contained within a defined range for each letter, there are occasionally odd examples which do not fall within the range. Accidental events, caused perhaps by a jolting of the pen or difficulties of control near the bottom of the page, or isolated examples for which there is no apparent reason, can result in a letter being written sufficiently differently from all the others to be outside their range. Such differences should not be taken as evidence of another writer. However, if the range within which all or nearly all of the examples of a particular sample fall differs from the range of variation of the same letter in another sample, this is evidence that the samples may be by different writers. Sometimes these differences, called consistent differences, are quite small, but their reproducibility within each sample and their consistency in being different between the samples is of greater significance than a larger difference of a single example which may well be 'one off' and untypical. It is very rare to find only one example of a consistent difference between two samples of writing. Normally, there will be far more than one in the writings of two people, and none in the natural writings of one person.

Use of different letter forms by one writer
As well as variations found within individual forms of letters it is not infrequently found that a writer will use more than one separate form of a letter. Perhaps both forms of the letter b described earlier (page 22) may be found in a single sample of the writing of one person. Other examples of this use of different forms can occur in capital letters where one writer may use both block capital and cursive capital forms apparently at random. Similar use of two or even more forms can occur with other letters, in some cases depending on their position in a word. One form may be found consistently only at the end of a word, while the other form is found in the middle or at the beginning of words. Where two forms occur there will be little relationship between them, and they are best regarded as different letters. As with other letters, each will have a range of variation within the examples present which will be different from the ranges of the same letters made by most other writers.

Personal and style characteristics
In the variations found between the writings of different people some features occur reasonably frequently and others only rarely. Some people introduce into their writing features which are very unusual. These are sometimes called personal characteristics, indicating that they characterise or, in other words, are a means to distinguish the writings of one person from that of others. This is largely true in that, because of their uncommonness, they are unlikely to be found in the writing of another person picked at random.

In the writings of many other people, especially those who do not have opportunity or need to write very often, there may not be much progression from the standard form originally learned. Many of the features found in their writings have a common source in the copy book of the style of writing taught. They are therefore not unusual, and are also likely to be found in combination with other such features which also have the same origin. These are characteristics of a style rather than of the method of an individual, and are therefore sometimes called style characteristics.

THE SIGNIFICANCE OF VARIATIONS BETWEEN WRITERS
All these considerations, in addition to overall factors such as size, slope, line quality, and smoothness of curvature, provide an enormous potential to separate the block capital and cursive writings of one person from those of another (Fig. 4). What makes this possible is the fact that with so many variables available in every letter and so many letters available for comparison between the writings of any two people, there is no practical possibility that one will resemble the other in every respect. Of course such a coincidence is in theory possible, but to encounter it in practice can safely be discounted. However, this states the ideal position and refers to writings of a person as a whole. To say, then, that any one individual has a uniquely personal method of writing may be true, but to say that every piece of writing made by that person could not be matched by another person is not. How true this is for any one piece of writing depends on the amount of material present and how unusual it is. Provided that a sufficient amount of material is present, the combination of features used by one person in his or her writing will be sufficiently different from the

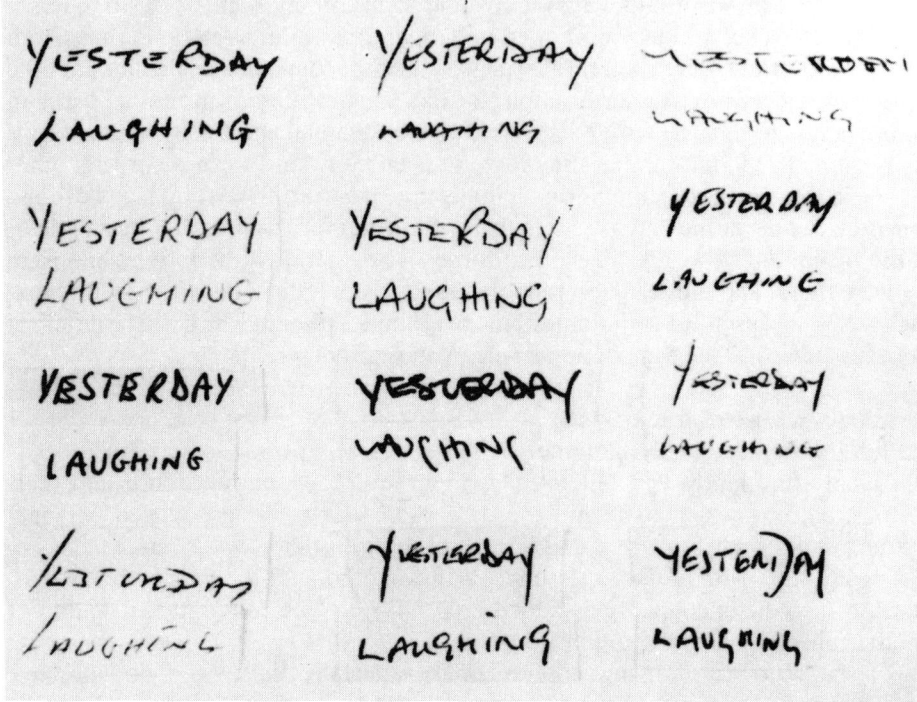

Fig. 4 — Two words written in block capitals by different writers. Different methods of construction and different proportions within each letter and written each word can be observed.

combination of features of any other person for any chance match to be found. If the amount of writing is smaller, the probability of coincidental match will be greater.

How these factors are considered in the comparison of writings for forensic purposes is dealt with in more detail in Chapter 4.

SPELLING MISTAKES, TEXT ANALYSIS, AND OTHER VARIABLES

When writings of different people are studied, much can be gained from aspects other than those of the writing and its layout on the page. Some people are not good at spelling correctly, and errors are found in their writings. Similar errors may occur in questioned writings suspected of having been written by them. This rather obvious feature is often given great weight by the layman, but those who examine documents regularly find that certain mistakes are so common as to provide little significant evidence. Words such as forty and ninety are often spelt wrongly, and the document examiner is more likely to warn that too much emphasis should not be put on them rather than point them out as similarities of importance. Generally, however, practitioners in forensic handwriting comparison do not regard themselves as experts in the frequency of occurrence of mis-spellings, and are therefore not inclined to comment on them. In court the jury may be told that the way certain words are spelt has played no part in the conclusions reached from a comparison of handwritings, and any evidence they choose to elicit from this is over and above that obtained from the writing.

The analysis of the textual style may also be of value, but is rarely attempted by document examiners. There is in certain cases much to be obtained from this by people who specialise in the analysis of text. The stylistic approach to comparing writings requires reasonably large samples, but is independent of the medium in which it is written; handwriting, for instance, can be compared with typewriting. Factors considered are length of sentence, ratio of sentence lengths, verb/adjective ratio, use of certain words ('however', for instance), and the ratio of syllables to words. Proper evaluation of such features can provide useful evidence in certain circumstances, and has been used when statements of defendants have been challenged.

NON-ROMAN SCRIPTS

The principles described above in relation to writings in English in Roman script also apply to writings in other languages and scripts. Whether the writings are made from right to left or left to right, whether they are based on phonetics or on characters representing words rather than letters, there are variations within and between writers and significant evidence can be drawn from these.

In writings made in non-Roman script which also use a phonetic alphabet variations occur within and between writers in the same way as they do in Roman scripts. Some alphabets have a greater capacity for variation and others a lesser one. In Arabic writings some letters are distinguished from each other by the number of dots, between one and three, above or below a feature common to all of them. There is, however, a difference between the same letter written at the beginning, at the end, or in the middle of the word, so a large amount of comparable material is available in most writings.

In Chinese, words are written as separate characters and not phonetically. The characters are built up from eight different forms of stroke, each of which is shaded, that is, made with a gradually changing width of the writing line. In traditional writing this is made with a brush. But even with ball-point pens some shading is possible, and can be used as a method of distinguishing between two writers.

As in other scripts, the method of construction, the order in which strokes are made, plays an important part in the distinction of writings of different people, but to a greater extent because of the complexity of the written characters. Differences in ratio between width and height are also important, as are the individual strokes themselves. These may be shaded or made with pen emphasis, giving a wedge shaped beginning or end of a line. Variations from what should be symmetrical or parallel strokes are also found in different degrees, and so are slope and spacing of characters. There is scope for 'spelling' errors because the same monosyllabic sound may be represented by many different characters, and the writer may not be aware of the correct one to use. The human condition of individuality and unmachinelike variability applies across national and racial boundaries [18].

CLASSIFICATION OF HANDWRITINGS

Certain features which are present in some writings but not others can be used to place writings in groups which contain them and differ from other groups which do not. The advantages of such classification of writings of different people are twofold. Firstly, some indication of the frequency of occurrence of certain features can be measured. Secondly, a system can be used with a collection of handwritings to retrieve a matching writing without searching through every example in the collection.

Such classification is not easy. Most of the features which distinguish one writer from another, though clearly different in the writings of two people, are continuously variable through the population. It is therefore difficult to define a line of separation, and this problem is increased because of the variability found within the writings of one person. The natural range of variability of one writer may span the chosen dividing line.

Despite these problems, a number of systems for the classification of writings have been devised including one which has been in use in West Germany for many years. This is based on overall features common to different letters of the alphabet rather than more detailed examination of the letters. Similarly, systems for classification of stolen cheques which are based largely on features of the word 'pounds' are in use in the United Kingdom. The method of construction of block capital letters is used in another method of classification developed in the Metropolitan Police Forensic Science Laboratory in London. The advantages of this are that the differences between writings are clear-cut and unambiguous, and that the features used tend to remain consistent between writers. This system has provided useful information about the frequency of occurrence of different methods of construction.

Other measurements have been made with cursive writing and signatures [9], [29]. Generally, however, there has not been enough quantitative data collected to have much impact on the work of the document examiner, who relies more on his own observations and experience.

Pattern recognition techniques

The development of methods to read handwriting by machine has led to the application of these techniques to distinguish between the writings of different people. Computer-based pattern recognition methods are extremely complicated, requiring specialist knowledge in a rather obscure field. Heights of upper loops and the areas within them can be compared and measured and data provided. Similarly, areas within circular letters and angularity can be calculated.

These methods have not yet entered the area of forensic document examination to any extent. It appears that they will provide a method of retrieval of a similar writing from a large number of samples in a collection; in West Germany this has already begun. In the United Kingdom research is being carried out into the use of such methods to authenticate signatures at points of sale. It seems unlikely that evidence in courts of law will be based on pattern recognition techniques for a long time, if ever.

REFERENCES AND FURTHER READING

[1] Ansell, M. (1979) Handwriting classification in forensic science *Visible Language* **8** 239

[2] Brown, M. (1985) Teaching handwriting in an English inner-city area *Journal of the Forensic Science Society* **25** 313

[3] Casey-Owens, M. (1984) The anonymous letter writer — a psychological profile *Journal of Forensic Sciences* **29** 816

[4] Conway, J. V. P. (1955) The identification of handprinting *Journal of Criminal Law, Criminology and Police Science* **45** 605

[5] Crown, D. A. & Shimaoka, T. (1974) The examination of ideographic writing (Chinese and Japanese) *Journal of Police Science and Administration* **2** 279

[6] Dawson, G. A. (1987) Internal consistency in handwriting *Canadian Society of Forensic Science Journal* **20** 57

[7] Eldridge, M. A., Nimmo-Smith, I., Wing, A. M. & Totty, R. N. (1984) The variability of selected features in cursive handwriting: categorical measures *Journal of the Forensic Science Society* **24** 179

[8] Eldridge, M. A., Nimmo-Smith, I. & Wing, A. M. (1985) The dependence between selected categorical elements of cursive handwriting *Journal of the Forensic Science Society* **25** 217

[9] Evett, I. W. & Totty, R. N. (1985) A study of the variation in the dimensions of genuine signatures *Journal of the Forensic Science Society* **25** 207

[10] Franks, J. E. (1982) The direction of ballpoint penstrokes in left and right-handed writers as indicated by the orientation of burr striations *Journal of the Forensic Science Society* **22** 271

[11] Franks, J. E., Davis, T. R., Totty, R. N., Hardcastle, R. A. & Grove, D. M. (1985) Variability of stroke direction between left and right-handed writers *Journal of the Forensic Science Society* **25** 353

[12] Foley, R. G. (1987) Characteristics of synchronous sequential signatures *Journal of Forensic Sciences* **32** 121

[13] Fryd, C. F. M. (1975) The direction of pen motion and its effect on the written line *Medicine, Science and the Law* **15** 167

[14] Gamble, D. J. (1960) The handwriting of identical twins *Canadian Society of Forensic Science Journal* **13** 11

[15] Gupta, S. K. (1979) Protecting signatures against forgery *Journal of the Forensic Science Society* **19** 19

[16] Hardcastle, R. A., Thornton, D. & Totty, R. N. (1986) A computer-based system for the classification of handwriting in cheques *Journal of the Forensic Science Society* **26** 383

[17] Kapoor, B., Kapoor, M. & Sharma, G. P. (1985) Study of the form and extent of natural variation in genuine writings with age *Journal of the Forensic Science Society* **25** 371

[18] Leung, S. C., Tsui, C. K., Cheung, W. L. and Cheung, M. W. L. (1985, 1987,

1988) A comparative approach to the examination of Chinese handwriting—the Chinese character, Parts 1–3 *Journal of the Forensic Science Society* **25** 255, **27** 157, **28** 149

[19] Levinson, J. (1983) Questioned document examination in foreign scripts *Forensic Science International* **22** 249

[20] Masson, J. F. (1988) A study of handwriting of adolescents *Journal of Forensic Sciences* **33** 167

[21] Miller, J. T. (1979) Writing machines *Forensic Science International* **13** 1

[22] Purtell, D. J. (1966) Modern handwriting instructions, systems techniques *Journal of Police Science and Administration* **8** 66

[23] Sedeyn, M.-J. (1988) Handwriting examination: a practical approach *Forensic Science International* **36** 169

[24] Snape, K. W. (1980) Determination of the direction of ball point pen motion from the orientations of burr striations in curved pen strokes *Journal of Forensic Sciences* **25** 386

[25] Strangohr, G. R. & Alford, E. F. (1965) Synthetic signatures *Journal of Forensic Sciences* **10** 77

[26] Taylor, L. R. & Chandler, M. (1987) A system for handwriting classification *Journal of Forensic Sciences* **32** 1775

[27] Totty, R. N., Hardcastle, R. A. & Dempsey, J. (1983) The dependence of slope of handwriting upon the sex and handedness of the writer *Journal of the Forensic Science Society* **23** 237

[28] Totty, R. N., Hardcastle, R. A. & Pearson, J. (1987) Forensic linguistics: the determination of authorship from habits of style *Journal of the Forensic Science Society* **27** 13

[29] Wing, A. M. & Nimmo-Smith, I. (1987) The variability of cursive handwriting measure defined along a continuum: letter specificity *Journal of the Forensic Science Society* **27** 297

3

Handwriting — accidental and deliberate modification of handwriting

In the previous chapter natural handwriting was described. The variations, and some of their causes, between the writings of different people and within the handwriting of an individual were outlined. The subject is further complicated by accidental and deliberate modification, and in this chapter these complications are discussed. In the next chapter the conclusions which can be properly drawn from the examination and comparison of two or more handwritings in the light of this background will be considered.

ACCIDENTAL VARIATION OF HANDWRITING

The variation within the writings of one person, mentioned in the previous chapter, occur however hard the writer tries to avoid them. A well practised calligrapher used to writing in a very consistent artistic hand may achieve a result where each example of any letter is nearly identical to all the other examples of the same letter, but no two will be exactly the same. A neat, careful writer will produce a consistency not far short of that of the calligrapher, but for most people, even in ideal circumstances, their writings will show quite noticeable differences between different examples of the same letter of the alphabet.

Writing conditions in the day-to-day course of business are often not ideal. They can be impaired by difficulties produced by physical causes, such as the quality of the pen or the writing surface, by the position of the writer, who may be operating in an abnormal position, or by the health (in the broadest sense of the word) of the writer.

Writing instruments

There is a wide variety of pens now available, ranging from those with wide nibs using water based inks, through pens which use a porous material such as felt or compressed fibres to apply a similar ink to the paper surface, to ball-point pens where a rotating ball rolls either a water based ink, or, most commonly of all, a glycol based paste on to the paper. Despite this variety of instruments, little difference is found in the writings of one person when using different types of pen. This is because nearly all pens now write from a single point source. This applies to a pointed fibre pen, to a ball pen, or even to a fountain pen which is tipped with a blob of hard metal rounded to an approximately spherical shape. When a broad nib or a wide fibre tipped or felt pen is used there may be differences produced that are due to the greater difficulty in moving a wide pen upwards at right angles to its wide length, but with most modern writing instruments the differences in friction which occur with with different pens and paper surfaces are hardly noticeable. Of course, a defective nib, or a very rough surface on which the paper is placed, will affect writing. Broken pen nibs, deformed fibre points, or a ball not rotating properly in its housing can all result in uneven flow of ink on to the paper. The line may be uneven both in width and along its length. In addition, the difficulty of guiding a point no longer smooth across the paper surface will affect the intended movement of the pen, particularly in the ease of changing direction. This may force the writer to lift the pen more often than he would normally, and will therefore give the appearance of a different method of construction. An extreme case of this was found when writing was made with a ball-point pen on a plaster wall. The writing was made with the pen pointing upwards, and this cut off the flow of ink; many ball-point pens depend on gravity to feed the ink to the ball. When the ink ceased to flow the writing was continued by making a deep impression in the plaster surface. This transferred metal from the ball housing to the wall like a pencil depositing graphite by friction, and it gave the same appearance as a pencil. The effect on the writer was to force him to reduce each letter to a series of separate strokes with no sharp angles or curves. In less extreme cases of unusually high resistance to movement of the pen, similar modifications of the writing are found.

When paper is placed on a rough surface the coarseness of the background will affect the writing line. Instead of a smooth flowing line there is one broken up by the irregularity of the underlying surface. If an unplaned wood surface is under the paper a regular pattern following the grain of the wood is formed. As the pen runs over the raised ridges, more ink is left on the paper, and when it passes over the troughs, less is deposited. This effect can be confused with that found in simulated writings, to be discussed later, but the regularity of the unevenness is a good indication of such a background surface effect.

A very glossy paper can result in poor take-up of ink, giving a similar appearance to that when a poor quality pen is used, but the writing line can often be seen as an uninked impression. In such cases double pen lines may be found because the writer tries to correct an unsuccessful attempt to put ink on the paper. This too can be confused with an attempt to simulate writing. The confusion may be increased if differences caused by difficulties of pen control are also found. In the act of writing the friction of pen on paper is allowed for. On a shiny surface the friction will be less, and the pen may be more difficult to guide in the intended path. This results in small differences from the normal writing.

Thick-nibbed fibre or felt tipped pens have little effect on the actions of the writer, but the examiner may find difficulty in establishing the pen movement from his examination of the writing.

Writing position

When writings are made in awkward positions such as standing with a pen in one hand and a note book in the other the control of the pen is less than when writing is made in ideal conditions. Examples of this may occur when a registered or recorded delivery is signed for at the door at the request of the postman. Again, a delivery of goods to a factory or building site is often receipted by signing the delivery note resting on anything conveniently available. Transactions completed or notes made in moving vehicles, aircraft, or ships may be the subject of an enquiry which requires a handwriting comparison. These writings, too, may show evidence of difficulty of position of the writer or the paper.

However, the effects are not always very great. Instead of a letter being carefully made with the normal degree of retracing along a line, the retrace will be less exact; for instance, instead of a letter 'a' being made with a reasonably closed circle there may be a gap where the top of the circle and the right hand upright do not meet. (The effect, of apparently stretching the line of writing and opening enclosed areas and retraced lines, is not unlike the effect of fast writing.) In addition, accidental effects occur. Odd pen movements resulting in poorly shaped loops or strokes which are too long are caused by lack of consistency in pen control. Difficult writing conditions can be variable, so the quality of the writing will also be variable. Therefore in these conditions some words will appear quite normal while others will be considerably deformed.

The position of the writing itself, rather than that of the writer, can affect the result. This is most likely when writing or a signature are made in a restricted space, at the bottom of a page, for instance. Basic features, such as the method of construction of letters, are unlikely to be affected by such difficulties. The subconscious act of directing a pen in a particular direction is too engrained to be easily deflected, but proportions of letters and words might be modified.

Health of writer

The health of the writer will affect his writing. Some conditions result in mental disorder, others produce a disability in the hand, while others cause a weakness which renders proper control impossible. The examination of patients' writing has been used to diagnose certain illnesses both physical and mental, but the study of the connection between illness and handwriting is too large a subject to be dealt with in detail in this book. However, in many cases requiring the examination of handwriting illness or the effect of drugs or alcohol play a part. Some signatures on disputed wills are either written at a time of severe illness or are claimed to be so. Comparison of these with signatures written in good health will reveal great differences either because of illness or because a different writer has been involved. It is important to consider the two possibilities.

Studies made on the writings of elderly or diseased people show that the effects depend on the degree of infirmity as well as the disease. Some complaints such as Parkinson's disease produce a tremor; others such as arthritis affect the ability to hold the pen or to move the hand or fingers easily. Impairment of eyesight also will handicap the writer. The effects found in the writings of people suffering these illnesses is fairly predictable. Tremor of the hand shows up in an even oscillation of the writing line, while poor coordination produces lines which are not smoothly curved, misplaced strokes, and poorly joined circles. There is also a consistency throughout the writing. Tremor found in one part of the writing will be found throughout, and lack of control will be even within the writing. An exception occurs on those occasions when the writer becomes tired during the period of writing and the quality worsens.

Although normally consistent within writing made at a single sitting, poor quality due to ill health is often not consistent over an extended period. Some illnesses, especially those associated with old age, worsen and a steady deterioration can be seen in the writings of a patient over a period. In some cases the deterioration may be arrested or reversed as the use of drugs controls the symptoms.

Guided hand signatures

In cases of extreme illness signatures are sometimes made with the assistance of another person. By holding the hand of the invalid and guiding it, a signature is constructed. In some cases the pen may be in the hand of the supposed writer, but little or nothing of his natural habits, which at one time controlled the movement of the writing line, are left. There will, therefore, be no evidence that the person whose hand was guided had anything to do with the writing of the signature. If the hand is entirely limp, the writing style of the person guiding it will be found in the signature.

Such signatures may be constructed from a number of ill-formed and separated strokes or may be in the fairly well formed writing of the assistant. There is little to be gained from any comparison with the original signatures of the invalid made when he was healthy.

In other cases where the assistant merely supports the arm, there is little departure from the normal signature. In between the two extremes the resultant signature could be a mixture of both the writings of writer and his helper. Here there is a tendency to find greater pressure on the paper, a poor line quality, and change in the direction of writing. In addition, accidental features quite different from the normal signature may be found.

The consideration as to whether or not a signature has been made by a guided hand is more likely to occur when a simulation is claimed to differ from the genuine because it was made with assistance. The distinction between the two methods of making a signature different from the normal signature of the writer is, therefore, of great importance. Those features, described later, which are normally found in a simulated signature, made by free hand or tracing, are clearly distinguished from those of the guided hand signature [19].

Drugs and alcohol

The taking of drugs in therapeutic quantities will affect the symptoms of many diseases and enable the sufferer to write with fluency and control which he could not produce without them. This has been found with treatment of diabetes, Parkinson's disease, and states of tension relieved by tranquillisers.

The effect of drugs taken by addicts on their handwriting has also been researched. Under the influence of narcotics and alcohol, writing is modified as muscular control deteriorates. Studies of controlled subjects have indicated that the effects are not the same for each person. In general, however, the writing becomes larger and less well formed and coordinated. The method of construction and relative proportions remain the same, but the latter can be modified by the enlargement and distortion. The writing of addicts and alcoholics will be affected by high concentrations of the drug and also by the discomfort caused by its withdrawal. The most natural writing is found when a state of well-being is induced by a lower concentration of the drug.

Impairment of vision

Another condition which affects writing is impairment of vision. Having learned to write with normal or near normal eyesight a person may be afflicted with a disease affecting the sight. Writing can still be made even with complete blindness, but the effect is to run lines together, or otherwise to misplace the writing line. Sometimes a ruler or other straight edge may be used as a guide line. This is easily discernible in the writing, with horizontal lines appearing at the bottom of many of the letters and lower loops absent. The use of a straight edge to keep writing in place is not confined to poorly sighted writers but is found elsewhere, often where it is necessary to place words and figures neatly into a limited space.

A further feature found in the writings of the visually handicapped is that some obvious errors which a sighted person would have noticed remain uncorrected.

DELIBERATE VARIATION OF HANDWRITING

Handwriting, then, can be abnormally varied by many conditions without the writer specifically giving thought to it. The acquired ability to express ideas by writing words made up of individual letters is exploited, with little consideration about how it is done or what it looks like, except for a general need for the writing to be readable and perhaps attractive in appearance. In normal writing detail is relegated to the subconscious and attention is not paid to every movement of the pen.

However, deliberate alteration of writing occurs on many occasions both for amusement and for deceit. Documents bearing such writings are frequently produced in both the criminal and civil court.

These unnatural writings, where deliberation has been employed to make differences, can be conveniently divided into two classes. The two divisions are (1) the disguise of writing to make it appear not to be by the person who wrote it, and (2) the simulation of the writing of another person. As in any such division, the border may not always be clear; copying the writing of another person effectively disguises the style of the copier.

Disguised writings

Each February many anonymous communications are sent by post. The object is for the recipient to be faced with the problem of identifying the sender of a St Valentine's Day card. This time of year probably represents most of the occasions on which writing is disguised. However, similar deception is attempted in many other circumstances for less innocent purposes. Vicious threatening letters, obscene missives, and explosive devices are regularly posted. Notes demanding money are passed across bank counters. In many of these cases attempts are made to make the writings less characteristic of their writers. Samples of writing given for comparison purposes are frequently disguised.

The most obvious feature of the writing of any person is its overall appearance. How large it is and how it slants are immediately noticeable without close examination. Therefore the most likely move in an attempt to disguise is to modify the appearance by changing the size or the slope of the writing. The effect can be to alter the apparent style quite dramatically. A pronounced forward slant is clearly different from a backward one when all the writing on a page is seen at a glance. Similarly, small cramped writing filling a page gives a different overall effect than that given by widely spaced, large, open letters. In the previous chapter the detail found in individual letters was discussed. This detail, produced subconsciously, will be little affected by changes in slope or size. The method of writing each letter and the general proportions used as a matter of habit will remain largely unchanged by a change of slope and size. Although small differences may be introduced to accommodate the deliberate alteration, not much will change. For instance, the ratio between the height of loops and the middle zone of the writing tends to remain much the same.

However, the disguiser may go a stage further and make deliberate amendments to the shape of loops or proportions of letters. He may also alter the features which he thinks are most characteristic of his own writing, or introduce new grotesque letter forms which are totally unlike anything he writes normally. The wrong hand may be used to write a disguised passage; the left hand for a right hand writer, and vice versa. This normally results in a poorly controlled, untidy, and irregular effect, larger than the writing made with the usual hand. Despite this, the same general features of movement and proportion are found, with the exception that a few letters may be constructed with a different direction of stroke.

Another method of disguise is, of course, to use a totally different form of script. Sometimes block capital letters will be employed, but this is not so much a change of handwriting as a change of writing method. Similarly, lower case unjoined letters might be used or a mixture of both. Other methods include writing with what happens to be less skill than is usual. A skilful writer can introduce evidence of lack of ability, imitating the poor quality and hesitancy of a near-illiterate. Any writer can revert to the basic copy book method which he was originally taught. He may write slowly, deliberately, and precisely, remembering each form and reproducing it consistently.

People who have more than one method of cursive writing can use the one which is not familiar to the recipient. This hardly counts as disguise in that both forms of writing can be made naturally, but the intention may be the same. These people find little difficulty in achieving a different method, but this is exceptional and contrasts with the problems encountered by most people, who do not have such ability.

Difficulties of disguising writing

The subconscious method of writing each letter is so ingrained that the conscious effort to change it is great. Less effort is required if only the slope or size are altered, but even then the rhythm which comes from habit and which gives a consistent angle of slope will not be there. This means that the newly chosen slope of the disguise may lack consistency. Some parts will slope more than others, and some parts may actually revert to the natural slant.

The same inconsistencies occur when differences of detail are introduced. For instance, in a particular case, an anonymous letter was written in a disguised hand.

Not only was the slope reversed but the lower loops of letters g and y were made with a double loop in the form of an 8. This contrasted with the single loops of the normal writing of the writer. However, not only were there some examples where the new form had been forgotten, but some had been written firstly as single loops and then retouched with extra strokes in an attempt to maintain the consistency of the different form. This is typical of disguised writing. Lapses of concentration cause reversion to the natural method.

As with every other human activity the ability to disguise varies with the individual. Some people are good at it, consistently changing many features, while others find it nearly impossible to make any appreciable change from their natural method. As in other activities, practice will no doubt enable better results to be obtained. A determined disguiser could spend days or weeks perfecting a different style which would have little in common with his normal method. Fortunately, this is rare. People committing crimes or other forms of deceit normally do not take the trouble to go beyond what seems to them to be an acceptable disguise. If the amount of writing is of reasonable quantity many of the features of their normal handwritings will remain, but if only a few words are written it is not difficult to maintain concentration sufficiently to change all the letters.

In the investigation of a crime it is common for the suspect to be asked for samples of writing. The opportunity for disguise is frequently seized, and the samples are written using a method very different from what is normal. This possibility has to be considered when such samples are taken, and also when they are used as comparison material. This will be dealt with more fully later.

Block capital writings are not so often disguised. Perhaps the common belief that they cannot be identified and are not characteristic of their writer leads people to regard it as unnecessary. When disguise is used it tends to take the form of carefully written 'copy book' letters, each letter made in as many different strokes as possible, or of letters ornamented with extra and superfluous serifs.

Disguised signatures

Some disguises encountered in criminal investigation are found in signatures. A common method of fraud is to sign a document and then disclaim the signature. Frequently, cheques are reported stolen when they have been used by their owner. Rather than attempting to claim that a normal-looking signature is a perfect copy, the fraudsman or woman (cheque frauds of this sort are often perpetrated by girls in their late teens) will introduce differences. These will often be sufficiently noticeable to be later pointed out when the signature is denied. 'I never write a J like that' is a typical remark. Much of the signature will remain unaffected, but the more obvious features like the capital letters are modified. It will be necessary in many cases to avoid too great a departure from the normal signature because the recipient will compare the result with an identifying signature on a cheque card, driving licence, or other document.

A common result of this ploy therefore is a signature written with normal fluency and with good match in detail of letter formation but with some clear discrepancies, especially in capitals. This does not present a great problem for the document examiner. When considering the possibility of simulation by another person he would find the combination of close match in detail together with obvious differences inconsistent and inexplicable. The other alternative of 'self-forgery' is far more plausible.

This is not the only way of writing a signature designed to be denied later. If no comparison is to be made with a standard a completely different design is chosen. It is not difficult to change a small amount of writing completely so that it shows little resemblance to the normal. This can present a problem. Often no evidence of the normal method of the writer remains, and there is no indication of his having made the signature. On other occasions the signature is reduced to a hardly readable scrawl. In these, movements of the pen corresponding to those of the normal signature of the writer are sometimes found. This would be unlikely to occur if another writer had copied the genuine signature; the attempt is likely to match in overall appearance rather than in detail.

A further method, one rarely found, is for the self-forger to produce what another person would when simulating a signature. The same features, described later, which are found in a drawn or traced signature can be introduced deliberately into the writing of one's own signature. In a survey carried out in Germany for research purposes it was found that a small proportion of a group of people asked to disguise their signatures chose this method [22].

Simulated writings

There are two main methods of copying the writing of another person. One is to 'draw' the writing as if one were drawing an object. This results in a freehand copy or simulation, so called because the hand is free from restraints such as previously written guide lines. The second method is to use such guide lines and to trace over them with a writing instrument. This is known as a traced copy or simulation. Although the two methods are basically different, an inaccurate following of a signature may be similar to an attempt to draw it. There is therefore a continuously variable range between the two methods. Normally, however, the choice is made between a drawing or a carefully followed tracing.

The result of both methods is likely to be a forgery, writing which deceives. However, the word 'forgery' implies intent to deceive and is best avoided when describing simulated writings, whether freehand or traced copies. They may have been written by another without any felonious intent and in full knowledge of the person whose writing has been copied. Alternatively, a signature written by another without any attempt to copy the normal style of its owner will be a forgery if it is made with intent to deceive.

Writing, as has been seen earlier, is not uniform and varies both between different persons and within the writing of one person. The quality is also a variable factor. To copy writing successfully does not require a precise match, because two pieces of writing by one person will not be precisely the same. It is necessary to place the result somewhere in the range of variation of the writing being simulated so that it is thought to be the same writing.

Freehand simulation

Freehand simulations can be made of signatures or of larger amounts of writing, but the former is more common than the latter. The signature appears to have been used as a means of authentication since the sixteenth century. Even then the danger of simulation was recognised, and extra flourishes unnecessary for reading the name were added to minimise the danger. The same practice is found today. Some people will introduce elaborate rubrics which pose an extra problem for the forger.

When a signature is copied the copier needs to reproduce its overall appearance sufficiently well to deceive the person who has to check its authenticity. This is all that is needed. The shop assistant, bank clerk, or car rental clerk will glance at both the signature presented and that on the cheque card or driving licence and be satisfied. Little attempt is made, especially if the counter is busy, to examine it closely, so there is little need to make a closely matching simulation. If greater care is required to be taken more effort is needed to produce a better copy.

The problem of achieving a good copy of a well formed and flowing signature is that two conditions have to be met. Firstly accuracy in shape and proportion within the signature is required, and, secondly, smoothness of line. Either one is not too difficult to manage, but, for most people, to satisfy both is nearly impossible. Normally, a copy is made either by writing slowly to achieve accuracy or by writing rapidly so that more fluency is obtained.

Slowly made simulations

Accuracy is best achieved by writing carefully and slowly, but this makes writing with smoothly graduating curves and loops difficult. Instead of the loops turning gradually from a lesser to a greater curvature giving a smooth appearance they change more abruptly with greater angularity.

When writing is made naturally the pressure applied to the paper is not consistent. Some lines are made quickly and the pen hardly touches the surface, while others, where more change of direction is required, are made with more weight. When the pen is lifted to begin the next word the pressure is progressively reduced and the end of the line tails off gradually. In trying to produce a careful and slowly made freehand copy such variations in pressure are difficult to reproduce. Because they arise from the speed of natural movement they cannot be produced when the hand is moving slowly and is consciously controlled to imitate an unfamiliar pattern. Instead, the slowly moving pen is maintained at a more constant pressure on the paper, and the written line is therefore more even in width and its end not 'feathered' but blunt.

Despite the care taken to copy accurately, a drawn simulation is often outside the range of variation of the genuine signatures in the shape of some or even all of the letters. The overall proportions of a signature may be wrong, the relative proportion of letters and the spacing between initials may not be reproduced accurately. The shapes of loops are often difficult to imitate, and so are complex underlinings and other rubrics.

In natural writing the pen is likely to write most if not all of a single word without leaving the paper. This is also the case for signatures; individual letters or words are made in one line or else a stop is made regularly in the same place. When copying a signature more accuracy is achieved when the pen travels for a shorter distance. The signature is then completed in more strokes than were present in the original, and breaks are found in the writing line. It is not always easy to determine whether or not this has occurred, but under the microscope, using a magnification of about 20 to 40 times, breaks in the line can usually be detected. When a genuine signature is 'drawn' to produce a simulation, the form will be reproduced as accurately as possible, but little attention may be paid to how the signature was constructed, how the pen moved to form the letters and to join them. The copy may therefore include a number of letters made in the wrong way. This is important evidence to indicate that simulation has taken place; such differences in letter or word construction are most unlikely to have been introduced by the genuine writer.

The 'drawing' of a signature rather than writing it naturally gives rise to the possibility that the forger may choose to copy it upside-down. Whether this is an advantage is doubtful, but it can happen. Similarly, a signature in Arabic or other scripts written from right to left may be copied by writing from left to right. Indications of lines made in the wrong direction provide conclusive evidence that the signature is not natural.

In copying a signature, or more commonly when larger amounts of writing are simulated, mistakes are made, noticed, and corrected. This means, for instance, that an addition may be made to close a gap which should not be there at the top of the circle in a letter a, d, or g. In other cases the length of the staff of a t or the loop of another letter might be adjusted by adding the necessary connecting stroke. This is known as 'patching'.

Another error occasionally made by a copier is to mistake one letter for another in a signature he is trying to reproduce. This will occur when the letters of the genuine signature are not clearly identifiable. The resulting copy may include obviously readable letters which do not occur in the name, the copier having erroneously thought that they were there.

Simulations of poorly made signatures
To make a freehand copy, then, is usually not an easy task. The difficulty is considerably reduced when the signature being copied is short, slowly written, and rather more variable than usual. Then the poor line quality of a copy will not be very different from the model, and the task of making the copy fall into the range shown by the genuine signatures will not be too difficult. Copied signatures of this type may be nearly indistinguishable from the genuine.

Rapidly made simulations
People vary greatly in their ability to simulate a signature by producing a freehand 'drawing'. Some improve considerably with practice, but others are never able to make a good copy. Unfortunately, it is not necessary to acquire any great skill in the art of imitating the writing of another person to obtain the benefit of forgery because the shopkeeper or clerk or official who has the task of verifying a signature or a document will usually give it only a cursory glance. In such transactions it may be necessary for the forger to produce his simulation in front of the person receiving it. He cannot sit down and carefully copy from a model, but has to learn the pattern first and then quickly write it, usually in a different place. This leads to a greater divergence from the genuine signature, but the result will on most occasions pass the brief examination by the recipient.

When such signatures are written, and the same applies to larger amounts of writing, inaccuracy rather than poor line quality is the most likely result. The problem of remembering all the features of the signature being forged, or observing them at the time of writing, is usually too great to enable a signature to be written within the range of variation of the genuine signatures. Practice may improve the prospects of making a good copy close to that range, but it is unlikely to enable the copier to avoid inaccuracies, especially in the relative heights of letters, spacing between capitals, and shapes of loops. In addition, the method of construction of the model signature or of its individual letters may not be noticed or not reproduced, and will provide clear evidence that the copy is not genuine.

Traced signatures
Tracing is widely used as a method of simulating signatures, especially when the object is to reproduce as exactly as possible the signature to be copied. In some cases writings apart from signatures are traced, but to do so requires the possession of sufficient writing from which to trace the wording required for the deception.

To trace a signature it is necessary that the shape of the model to be copied is placed in the right place on the appropriate document. This can be done in a number of ways. A piece of carbon paper can be placed on the document and the signature to be copied placed over it. Light pressure of a pen following the line of the signature will produce a 'carbon' impression on the lower document. This can in turn be overwritten with ink to produce a realistic simulation of the original.

Another way is to place the original on the document where the copy is required and to trace heavily along the line of writing so that impressions are made on the paper below. These impressions can in turn be inked in by following the indented line with a pen. The difficulty is to make the written line coincide exactly with the impressions, but the general shape of the copy can be reproduced adequately.

A different method is to place the document on which the copy is needed over the genuine article. The two are held on to a window so that the lower signature can be seen through the top paper. The lower signature can then be traced directly by writing on the upper document. A light box, a device used to examine transparencies or photographic negatives, can be used to provide a similar means of showing the lower signature through the top piece of paper.

Tracing paper can be used for the same purpose. It is placed over the genuine signature which is then traced on to it. The other side of the tracing paper is then covered with graphite by rubbing a soft pencil lead over the surface. By writing exactly over the first tracing a graphite impression is left on the paper below. This can be overwritten to produce a simulated signature written in ink or with any other medium. The graphite can be removed with a rubber eraser.

There are other ways to reproduce a signature artificially, but these are less commonly used. Tracing a signature by any of these means produces similar results. The simulation will be a close match of the copied original. It will, in fact, normally be closer to the model copied than another genuine signature would be. It will show same signs of slow, laborious production as a slowly written freehand 'drawn' simulation. It may show lifts of the pen, poor line quality and even pressure, in contrast to the smoother line with varying downward pressure caused by the speed of movement of the pen found in natural writing.

Unlike a freehand copy it will be free or nearly free of the inaccuracies caused by imperfect observation or powers of reproduction. It will fall within the range of variation of the genuine signatures apart from dots or other small features which may not be noticed during the tracing. Unless it is a direct copy made by means of transmitted light it will show evidence of the guide lines from which it was traced, and these can be detected by close examination in the correct light conditions. It is nearly impossible for the forger to follow the guide lines exactly, so the writing line will be found not to coincide with the guide line in several places. Guides lines will be detectable under oblique light or by electrostatic detection if they are indented impressions, or by low-power magnification and infrared examination if they are pencil or carbon. Despite the erasure of pencil or guide lines, traces of these may be discovered. Erasure may cause the simulation to smear and may damage the paper surface.

Introduction of features of the copier

When making an attempt to copy writing the copier has to control his hand in order to reproduce the original as accurately as possible. However, the hand is accustomed to writing in its own natural style, so if concentration is reduced a tendency to write in the usual way takes over. Therefore copied writings will often exhibit features which are not present in whatever is being simulated but are found in the normal habits of the writer. This is more often the case where a reasonable quantity of writing is copied, and occurs less often if only a signature is simulated.

In some poorly made copies there will be a mixture of the writing styles of both the copied and the copier. The more obvious features of the writing of the former are noticed and reproduced, but much of the writing is close to that of the copier.

Where the natural writing of the copier intrudes into the copy he is making, evidence is provided to indicate his identity. Without such evidence, there is nothing to indicate who is the writer because each letter and feature of the writing has been based on the model copied. This situation is usual when signatures are simulated by careful drawing.

Copies of writings other than signatures are more likely to provide evidence of their writer. If certain letters are missing from the material being copied, they may be written in the natural writing of the copier, because he has no model to copy. Rapidly written simulated signatures, which contain a relatively small amount of writing, sometimes provide evidence of their writer. When a number of such simulations are made by one person copying a particular signature, there is a tendency for them to show consistency between themselves and a difference both from the genuine signature and also from copies made by other people.

Traced signatures contain no evidence of their writer; the following of an indented impression or a written line has nothing to do with natural writing. The fact that naturally made signatures are never exactly the same means that the particular signature from which the copy was traced will be closer to it than any other natural signature, unless signatures of the genuine writer are remarkably consistent. Therefore, if the model signature is found and compared with the copy it can be shown to be the source. Apart from close similarity in size and shape it may contain ink from the pen which traced it or impressions of the simulation if this was made directly following the line of the underlying original. If multiple tracings are made from one genuine original, their closeness in proportion and shape will indicate that they have been made by this method. The finding of several such signatures may provide added proof that they are not genuine.

FURTHER READING

[1] Alford, E. F. (1970) Disguised handwritings: a statistical survey of how handwriting is most frequently disguised *Journal of Forensic Sciences* **15** 476

[2] Alford, E. F. & Dick, R. M. (1978) Intentional disguise in court-ordered handwriting specimens *Journal of Police Science and Administration* **6** 419

[3] Beacon, M. S. (1976) Handwriting by the blind *Journal of Forensic Sciences* **12** 37

[4] Beck, J. (1985) Handwriting of the alcoholic *Forensic Science International* **28** 19

[5] Blueschke, A. (1986) Regression and/or attempt simulation of handwriting by hypnosis *Canadian Society of Forensic Science Journal* **19** 103

[6] Boisseau, M., Chamberland, G. & Gauthier, S. (1987) Handwriting analysis of several extrapyramidal disorders *Canadian Society of Forensic Science Journal* **20** 139

[7] Buquet, A. & Rudler, M. (1987) Handwriting and exogenous intoxication *International Criminal Police Review* No. 408 9

[8] Foley, B. G. & Kelly, J. H. (1977) Guided hand signatures research *Journal of Police Science and Administration* **5** 227

[9] Foley, R. G. & Miller, A. L. (1979) The effects of marijuana and alcohol usage in handwriting *Forensic Science International* **14** 159

[10] Frank, F. E. (1988) Disguised writing: chronic or acute *Journal of Forensic Sciences* **33** 727

[11] Gilmour, C. & Bradford, J. (1988) The effect of medication on handwriting *Canadian Society of Forensic Science Journal* **20** 119

[12] Herkt, A. J. (1986) Signature disguise or signature forgery? *Journal of the Forensic Science Society* **26** 257

[13] Hilton, O. (1962) Handwriting and the mentally ill *Journal of Forensic Sciences* **7** 131

[14] Hilton, O. (1969) Considerations of the writer's health in identifying signatures and detecting forgery *Journal of Forensic Sciences* **14** 157

[15] Hilton, O. (1969) A study of the influence of alcohol on handwriting *Journal of Forensic Sciences* **14** 309

[16] Hilton, O. (1977) Influence of age and illness on handwriting, identification problems *Forensic Science* **9** 161

[17] Hilton, O. (1984) Effects of writing instruments on handwriting details *Journal of Forensic Sciences* **29** 80.

[18] Jamieson, J. A. (1983) Effects of slope change on handwriting *Canadian Society of Forensic Science Journal* **19** 117

[19] Jones, D. G. (1986) Guided hand or forgery? *Journal of the Forensic Science Society* **26** 169

[20] Konstantinidis, S. I. V. (1987) Disguised handwriting *Journal of the Forensic Science Society* **27** 383

[21] Masson, J. F. (1985) Felt tip writing. Problems of identification *Journal of Forensic Sciences* **30** 172

[22] Miller, L. S. (1987) Forensic examination of arthritic impaired writings *Journal of Police Science and Administration* **15** 51

[23] Michel, L. (1978) Disguised signatures *Journal of the Forensic Science Society* **18** 25

[24] Michel, L. (1982) Assistance by third parties in writing signatures and wills *Archiv für Kriminologie* 173

[25] Morton, S. E. (1980) How does crowding affect signatures? *Journal of Forensic Sciences* **25** 141

[26] Purtell, D. J. (1965) Effects of drugs on handwriting *Journal of Forensic Sciences* **10** 335

[27] Savage, G. A. (1978) Handwriting of the deaf and hard of hearing *Canadian Forensic Science Society Journal* **11** 1

[28] Skelly, J. D. (1987) Guided death bed signatures *Canadian Society of Forensic Science Journal* **20** 147

4

Handwriting — the purposes and principles of scientific examination

INTRODUCTION

The previous two chapters have considered the features of handwritings of different people and their natural, accidental, and artificial variations. In this chapter the conclusions that can properly be drawn from these observations are discussed in outline. It is not possible in the space available to consider every factor which contributes to the final outcome of an examination of handwritings but only the basic principles

Amateur experts

Virtually everyone recognises the writing of at least one person as well as his or her own. It is common practice to examine the writing on an envelope before opening it; workers in offices are familiar with each other's writing, so are members of families and other small social groups. This recognition, due to acquaintance with the writings, is not unlike the recognition of faces. At a quick glance everyone can identify one of a large number of people by his or her appearance, comparing what is seen with a gallery of faces in the memory. This ability, however, is not so great when handwriting is concerned. Too many writings will be too similar in appearance to allow an efficient separation. The memory bank of handwritings will not be as large as that of faces, and the power to discriminate between them is lower.

In another capacity many people examine handwritings on a regular basis. Bank clerks and shop assistants compare signatures on cheques with those on cheque guarantee cards. Similarly, travellers cheques are paid on the strength of a similar cursory examination. The problem with identification or verification by a quick glance is that too much can be missed. The small but significant differences and the poor line quality of the simulation are not noticed; the subtle distinction between the false and the genuine are not appreciated.

In other areas small but noticeable features may be attributed great significance. In Shakespeare's 'Twelfth Night', Maria recognises that she writes very much like her mistress Olivia. 'On a forgotten matter we can hardly make distinction of our hands'. She writes a letter which Malvolio finds, and falls into a trap 'By my life this is my lady's hand! these be her very c's, her u's and her t's, and thus makes she her great P's. It is, in contempt of question, her hand'. But it was not Olivia's writing but that of Maria.

The layman, then, will be impressed by overall appearance or by individual features which match closely. He will tend not to notice quite clear differences which are present. It is the experience of those who study handwriting that writings which they find to be clearly and significantly different are regarded by the inexperienced as the same. Time and time again the expert is presented with writings which are thought to be by one person, and he has to inform the client that they are not. The similarities which appear so convincing to the layman are either common forms of letters typical of a style, sometimes called class characteristics, or less common features which can still occur by coincidence. With twenty-six letters of the alphabet there are twenty-six chances of a coincidental match between one of them in two writings. When capitals and numerals are counted, the chances are increased. Again, styles widely taught or in fashion will often give the same appearance to writings of different people from the same background or nationality.

In addition to confusion between different writers the inexperienced observer may fail to realise that two totally different-looking writings can come from the same hand.

SCIENTIFIC METHOD

The study, classification, and recording of natural laws of science has built up a background of knowledge which is consistent and repeatable. From this background, methods of determining the qualitative and quantitative make-up of materials have been devised. Analysis of such substances is based on performing a test, the results of which can be related to background knowledge about the material. Similar principles apply to the comparison of handwriting.

In reaching any conclusion on the basis of a comparison of handwritings it is necessary to make accurate observations of those factors referred to in the previous two chapters, and to weigh up the evidence found in the light of this background knowledge. This corpus of knowledge, built up by the study of many different handwritings in a scientific and analytical way, is essential for the examiner and distinguishes his approach from that of the layman.

To prove that two writings were made by one person it is necessary to show that no other explanation is possible. It is not sufficient to note that the writings are similar, assume that everyone writes differently, and therefore conclude that they must be written by one person. To do this is to ignore the possibilities of coincidence and of simulation. Only when these can be ruled out as practically impossible is the conclusion justified. This is the fundamental principle of the identification of questioned handwriting; the same principle applies throughout forensic science.

Other aspects of forensic science

In the comparison of fingerprints, blood, and other materials the property which varies most within the population and least within an individual source is compared.

The significance of the match is either calculated or estimated by the likelihood of finding a chance match elsewhere in the population.

When fingerprints are examined the same method applies. A chance match is regarded as impossible when a certain number of features are found to agree, because the randomness of the ridge characteristics is well established. The comparison of marks made by shoes is, however, somewhat different. Mass-produced shoes in new condition will not provide different patterns, so coincidence cannot be ruled out. When damage, cuts, holes, imbedded stones, etc. affect the marks their random shape and position will not be reproduced in another shoe.

The consideration of chance match in handwriting falls between that of fingerprints and of shoe marks. Many of the features are not unique but, like ridge characteristics, their combination is significant, and some are very unusual, like a cut mark in a shoe.

In the comparison of blood, reliable data are available for the frequency of occurrence of different groups. It is established that the proportion of the caucasian population of the United Kingdom with group AB blood is around 3%, and that the proportion with group N is 22%. These are groups within different independent systems, and so by multiplying the proportions it can be calculated that 0.66% of the population have blood containing both AB and N groups. Such accuracy cannot be determined where fingerprints are concerned, but the features found are also random and independent. To establish an identification a number of features are compared. In the United Kingdom 16 matches are required before it can be assumed that no other person could have left an identical fingerprint.

This mathematical calculation is not possible in handwriting comparisons. In the first place it is not clear what is being counted, as each letter may have more than one feature of note. In the second place it is very difficult to define a particular property or class equivalent to a clearly identifiable blood group. Thirdly, while blood groups and fingerprint details are independent of each other and their frequencies of occurrence can be multiplied, many of the features found in handwritings are related, and therefore such mathematical treatment would be unsafe.

COMPARISON OF HANDWRITING

The initial examination of handwriting must be to determine if the writings are in fact similar, and, if this is so, consideration must then be given to the reasons for it. It has already been made clear that no two writings will be exactly the same; so it is necessary to decide whether the variations which are found are typical of those of one writer or two. To do this, each letter of the alphabet is examined to determine its method of construction and proportions, or shape. Although each will be different, its variations will fall into a range which will have limits. The letters could be measured for height, width, angle, and other parameters, but little is gained from this. Observation of a number of examples will soon establish the average pattern of the letter. The shape of curves, angles, or ovals, openness of circles, length of lead-in strokes and connecting strokes, and the height of the point where the letter begins can all vary within a small range for one person and can be distinguished from the different range of another.

Consideration of similarities

As the comparison of individual letters proceeds it may become apparent that the range of each letter is found to match. When all the letters have been examined, when other factors such as size and slope, the distance between letters, their connecting strokes, the distance between words and lines, the margins and pen pressure, have been compared and found to be similar, consideration is given to the significance of the findings.

Is it possible that a chance match has occurred? Could the similarities be due to the possibility that two people write these letters in an ordinary, frequently occurring way? Could the resemblances be due to the questioned writing being a simulation? Are the differences merely the variations expected in one person's writing? Are the similarities rare or characteristic?

The possibility of chance match

These questions cannot as yet be answered by quantitative data, and perhaps never will be. However, the wide range of variation found for each letter of the alphabet between different writers, the presence in many writings of unusual forms, and the number of characters present in writings being compared, means that the chances of finding a match between all the features in combination must be very remote or impossible.

Despite the fact that no mathematical data are available for the frequency of occurrence of different forms or the correlation between them, the basic statistical approach is applicable and logical. By relating his observations to his corpus of knowledge the document examiner can assess whether or not the resemblances between the writings are sufficient to rule out a chance match.

The possibility of simulation

In a comparison of a good fingerprint the practical elimination of the possibility of coincidence would be sufficient for a conclusion of common origin. The same applies in other branches of forensic science; typewritings, shoe prints, tool marks, or striations on bullets can be positively linked to their origins. In handwriting, however, another factor has to be considered. It is possible to produce all the characteristics of a writer, however rare, by simulation. The criminalist comparing other materials is not concerned with this, but proper attention to it is vital for the handwriting expert.

Therefore, in addition to looking for similarity in method of construction, proportions, and general shapes of letters the examiner must look for evidence of simulation. Inaccuracy, where letter forms will be close but consistently different perhaps in method of construction, poor line quality, indentations or remains of pencil or carbon lines which have been traced on to the paper, are all indications of copied rather than natural writing. If these are found there is clearly reason to believe that the resemblances are due to simulation and not common authorship. If they are not found and the line quality is good, or at least similar to that of the known writing, and if the resemblances are sufficiently close, then there is no evidence that the writing is other than normal.

This, in itself, does not totally exclude the possibility of simulation. Again, an assessment has to be made as to the likelihood that a person can copy the writing of another so closely that no evidence remains. In the case of a large quantity of well formed, smoothly and rapidly written text this would be virtually impossible. At the other extreme, if a small amount such as a single poorly written word is the only questioned writing, the possibility that this is not genuine but is a copy made by another person cannot be excluded. In other comparisons a situation between these two positions is found.

The same principles apply whether the writing in question is a quantity of writing or a signature; both alternatives must be ruled out as a practical possibility. While a signature contains only a small amount of writing it will usually show other 'personal' features such as choice of names or initials, underlining and unusual letter forms which will provide adequate evidence against the possibility of chance match. The main consideration in the examination of signatures is the possibility of simulation.

Subjectivity

In any assessment of evidence derived from examination of documents which depends not on mathematical calculation but on the evaluation of the significance of all of the findings taken in combination there must be a subjective element. As well as a possible variation in observation of the documents in question and in awareness of the background knowledge of the subject, there may be elements within the personality of the expert which play a part, a tendency to caution or to the opposite, perhaps. In addition there will be variations in the competence of the different examiners.

It is important that any person practising the science of document examination is aware of this. It is part of the training of a student in any scientific discipline to be aware of the limitations of the methods he is using. He must know how exact his methods are and report his results within those limits. Inexactness is normal in many disciplines, an 'exact science' hardly exists, and a qualified scientist is well able to allow for it. The conclusion of the examiner must be made allowing for any lack of precision which is inherent in the methods used. The subjectivity of the reasoning process must be recognised, and in the circumstances leading to a criminal trial the benefit of any doubt given to the defendant.

It is a long way from the careful, well based consideration of the evidence and its reasoned evaluation in reaching a conclusion to the guesswork which is sometimes implied when the word 'subjective' is used. The idea that a degree of inexactness of method is equated with a random or ill-considered personal choice is erroneous. The use of the word 'opinion' as the technical term in legal circles to describe the conclusion of an expert may give rise to this. In contrast, the conclusions of a properly trained and competent document examiner are found to be consistent, accurate, and sound. The subjective element, recognised and allowed for, is reduced to an absolute minimum, and there is, with few exceptions, close agreement between the findings and conclusions of different competent practitioners.

Identification

When two handwritings are compared, and both coincidence and simulation are ruled out, the conclusion of the expert is that both the known and questioned writings are by one person. The degree of certainty is very high; it is not merely an expression of likelihood or a vague indication of similarity; if it is properly arrived at it is a conclusion that has taken into account all the variations and similarities in the writings and their significance. They have been related to the background knowledge on the subject amassed by both the examiner and his colleagues, and all other possibilities have been considered. Only one conclusion has remained, and that is one of identity. It is as if the expert has unwillingly come to this conclusion, having diligently sought and failed to find evidence for some other explanation. The only other inferences are that by some remarkable coincidence, well outside his experience, someone else writes like this, or someone with an extraordinary skill can produce the perfect simulation, leaving no evidence that it is so. These possibilities are so remote as to be negligible. No practical chance that they have occurred exists. This is what is meant by the identification of handwriting with a writer by comparing known and questioned writings.

Qualified conclusions

In some circumstances questioned handwritings are small in quantity. The same principles apply to these cases as to those where more writing is available. Each letter of the alphabet is compared with the same letter in the known writing, and if all are found to be similar, within the expected range of variation, and there is no evidence of simulation, there is no reason to believe another writer is involved. However, the possibility cannot be excluded, because the amount of material available for comparison is insufficient to exclude a chance match. If the quantity of similar writing, though less than that sufficient for a conclusion that it was made by one person, is nearly so, the evidence is still strong. The chance of coincidental match may be not quite negligible but very unlikely, because there is a reasonable amount of writing or a smaller amount with some uncommon features. It then becomes highly unlikely that another writer could be found who, by chance, writes in the same way; there is therefore a high probability that the two writings were written by one person. This conclusion, not so strong as identification, but stronger than mere consistency, is of considerable value.

In other cases there is a smaller amount of writing without sufficient unusual features, so coincidental match can neither be ruled out nor regarded as very unlikely. There will be many people whose writings will not match the writing, but a real chance that some will. This is especially so when the writing is poorly formed and likely to be somewhat variable around a common style not far removed from that of a copy book. In these cases the evidence indicates that there is no reason to believe that the writer of the known writing did not write the small amount of questioned material, so the appropriate conclusion is that the writings could have been made by one person, but that the evidence is insufficient for a more certain conclusion. This may be of no use to a court, and certainly would not be sufficient, if produced by the prosecution without any other evidence, to secure a conviction in a criminal trial. However, if other evidence is present the conclusion could be corroborative to the prosecution case. Similarly, it could assist the defence if it suggested that a prosecution witness was not telling the truth.

Limited populations

The method of identification of writing depends, as fingerprint evidence does, on the consideration and rejection of a large population — separating one person from an extremely large number. However, in some handwriting cases the circumstances might indicate that only one of a small number of people could be involved, and samples of writing of all of them may be available. Clearly, if one is found to match and the rest are different, significant evidence is obtained. Simulation must be ruled out because a particular individual could have been 'framed', but in situations like this conclusions of great importance can be obtained from a small amount of writing.

CONSIDERATION OF DIFFERENCES

The comparison of any two pieces of handwriting will show that there are differences between them. They may be large or small, be significant or consist of only those variations which are expected to occur in the writings of one person. Whatever form they take, it is important that they are properly considered.

In some cases there may be similarities, sometimes quite striking ones, but also differences which consistently occur. Each time a particular letter of the alphabet is found in the questioned writing it is very different from those of the known writings. The range of all the examples of that letter found in the questioned writing is outside or separate from the range of the letter found in the known writing. The same may be true for other letters. Some letters may appear at first sight to be very similar, but when all those in the known writings are examined together they are found to be consistently different from those in the questioned writing in some small feature, the position of the cross bar of a t, for instance, or the height at which the downstroke of a block capital A begins.

The presence of these differences is worth consideration. Why should one person write a number of letters in one way on one occasion and in a totally or slightly different way on another? If the known writings have been collected from examples written over a period including that of the questioned document and are found to be consistent in themselves, why should the questioned writings differ in these respects?

Consistent differences

When variations are found in a letter or figure, they can be considered as falling into a range represented by an enclosed area such as a circle. The variations of the same letter written by another person can be regarded as being enclosed in a different area or circle. These areas may be large or small, depending on the variability of the writer or the particular piece of writing. If the two writers make the letter in a similar way, the circles will completely or partly overlap. If they are consistently different, the circles will remain apart. Using this analogy it is easy to visualise that although one person could use a wide range of variation, occupying a large circle, it is difficult to see why he or she would use two separate, discrete ranges represented by two circles which do not overlap. Occasionally this will happen with one letter; it is not uncommon to find a letter b written both with an anticlockwise base opened upwards and also with a closed clockwise circle in the same piece of writing. Some-times the right hand vertical stroke of a block capital letter N will be made in either an upwards or downwards direction in the same writing. But generally there is no reason to expect consistently different forms from one writer.

The consistency of the differences between two writings is, then, a most important factor. It is usually unwise to attribute two writings with such a discrepancy to one person. It is, however, rare to find only one such difference if adequate writings are available for comparison. Normally there will be several or many consistent differences between writings of any two people, even when they appear to be similar in overall appearance. The presence of these differences, despite some similarities in style or between certain other letters, is an indication of a different writer, and there is therefore no reason to believe that the questioned writings were written by the writer of the known writings.

Other reasons for differences

It is not possible in most cases to say with certainty that two different writings must have been written by different persons because there are various ways in which a person can write, so that one sample of his writing is different from another. Some people, a very small proportion of the population, can write in more than one style. They can write quite naturally in totally different modes. Perhaps one is an italic style, and another one more conventional; perhaps both are in the same basic style.

Disguise is another possible cause of differences in the writing of one person. Although it is difficult for most people to introduce into their natural writing differences so consistent that they are present in each example of the chosen letter, this is not entirely impossible. If the amount of writing is small, a signature perhaps, the task becomes easier.

A not uncommon method of disguise, writing with the 'wrong' hand, produces a badly formed and poorly controlled writing. This could be thought to be the normal writing of the subject if the possibility is not allowed for, but can be excluded by adequate samples of 'course of business writings' (see Chapter 5).

Again, by copying the writing of another person by a variety of means such as simple drawing or tracing, the writer will produce a result totally different from his own normal product. These factors make it unwise to conclude that two different writings must have been made by different people. Normally, this will be the case, but the degree of certainty is reduced by these possibilities; without any knowledge of the ability of the subject to write in different styles or to disguise effectively, the likelihood of this cannot be assessed.

Nevertheless, there are many cases where the known writing is found to be of a generally poor quality, showing clear evidence of lack of skill, and it is sufficient in quantity for certainty that it represents the normal writing of the person. In these cases, if the questioned writing is not only different but of higher quality, it can safely be assumed that the writer of the poor quality known writing would not be able to achieve the standard of the questioned writing, and so could not have written it. There are other occasions where the construction of letters is consistently wrong, so that the evidence suggests it is most unlikely that one person has written two writings. Caution here is also advisable. Ambidextrous writers, a small but not insignificant proportion of the population, might find one method of construction less convenient with one hand than with the other and so change methods with a change of hand.

Therefore in most cases where writings differ from those with which they are being compared it is usually best not to conclude that they must be by different people, but that there is no evidence that they were written by the same person.

Similarities with differences

So far, discussion of possible results of handwriting comparisons has assumed that there is either no significant difference between the known and questioned writings or that such differences are sufficient to indicate no evidence of common authorship. In practice this is often the position, and the assessment of the value of evidence is dependent on the amount of writing available for comparison. Sometimes, however, the situation is complicated by differences which are not so clear-cut as to be significant in a negative direction. There are many reasons why these might occur; they have been discussed in the previous chapter. Disguise, simulation, ill health, difficult writing conditions, all contribute to differences from what might be regarded as normal natural writing.

Features generally found in disguised writing are described in the previous chapter. There is a tendency for a distortion of overall appearance with the retention of the detail of method of construction and proportion. Also, the disguiser finds it difficult to maintain consistency for a lengthy period of writing. Similarly, the tired, or ill, or intoxicated writer, as well as a person writing in difficult circumstances, will also keep those same features. The subconscious movements of the arm, hand, or fingers produce the same method of construction of each letter, and the propensity to write with the same proportions. Such detail will be little affected by deliberately altered appearance or by difficulties of less than ideal conditions. In contrast, an adequate sample of writings of another person will be certain to include some letters made in a consistently different way. Provided that enough material is available for a comparison the differences found can be established as consistent in form and detail, or alternatively, variable only in the more general features but similar in the finer points of construction and proportion.

From the determination of which of the two situations is present in the questioned writings the appropriate conclusion is derived. It may be possible, despite the differences, for the expert to conclude that both writings were made by one person. It may also be the case that some doubt has been introduced, and a qualification to the conclusion should be employed.

Disguise

Where differences occur which are typical of those found in disguised writing, this can be reported. It may be of interest to a court that some form of deception has been attempted. However, only those features which can only be attributed with certainty to attempted disguise should be reported. It would be wrong to accuse the writer of disguising his writings if differences from normal were due to other reasons, such as ill health or the influence of alcohol.

However, the most serious error is to attribute consistent differences to disguise and therefore to pay insufficient attention to their cause.

SIMULATION

A further cause for apparent similarities occurring alongside difference is that one of the pieces of writing being compared is a simulation. The methods used to simulate writings, mostly signatures, of other people were discussed in Chapter 3. Whether the method chosen is a rapidly drawn copy, a slowly made freehand simulation, or a tracing, evidence will normally be found. Such evidence, poor line quality, pen lifts and retouching, inaccuracy, evidence of guide lines, was referred to there. In many cases the observation of such features provides clear evidence that simulation has occurred (see Fig. 5).

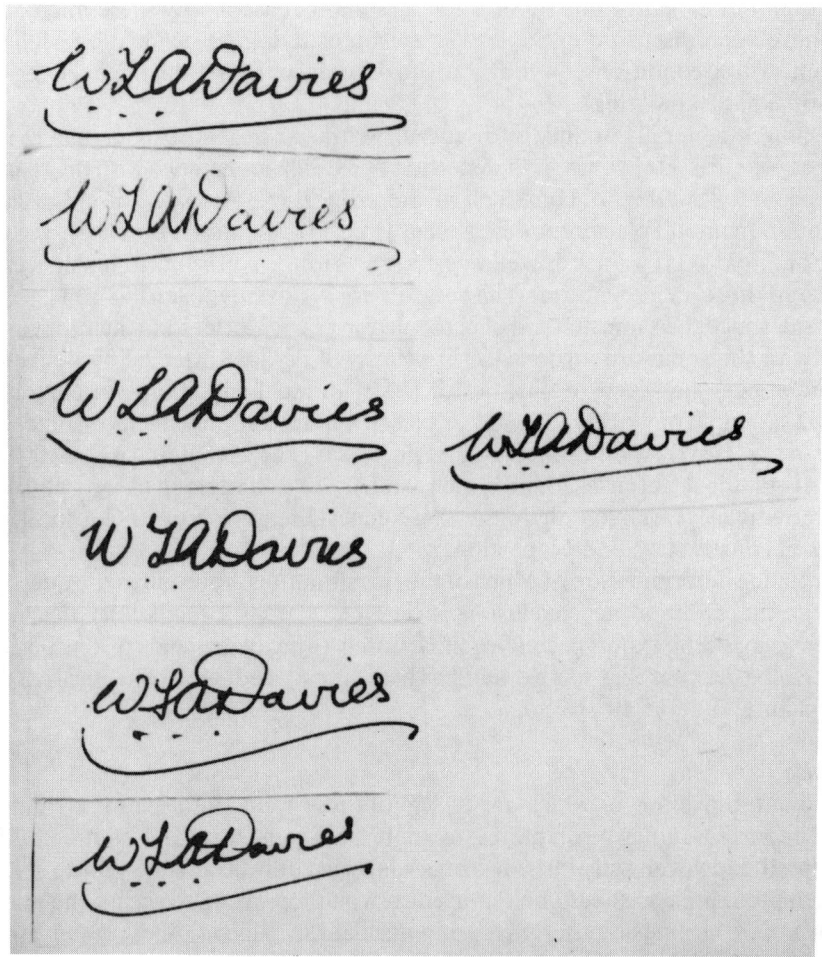

Fig. 5 — On the right hand side of the picture a genuine signature is shown. On the left are two attempts at a freehand simulation made by three different people. Note (1) the inaccuracies, (2) the poor line quality and (3) the similarities of the deviations from the genuine letter D within each pair.

This, however, is a simplification of the position. The natural variations found in the writings of one person can be mistaken for evidence of simulation. If inadequate samples of signatures known to have been written by the person whose signature is in question are available for comparison, the whole range of variation will not be apparent to the examiner. This means that what appear to be significant differences due to inaccuracies in copying may be variations not represented in the known writings. It is not possible to say what is the minimum number of signatures needed to establish the range of variation, but between ten and twenty made over a period preferably including the time of the signature in question are usually adequate, but fewer could be sufficient if there is clear evidence of simulation in the suspect writing, or consistency of difference between a number of simulations and the genuine signatures.

When significant differences typical of those found when signatures or other writings are copied are discovered in a questioned signature, and are not present in any of an adequate number of those known to be genuine, it can safely be concluded that the signature is not the normal signature of the subject. If it also shows a clear overall similarity to the genuine signatures, too close to have arisen by chance match, it can be reported as a simulation, and that there is no evidence that it was made by the writer of the genuine signature.

In such cases it is usually unwise to report that because it is a simulation it was not made by the person whose writing has been simulated. Although it is not uncommon for a person to write a signature with the intention of later denying it, he will usually adopt a more obvious method to disguise his writing. While the more usual method of simulation, by another person, seeks to match the writing being copied as closely as possible, the person 'simulating' his own writing will normally make sure that he can point out a difference when he later claims not to have made the writing. However, this is not always the case. There is nothing to stop him adopting the usual methods of simulating writing, including tracing, when writing a signature later to be denied. It is for the document examiner to point out the possibility of these practices, but as with writings which are both natural and different, he is not able to be certain that the simulated writing was not made by the apparent victim.

There are exceptions to this; a clearly superior standard of writing in a simulation may show that the questioned signature could not have been made by the person who should have written it.

Qualified conclusions
Not every simulation has clear evidence of poor line quality, retouching, and those other 'classic' features which demonstrate its deception. Others, especially those made when copying simple short signatures, may have a line quality not very different from the genuine signature and be formed without pen lifts, retouchings, or tracing. In these cases it may not be possible to say with a high degree of certainty that the questioned writing is a simulation, but, depending on the degree of inaccuracy which may be present, it may be possible to indicate that it is probably so.

If a number of questioned signatures are available for comparison and they show consistency in their differences from the genuine signatures, this will increase the evidence that they are simulations. In a single signature a departure from the genuine signatures available for comparison may be accidental, but in a number, especially if they are made on different occasions, any consistent differences are far more likely to be caused by a habitual error of the simulator.

Simulations or ill health

In other circumstances concerning writing of inferior quality a poor line quality could be mistaken for evidence of simulation, especially if some accidental differences are present. In cases where a signature of a person is affected by infirmity the same slowness and shakiness which are associated with copying are found. The most apparent difference between the two causes is that while the tremor of illness is even and of uniform amplitude, the poor line quality of a slowly moving pen attempting to reproduce the writing of another person is irregular and jerky. In addition, the resemblance in method of letter construction and proportions both within and between the letters is likely to be close to those in the known signatures if the questioned signature is genuine. It is more likely to be poor in a copy. However, a good copy may be difficult to detect in these circumstances, and a firm conclusion on the genuineness or otherwise of the signature may not be possible. In this event, a qualified answer may be given to the client or court.

In cases where signature are compared it is important to notice changes which may occur with passing time. Even without ill health playing a part, a person may modify his or her signatures gradually over a period of years or even months. After the onset of illness the signature may deteriorate rapidly. If a questioned signature is purported to have been written on a particular date, it is important to have material to compare which is contemporary with it, otherwise differences may be attributed to forgery when they are in fact caused by change of habit or failure of health.

Of course the copier might choose as his model a signature made at about the same time as that of the poorly formed signature of the invalid. This is particularly likely if he decides to forge a will which he dates near the end of the life of the testator. Here the simulation of a signature might be easier. Instead of the difficult task of trying to reproduce a smooth line and an evenly graduating curve he has to copy a poorly written signature with a shaky appearance. But the task is still not easy. The proportions of the poorly written genuine signature are more likely to be consistent with each other than with those of a copy. The frequency of oscillation of the line of writing is likely to be even, while the line quality of the copy will possibly break into a smoother phase if concentration lapses. Such a smooth line could not be written by the genuine writer in his condition.

Traced writings

A common form of simulation is by tracing. The traced signature or, occasionally, other writings may be associated with guide lines such as indented impressions or graphite or impressions from carbon paper (see Fig. 6). Examination under oblique lighting or by electrostatic methods will detect the impressions, and microscopical examination or the use of infrared radiation (see Chapter 7) will discover any graphite which may be present. Attempts to remove graphite guide lines by using an eraser may leave damage to the surface of the paper, and may smear the ink of the traced writing. The use of lycopodium powder may detect evidence of erasure. Examination for all these guide lines is therefore made, and their discovery is clear evidence for tracing.

There are, however, other considerations to be made. Some genuine signatures are written over light pencil writings made to indicate where the signatures are to be placed. To be sure that a signature has been traced, therefore, it is essential that the

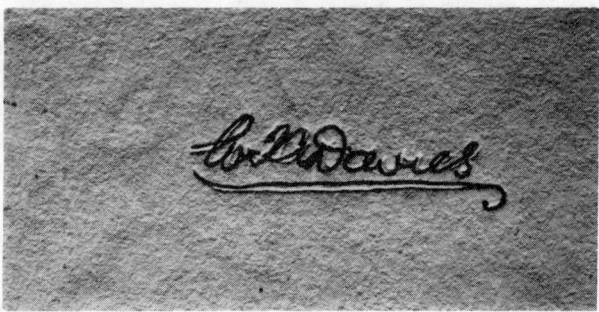

Fig. 6 — A signature traced from the same genuine signature shown in Fig. 5, photographed using oblique light. The indentations from which the signature has been traced can be clearly seen.

closeness of match between the signature and what appear to be guidelines is sufficient to rule out coincidence. There will always be places in a traced signature where the tracing does not coincide with the guide lines, but for the most part there is normally a close match. Care must also be taken to avoid erroneous conclusions when what appear to be written guide lines are discovered. Some pens when held at a certain angle will make indentations parallel to the line of writing, very near to it, and usually only on one side of the line. These are too closely associated with the written line to be regarded as indentations made before the line and subsequently followed, but there is some danger of a mistaken interpretation. Sometimes a defective pen will write with an uneven intensity of ink, a darker striation appearing within the line. This can be mistaken for a tracing line, but, again, it is too consistent in position for it to be a guide line.

It is sometimes the practice for genuine signatures to be made successively on a series of documents in a very similar position on the page. Indented impressions of one will then be found close to the next signature to be written. These could be wrongly thought to be guide lines. It would, however, be a remarkable coincidence if they matched at all closely; normally, they would be too far away from the written signature to be mistaken for guide lines. Some people write their signatures very consistently, but to find another signature whose impressions match both very closely in shape and in position, diverging only slightly from the written questioned signature, would be virtually impossible. In addition to the presence of guide lines, the line quality of the signature itself will be poor, similar to that of a slowly written freehand signature.

If a signature has been traced directly from another, no guide lines will be found round it. It may therefore be indistinguishable from a slowly written freehand signature. If, however, the signature from which it is copied is found, its origins will be established by the closeness of match and by the discovery of indented impressions associated with the original. Even without the original master signature, tracing can be established if two or more traced signatures are found which match each other too closely to be genuine.

Identification of the writer of simulations

Simulated writings can be compared with writings of people suspected of writing them, but only where the simulation has been unsuccessful and has not been accurately copied is there any evidence of the natural writing of the copier. In a short piece of simulated writing such as a signature there is likely to be very little if any evidence to indicate who wrote it, especially if it has been made slowly. With longer passages of writing there is a greater chance of finding characteristics of the writer. If the writing being copied is deficient in some letters of the alphabet the copier will probably use his own writing of them to complete the simulation. In such cases there is a considerable difference between some letters which match those of the known writings and those which are totally different, because they are based on the writings being copied.

Traced writings are unlikely to show any evidence of the writing of the tracer. Nevertheless, the discovery of the signature which has been traced will be of considerable importance; it may indicate with certainty who made the tracing from it.

Freehand simulations of a signature made by one person will generally be found to be consistent with each other, differing both from the copied signature and simulations of the same genuine signature made by other people. This is not only because the copier may leave evidence of his own writing, but also because people appear to be consistent in the way they make copy writings (see Fig. 5).

When a number of transactions are made by several people using the same stolen credit card the simulations on the vouchers can be placed into clearly defined groups, each group containing copies made by one writer. In these cases the variations are not necessarily related to the writing characteristics of the forgers, but rather to their methods and skill in simulation.

INCONCLUSIVE EXAMINATIONS

In many cases, where only a small amount of writing is presented to the examiner, little of value can be deduced, or the evidence is totally inconclusive. There is no reason why the handwriting expert should not state that the evidence is insufficient for any useful conclusion. If he is unable to indicate in which direction the truth lies it is right that he does not give vent to his suspicions or his feeling about the matter. When there is no hard evidence either way no conclusion should be given.

COMPLEXITIES OF HANDWRITING COMPARISONS

In many cases a comparison between one piece of questioned handwriting and one sample of known writing is all that is required. In other cases there may be a number of documents, sometimes very many, each with writing to be compared. A further difficulty could be that each document has more than one entry on it, and different writers have made them. There may be more than one suspect, indeed in some cases a large number. These cases require more than a simple comparison; they require management as well.

In the experience of every document examiner there are cases where the information with which he has been supplied is inaccurate. He may be told, usually in good faith, that a particular document bears the writing of a certain person, but finds later that this is not so. The investigator may not have taken sufficient care to ensure that because writing is found in a certain place it is by a particular person. It is therefore a sensible precaution for the examiner to compare all his known writings with each other before comparing them with the questioned material. This need not take a long time; it will usually be quickly apparent if writings are not consistent in themselves.

Inconsistent known writings

It is not always easy to be sure that two apparently different writings described as known writings of one person are not by different people. In the first place, as has been referred to earlier, some people can write naturally in more than one style. Secondly, if an effective disguise has been employed in the samples given on request, these may be very different from the course of business writings. In cases where there is doubt that the known writings are not by one person the examiner should return to the investigator and ask how sure he is of the authorship of the writings. If the complication is not cleared up by this action the questioned writings should be compared separately with each batch of 'known' writings. If the 'known' writings are by different people, only those which can be attributed to the subject with certainty will be of value in the investigation.

In any one document it is possible that the writings are by a number of different people. An address book or a diary may include entries written by various writers, and this may cause problems in establishing what are truly known writings. The same considerations can apply to questioned writings. If there are original entries to which are added small amounts of writing, the additions may not be so different that it is apparent that they are by another writer. They can then confuse the comparison of the whole. In some cases the additions will be made with a different ink and can therefore be recognised as not part of the original. It is a wise precaution to use the methods involving absorption and fluorescence of infrared radiation, described elsewhere in this book, to investigate this possibility.

Complex cases

In complex cases involving many documents there is much to be gained by comparing the questioned writings with each other before comparing the whole with the known writings. Although there is a danger that some of them may not be used in later proceedings and therefore may not be available then, this exercise is worthwhile. In the investigation of a large cheque fraud involving a number of cheque books it may be found that one writer has varied his writing to match the signatures which he has simulated. Despite these differences the detail is likely to be similar, and there will be much in common between the writings of each book. They will share the same words, figures, and layout. Cheques which in themselves show little resemblance to the known writing may be positively connected through others when it is clear that all are by one writer.

Signatures are often treated separately from other writings on a questioned document when being compared with known writings. Often an attempt is made to simulate the signature of the loser while the rest of the writing is written naturally.

Evidence of the writer is then found only in the main body of the writing. It is normally not possible in these cases to find appreciable evidence in the simulated signature for any indication to be given as to whether the writer of the rest of the writing was responsible for the simulation or whether another person made it. In other cases, where no simulation has taken place and the signature and the other writings are consistent in themselves, they can be regarded as one piece of writing.

Sometimes in a large fraud the perpetrator will use a variety of different names and will leave his writing in small quantities on many documents. Provided that there is clear evidence of a connection between all these fragments of writing they can be accumulated and compared as a whole with the known writing. If they, both in parts and together, are found to match the known writing, an identification may be made despite the fact that this would not have been possible with only one signature. The reason for this is that, although coincidence could not be ruled out with any one signature, it can be if all are taken together. If objection is made to this assumption then the only other possibility is that a series of different people, who all write in a manner very similar to the known writings, are responsible. This too is not a viable explanation, and only one conclusion, that of common authorship, remains, provided that simulation has been ruled out.

Multiple suspects

There are occasions when it is necessary to compare a particular piece of writing with known writings of many people, all of whom might be possible suspects. This has been done in the United Kingdom in several murder investigations, when the writer was thought to come from a particular location. Thousands of samples were gathered, and compared with the questioned writing. To do this, certain features of the writing were chosen, and only these were compared. If they did not match, the sample was discarded. It would have been impossible and unnecessary for more than this to be done. If the features matched, the writings were compared more fully. Although the culprits were not detected by this means, they would have been had their writings been in the samples originally examined. In two of the cases the writers were found by other means, and their writings were identified with the questioned documents [10].

PHOTOCOPIED WRITING

Difficulties can arise in handwriting comparisons for reasons other than complexity. So far, only writing written directly on to paper has been considered, but it is often reproduced by some photographic method such as the photocopying process. Although some of the detail will not be apparent, in many examples of good quality photocopies there will be adequate material for a useful comparison to be made. What will not be reproduced are indented impressions which have been used as guide lines in a simulated signature. Similarly, erased pencil lines will not be detectable. However, provided that these possibilities are allowed for, there is no reason why an appropriate conclusion should not be reached. If sufficient detail is visible on the photocopy, much can be adduced. It is possible to identify photocopied writing as having been made by the known writer. Care must be taken to distinguish between the writing and the document on which it appears to be written. The writing could be genuine but the document may not. The photocopy could be a composite of two or more documents, and so the writing appears in a context different from that in which it was written. This is especially true when a genuine signature is photocopied on to a fraudulent letter. This process is dealt with elsewhere in this book (Chapter 8).

Similar situations of 'secondhand' writings occur in prints from microfilm, carbon copied writing, and indented impressions detected by oblique lighting or by electrostatic detection. In all these processes it is possible in some cases to find enough detail for identification to be made, but in other cases there will be insufficient. In particular, with carbon writings of poor quality it may not be possible to rule out the possibility that the writing has been traced from a previously written model. When sufficient precautions are taken to allow for the possibilities of error, useful evidence can be obtained. It is unwise to reject photocopies, carbon copies, photographs, or any other reproduction without attempting to discover what evidence they contain.

UNFAMILIAR SCRIPTS

Document examiners normally work on writings in their own language, and have little difficulty in recognising each letter; they can refer to their experience of variation found within and between writings of styles familiar to them. When writings originating from other countries are examined, even though they may be in the same language, features which are common in that culture could mistakenly be thought to be unusual. A greater difficulty arises when unfamiliar languages are encountered. Although many of the features found will be recognisable as untypical of writings with which he is familiar, he will be unaware of which of those features are common or uncommon in that style. In these cases caution must be exercised so that what may be considered unusual is not given too great weight.

If the script as well as the language is unfamiliar to the examiner, he will require both the assistance of an interpreter to enable him to recognise the letters of the alphabet and a number of different writings in the same script to enable him to assess the variation found in them. Although he is unlikely to be able to identify any unusual or characteristic features, some estimation of the likelihood of coincidental match can be obtained from such a study. Writers in any language or script show the same sort of variations within and between their writings.

Similarly, the methods of simulation are the same in any language or script. The same evidence of poor line quality, inaccuracy, and other features described earlier are found because the same reasons for them apply. In addition, tracing may be used, and guide lines and other evidence for this can be found. Again, even with stylised signatures where every letter of the name is not written, the assistance of a translator to identify letters which are present is desirable.

STATEMENT

Having reached his conclusion the forensic document examiner has to report it. This can be done verbally, or informally in a report or a letter, but for possible litigation a statement or affidavit is prepared. Statements are normally made in the first person.

Unlike scientific papers and reports where the passive mood is used, the court requires the witness to take personal responsibility for what is said. The conclusion must begin with the personal pronoun. Statements and affidavits, therefore, must be worded in the same way, and reports not intended for submission directly to the court are best worded similarly.

It is necessary in testimony, and therefore in statements, to indicate that the witness has some grounds for being allowed to give expert evidence. His qualifications should therefore be stated. Academic attainments and length of experience in the examination of handwriting are usually of interest to the court. Some examiners add that they have published papers, attended conferences, and presented lectures. None of these guarantees that the expert is competent; even length of experience is not a certain indication of this. Those employed in forensic science laboratories usually put less on the statement than those practising independently; the reputation of the laboratory may be accepted as a guide to the validity of the witness.

Having introduced himself as one whose conclusions should be taken note of, the substantial part of the statement begins. This may be long or short depending on the need of the recipient. One method of writing a statement is to describe in considerable detail all the features found and their significance. The conclusion is then added at the end. In others the findings are summarised briefly and the conclusion added. If photographic charts, which are dealt with more fully in Chapter 11, are used, their content may be described in great detail. Alternatively, they may be briefly referred to, and the description of the features found be reserved for the court, should it be necessary.

Expressing conclusions

The most important part of any report or statement of findings of a handwriting examination is the conclusion. It is imperative that this is clearly expressed and is not written in a way that can be misunderstood. The conclusion of an expert witness is referred to in court as an opinion. The word has a meaning special to the legal process: experts giving evidence deliver an opinion. Its meaning is different from that normally used outside the confines of a court and its surroundings. To have an opinion about anything, a play, a musical performance, the views and actions of a politician, or whether or not it will rain shortly, is a prerogative of anyone. The opinion of one person will differ from that of another; everyone feels that he or she is entitled to his or her own opinion, whatever anyone else may think. This use of the word 'opinion' should not be confused with that of the expert witness in court, either by the witness or by the receiver of the report.

The technical term 'opinion' in court is synonymous with 'conclusion'. Whether that conclusion is firm or qualified, it is the expert opinion of the witness. Unlike the wider use, it does not convey a degree of doubt implied in the phrase 'it is only a matter of opinion'. This is not always realised by the writer of the report or lawyers reading it. Although the phrase 'in my opinion' followed by the result of the examination is a perfectly adequate method of expression, the fact that misunderstanding may take place as to its meaning is good reason to avoid it. Otherwise it might be confused with the opinions of those who regularly predict the winners of races in the newspapers. It is best to use the expression 'I concluded that . . .' or 'It is my conclusion that . . .'. This is less likely to be misunderstood.

Qualified conclusions

There is some difference of view between those who practise forensic document examination as to how handwriting conclusions should be reported. All who compare handwritings are agreed that they should report that, where the evidence warrants it, the two writings were written by one person. They are also agreed that comparisons of totally different writings should be reported as such. Where they disagree is in those grey areas where the evidence is insufficient for identity and not so clearly different to indicate that there is no connection between them. There is a school of thought that holds the view that all these comparisons should be reported as inconclusive. In other words, if the evidence is sufficient for an identification or is totally negative, this should be reported; if not, no conclusion should be offered.

The positive, negative, inconclusive method of comparison is attractive in its simplicity. The same method is normally applied to fingerprint examination where an identification is reported when a fixed number of characteristics is found. No problems exist in explaining what is meant by any uncertainty in the conclusion, and the amount of work can be reduced as soon as it is realised that the evidence will not reach that required for identification. The client receiving the report may not be interested in half measures. With an identification he can take some action; with anything less he can do nothing. In some countries the courts will not accept any conclusion which is qualified by an expression of uncertainty.

Another method of expressing conclusions is one usually favoured by those working as part of forensic science laboratories where comparisons of other materials such as glass, paint, fibres, and blood are also made. In most of these fields it is usually not possible to identify the source of a transferred trace with certainty. The variation in their populations is rarely sufficiently great to exclude a chance match. Nevertheless, useful evidence is provided if traces of these materials are transferred to or from the scene of a crime. The fact that the traces can be shown to be consistent with the source rather than positively identified with it is of considerable use to the investigator and the court. To ignore it because it was not completely certain would be to throw away significant evidence.

In the same way, handwriting which is not able to provide conclusive proof of its origin should not be ignored. There will be cases where the evidence is insufficient to give any indication, but in many there will be good reason to believe that the questioned writing was written by the writer of the known writing even though this is not certain. To say that this is inconclusive, although true, is not the whole truth. The fact that there is some indication of who wrote it should be reported in terms that express the strength of the evidence. If the court chooses not to use it, that is its right, but not to offer what can be said, merely because it is not in itself conclusive, is to deprive the investigator or the court of information which they might find of value.

Where there is evidence that handwriting is likely but not certain to be by a defendant, and there is other evidence such as a visual identification which requires corroboration, the handwriting will provide this. In virtually every circumstance and every court hearing there will be more than one piece of evidence. That of the handwriting expert, whether conclusive or not, will provide a part of the total testimony in the case. It could be a substantial part or merely a small piece of corroboration, depending on the strength of the conclusion and the weight of the other evidence. In some cases a qualified indication may be given that the questioned writing was written not by the defendant but by, say, a prosecution witness who has denied it. If this evidence is ignored because it is not completely positive the defendant will be denied justice.

Scales of conclusions

To express conclusions of varying degrees of certainty, appropriate words need to be chosen to convey the meaning intended by the examiner to the reader of the statement or to the court. The range of conclusions could, if quantitative measurements were possible, be numbered between 0 and 100, or with greater discrimination between 0 and 1000. This, however, is not possible. No such numerical precision is available in the assessment of the probability of coincidental match as it is in blood grouping, nor is it available in the calculation of the likelihood of simulation. Instead, the document examiner will use the words he considers most appropriate to the conclusion he has reached.

There is not much to be gained from using a large number of expressions giving finely distinguished differences between conclusions. It is better to keep to relatively few categories so that each will represent a range of degrees of certainty rather than a point. There are two reasons for this. The first is that it is not possible to assess a point on a scale or within a narrow range with sufficient accuracy. The second is that, if two different conclusions are expressed in terms which make only fine distinctions between them, the differences will make little impact on the court. It is better to confine the expression of conclusions to a short scale where different words represent real differences from each other.

The various terms used to express degrees of certainty in handwriting conclusions can therefore be summarised into a scale, each place on which represents a different level of certainty of the identity of the source of the questioned material. Although there is some variation between document examiners in the terms in which they word their conclusions, most use a short scale of perhaps five or six points, expressing identification, a high degree of probability, a lower degree of probability, an area where no conclusion of any value can be given, and a negative conclusion. If genuineness or simulation is the issue, a different scale indicating near-certainty, probability of genuineness, total uncertainty, probability of simulation, and near-certainty of simulation is commonly used.

Clarity of expression

When expressing any qualified conclusion it will be apparent that more than one possibility is allowed for, although one is more likely than the other or others. It will make the report more clear to those for whom it is written if these are spelt out and the greater probability of one rather than the others is stated. For instance, if the conclusion that there is a high probability that the writings are by one person, the converse is that coincidental match cannot be ruled out but is nevertheless very unlikely. This should be referred to in the interests of clarity in the report.

In any report the most important factors are that it should be accurate and understandable. There may be good reasons to give an account of the similarities and differences found in great detail. If this is so it should be done without recourse to unnecessary technical terms. These may sound impressive, and some experts will use them merely because of that, but it is far better that the report is understood. If technical expressions are employed they should be explained immediately.

In many legal systems evidence is allowed to be read if both sides agree. There are advantages in this in that no time is wasted giving undisputed testimony, but some of the impact may be lost if the statement is read by a court officer with no interest in, or no understanding of it. To counter this it is important that the statement is clear, understandable, unambiguous, and incapable of being misinterpreted.

FURTHER READING

[1] Baxendale, D. & Renshaw, I. D. (1979) Large scale searching of handwriting samples *Journal of the Forensic Science Society* **19** 245

[2] Brandt, V. (1977) The significance of partial handwriting features in location of an author *Kriminalistik* **11** 489

[3] Cabanne, R. A. (1975) The Clifford Irving hoax of the Howard Hughes autobiography *Journal of Forensic Sciences* **20** 5

[4] Cole, A. (1980) The search for certainty and the use of probability *Journal of Forensic Sciences* **25** 826

[5] Ellen, D. M. (1979) The expression of conclusions in handwriting examinations *Canadian Society of Forensic Science Journal* **12** 117

[6] Galbraith, N. G. (1981) Initials: a question of identity *Forensic Science International* **18** 13

[7] Gencavage, J. S. (1987) Recognition and identification of multiple authorship *Journal of Forensic Sciences* **32** 130

[8] Hanna, G. A. (1988) Microfilm documents: what are the boundaries in document examination? *Journal of Forensic Sciences* **33** 154

[9] Harris, J. J. (1986) The document evidence and some other observations about the Howard R. Hughes 'Mormon will' contest *Journal of Forensic Sciences* **31** 365

[10] Harvey, R. & Mitchell, R. M. (1973) The Nicola Brazier murder. The role of handwriting in large scale investigation *Journal of Forensic Sciences* **13** 157

[11] Hilton, O. (1952) Can the forger be identified from his handwriting? *Journal of Criminal Law, Criminology and Police Sciences* **43** 547

[12] Hilton, O. (1970) Identification of numerals *International Criminal Police Review* **241** 245

[13] Hilton, O. (1983) How individual are personal writing habits? *Journal of Forensic Sciences* **28** 683

[14] Hilton, O. (1987) Line quality — historic and contemporary views *Journal of Forensic Sciences* **32** 118

[15] Huber, R. A. (1978) The treatment of evidence in law and science *Canadian Forensic Science Society Journal* **11** 195

[16] Huber, R. A. (1980) The quandary of qualified opinions *Canadian Society of Forensic Science Journal* **13** 1

[17] Lindblom, B. (1983) Identifying characteristics in the handwriting of the visually impaired *Canadian Society of Forensic Science Journal* **16** 174

[18] McAlexander, T. V. (1977) The meaning of handwriting opinions *Journal of Police Science and Administration* **5** 43

[19] Masson, J. F. (1988) Depiciphering the handwriting of the recently blinded: a case study *Forensic Science International* **38** 161

[20] Moore, D. S. (1983) The importance of shading habits in handwriting identification *Journal of Forensic Sciences* **28** 278

[21] Muehlberger, R. J., Newman, K. W., Regent, J. & Wichmann, J. G. (1976) A statistical examination of selected handwriting characteristics *Journal of Forensic Sciences* **12** 206

[22] Purdy, D. C. (1982) The requirements of effective report writing for document examiners *Canadian Society of Forensic Science Journal* **15** 146

[23] Schima, K. (1977) Probability judgement and handwriting comparison *Kriminalistik* **9** 1

[24] Totty, R. N. (1981) A case of handwriting on an unusual surface *Journal of Forensic Science Society* **21** 349

[25] Vastrick, T. W. (1982) Illusions of tracing *Journal of Forensic Sciences* **27** 186

5

Handwriting — the collection of samples

INTRODUCTION

In the previous three chapters the technical aspects of the comparison of handwriting, its principles and methods were discussed. Here, consideration is given to what the document examiner needs in order to carry out his work effectively in the comparison of handwritings. Adequate authentic writings are vital to a successful examination.

KNOWN WRITINGS

The major use of forensic examination of handwriting is the comparison of the questioned writings with those known to be by certain people. The term universally applied to writings known to have been made by a particular person is 'known writing'. The epithet 'known' is transferred for convenience of expression from the writer to the writing. The acquisition of these standards may pose a number of difficulties to the investigator.

There are two essential requirements before any material is of use as a standard or specimen of known writing. One is that the writing must be adequate in quality and quantity for the examination to be carried out, and the other is that it can be proved to be by the person from whom it purports to originate. Depending on the circumstances of the investigation it may be easy or difficult to fulfil these conditions.

Request specimens

In criminal investigations, the suspect can be asked to provide samples of his handwriting. In many countries he cannot be forced to do so, but he may well decide that to refuse would not be for the best. It is common in the United Kingdom for people questioned about certain offences to give specimens without any objection. In these cases, no doubt exists about the origins of the writing; the police officer or investigator who takes them can authenticate them as having been made by the particular person.

When samples are taken there are two essential and easily remembered principles which have to be observed. It is necessary to compare like with like, and there must be adequate material.

Like with like

From the previous chapter it can be seen that the comparisons made are of each letter of the alphabet with each other. Nothing is gained by comparing letter ɑ with letter k. Similarly, there is no purpose in comparing a block capital A with a lower case cursive letter ɑ. Because each letter has to be compared it is important that all those present in the questioned writings are represented in the known writings. It is also important that figures are not forgotten. They, too, can provide useful evidence.

Besides the presence of actual letters in both writings there is advantage in comparison of other factors such as the joins between the letters, the spaces between words and lines and the layout of the words on the page. The latter includes the spacing of sentences and paragraphs, the size of the margins, and the position of the writing relative to printed words and lines which it follows. An example of the importance of layout comes in the writing out of cheques. The forms provided by the banks give spaces for the date, the payee, the amount in words and figures, and the signature. There is great variety in how these spaces can be filled. Writings can be started close to the left hand edge of the area allowed for the entry, or a gap can be left between the edge and the beginning of the writing. When a line is provided for them, writings or signatures may be well above the line or even partly below it, they might stay parallel to it, or slope away from it or towards it. Because these features might show significant similarities to or differences from the questioned writings, samples taken on a plain piece of paper with no guiding marks may lose some points of useful comparison. In the United Kingdom special forms which simulate cheques are used by police forces to enable samples to be taken which contain all these components as well as those of the handwriting itself.

Adequate material

The quantity of writing available for comparison is also of great importance. It is important to have adequate material, and it is easy for samples to be taken which do not provide this. Writings of one person are variable, not only because deliberate or accidental causes exist, but because human beings are not able to produce consistent results in the execution of such a complicated exercise. If adequate writings are not taken, the questioned writing may show what appear to be significant differences. Some writers use more than one form of a letter as well as a considerable variation in the proportions of a single form. If several or many examples of the subject's writing are available, there will be plenty of opportunity for the whole range to be exhibited. Writing given at the request of an investigator cannot, of course, contain all the variations used over a period in all the various conditions in which the person can write. Nevertheless, in the samples there may well be sufficient material for an identification to be made, if there is significant detail present which is similar to that of the questioned writing. It is in this detail that the greatest evidence for determining authorship lies.

Taking of samples

When samples of the writing of a person are taken it is necessary, then, to obtain adequate amounts of usefully comparable writing. Too little can be taken, but it is impossible to take too much. The subject should be asked to write the same wording as that in question in the same style of writing, block capitals, cursive, or disconnected script. He or she should be asked to write the required passage between five and ten times. The pen used could play some part in the quality of writing, and certain writing instruments should be avoided such as fibre-tipped pens which tend to make a rather wide line. A difficulty with this type of pen is that the ink of one line will sometimes merge with that of a line just written, which makes it hard to determine the movement of the pen when the writing is examined. The ball-point pen is the most widely used instrument, and is the best for taking samples. For the most part, the structure of the writing will be clear, and the subject will find no difficulty in using it. If the questioned writing is written with a particular type of pen, that type can be used for some of the samples; but, because a ball-point pen is generally better, samples should also be taken with one.

There are occasions when it may be necessary not to disclose that the particular questioned writing is under investigation, so that its wording cannot be copied. In these, rather unusual, cases it is useful to prepare a paragraph of sufficient length to contain the same letters or, preferably, words of the questioned writing. A more convenient method is to reproduce sections printed in a newspaper. Provided that a long enough passage is written, most, if not all, of the letters of the questioned writing will be in the samples. If figures are an important part of the writing suspected of having been written by the subject, the sports or financial pages of the newspaper will provide a source for them.

There is a temptation to use the phrase 'The quick brown fox jumps over the lazy dog' because it contains all the letters of the alphabet, but there is likely to be only one capital letter in the sentence. It may be of some use for samples of block capital writings, but generally it is inferior to the use of the same material as that in question. One passage to be avoided is 'Now is the time for all good men to come to the aid of the party'. There is little to be said for this. Again, it does not contain more than one capital, and a number of letters, b, j, and k, for instance, are missing. In both passages there is no opportunity to write numerals or other characters such as ampersands. Other passages have been devised to contain all the letters of the alphabet, both in capital and lower case form, several times. These tend to be rather lengthy but have undoubted value in their completeness. In most cases, however, like with like is the best policy, and the wording of the questioned document provides the most suitable material.

Avoidance of disguise
The person who is asked to give samples will sometimes think that if he disguises his writing he will confuse the expert making the comparison; on some occasions he will attempt to deceive the examiner whom he has engaged. People are very variable in their ability to disguise, and those who are not good at it provide few problems for the examiner. Others, however, can make their writing sufficiently different by introducing features which might also be found in the writing of another person. It is therefore advisable to avoid or counteract disguise if possible.

To change natural writing consistently requires concentration, and this is more difficult for longer periods than it is if it is necessary only to write a short passage. Therefore when samples of writing are taken a reasonable quantity should be obtained. Earlier, the questioned wording written five to ten times was recommended. If disguise is suspected by the investigator, and an unusual slowness or rapidity of execution is evidence of this, ten or more samples should be taken if possible. Another precaution is to remove the pages of samples as soon as they are written. Disguise is more effectively maintained if the altered forms chosen are copied from examples already written. Concentration can sometimes be broken by asking for a sample of writing which is not described as such. The subject can be asked to write his name and address and the date. He may then forget to apply his disguise. Although this may not provide much material for comparison, it may provide evidence that disguise has taken place in the main sample.

Other reasons may exist for the samples given on request to be unnatural; the subject may be nervous or uncomfortable. Steps should be taken to prevent this happening. There are two reasons for this apart from considerations of dignity and courteousness. One reason is that the most natural writing written by the subject sitting comfortably is the most useful for the proposed comparison. The other is that differences introduced deliberately might later be attributed to other factors. It is of value to be able to refute this as far as possible.

The wording of samples should be dictated to the subject. On no account should the questioned document be put in front of the writer for him to copy. Similarly, the wording should not be written by the investigator and given to the writer to copy. This will give him the opportunity to effect a disguise by copying not only the wording but the writing itself. Alternatively, he may not do so but later claim that the resemblances between the questioned writing and his samples are due to this. Typewritten or printed text can be used as a source from which the written passage can be copied, but again the style of the typeface could be imitated. The preferred method is that of dictation, even if it takes the investigator more time than do the other methods. The proper taking of samples is one of the most important facets of an inquiry involving handwriting, and it is well worth giving the attention needed to do it properly.

In cases where the subject is suspected of forging a signature or other writings, the samples taken should be of the name of the signature or of the wording of the questioned writing. It is pointless to try to get so close to the circumstances of the crime that the subject is asked to simulate the signature or other writing. The attempt is hardly likely to be authentic. Samples of his natural writings could be of value to compare with those places where the copying of the genuine writing is not accurate, rarely for signatures and more commonly for longer writings.

Samples of writing of the copied

In such cases where writing has been copied it is important to take samples from the person whose writing has been copied. This is clearly necessary to enable the examiner to compare the suspected simulation with what it should be, to look for significant differences in line quality and structure. In these cases, samples will be expected to be free of disguise; it is not likely that the victim of a forgery will obstruct the investigation.

Not every case of this type is recognised as such at an early stage. In one case the report that the writing on a cheque was different from that of the suspect surprised the investigator because he had strong evidence supporting his suspicion. A second cheque appeared on which the writing was also different, both from that of the first cheque and of the suspect. When the writings of the loser of the cheques were obtained the position became clearer. A good copy of the writing of the owner of the cheque as well as the signature had been made in each case. Although it did not indicate that the suspect had written the cheques, the evidence from the handwriting no longer pointed in the other direction.

After the enquiries into a criminal matter or one of interest to a civil court, comes the hearing. When one side suspects or seeks to prove that a document was written by a particular person, the other side may argue not that anyone else may have done it, but that one person or one of a small number was responsible. It is worthwhile, therefore, to anticipate this situation and test the hypothesis first. Samples of writing of those not suspected but who are possible perpetrators of the crime should be taken if their number is limited. This policy sometimes has surprising results. It is not necessarily the suspect that is found to be responsible. Recipients of anonymous letters, for instance, are sometimes the senders.

Course of business writings

It is not always possible to obtain suitable samples of writing of the people involved in an investigation by simply asking them to write whatever is requested. They may be dead, ill, or otherwise unobtainable; they may be unwilling or willing but able to disguise effectively. In any case the writings obtained on request may not represent the whole range of which each subject is capable. There are other sources of writing, made in the normal day-to-day activities, which will suffice and perhaps be better than samples given by dictation. These, referred to as 'course of business' writings, can play an important part in the enquiry and any subsequent hearing.

Sources

There are many sources of course of business writings. Not all of them will be available in any one case, and in some it will be impossible to find any. Police officers have greater powers than private investigators, and are in a better position to search for what is required. Among sources which have been used in criminal cases are passport application forms, driving licence applications, job applications, letters, diaries, account books, claims for reportedly lost payments, previously written cheques, witness statements, and bail forms.

Signatures

Signatures are important as known writings written in the course of business. A wide variety of these written without the knowledge that they may be later used as comparison material gives a better indication of the whole range of variation used by the writer than a small sample taken at one sitting. The documents listed above will provide useful sources for signatures, which can also be found on questionnaires, charge sheets, labels on exhibits, credit cards, and driving licences.

In some cases writings on documents which are themselves the subjects of offences are admitted by a suspect or are seen by a witness to have been made by that person. These can be used for comparison with further documents. A typical example of this occurs when a person is arrested or detained whilst writing a stolen cheque. One cheque in itself might be regarded as a minor fraud, but later other cheques from the same book as well as others from different accounts may come to light, all bearing the same writing. The comparison of this admitted or witnessed writing with that on the other cheques will be of value in establishing that a much more serious involvement in major fraud has taken place.

Similar frauds involve the repeated use of credit cards. Here the card may have been stolen unsigned or may have had its signature chemically removed. A signature, not of the loser but in the writing of the fraudsman, will then be added to enable it to be used. Comparison of all the vouchers used to obtain goods may indicate a close similarity between the signatures on them. If the culprit is caught signing one, the rest can be added to the charge, provided that the comparison provides a positive link. In other cases of this nature the previously written signature of the loser may be left on the card and simulated each time the card is used. Sometimes writing the signature accurately is assiduously practised, so that no great effort is needed to get a reasonable likeness. In these cases, although comparison is not of natural writings but of simulation with simulation, useful evidence of a single writer can be obtained. If another person copied the same signature the result is likely to be markedly different even if both were similar in overall appearance to the signature of the loser.

Practising of simulated signatures can provide important evidence. Attempts to get the simulation right are sometimes found by the investigating officer. The document examiner may be asked to comment on these in court. If he can establish them to be simulations, he can advise the court of their likely purpose. The court will be able to assess the significance in the light of other evidence.

Verification of course of business writings
Course of business writings taken as known writing for comparison purposes have to be established as such before the evidence is of any value to the court. It is not always written by the person who is most obvious. Sometimes a letter apparently by a man will be written by his wife. On occasions one person will write a letter for another to sign. In other cases it is clear from the content of the form or application who has completed it. The subject of the enquiry should be asked if the writing to be used as course of business known writing is his. It will often not occur to him to deny it; to do so might appear rather foolish if it is clearly by him. Nevertheless, his verbal admission will be of assistance to the court.

Care should be taken to ensure that the known writing is not by its nature inadmissible in court. References to previous offences may be disallowed because the jury could be influenced by them. Similarly, writings which are themselves the subject of previous offences already dealt with may not be allowed for the same reasons. Letters from prison will indicate a previous conviction, or else that the accused is remanded in custody. In these cases it is sometimes possible to use the writing without revealing its source. If photographic charts are used to demonstrate the findings of the expert the writings can be shown to the court without revealing its content.

Request and course of business writings
In both request samples and course of business writings there are advantages and disadvantages. Request samples can be easily proved to have come from the person in question, they can be of the right method of writing, and contain the right letters and words. They can, however, be disguised or refused, either completely or after only a small amount has been written. On the other hand, course of business writings

may be difficult to associate with their writer with a degree of certainty sufficient for a court to be satisfied, or they may be of the wrong type of script, for example, block capital not cursive writing. Their advantage is that they are likely to be natural, without any disguise, and possibly large in quantity. There is nothing to be gained in debating whether or not request samples are better than course of business writings; in most investigations it is much more useful to obtain both. In this way it can sometimes be shown that the request samples are disguised when this was not previously suspected or certain. By comparing the two sources, sufficient similarity may be found to show this, despite the differences caused by deliberate deception. This sample to sample comparison can be of value where the origin of course of business writing is not provable. It may be that it provides a link between the questioned writing and the disguised request samples. It is possible in certain cases to link two writings only by comparison with a third. There may be insufficient usefully comparable material between the two pieces of writing, but when each is separately compared to a third and larger sample there is enough in common to establish a common writer. Request and course of business writings are therefore complementary.

FURTHER READING

[1] Bohn, C. E. (1965) Admissibility of standard handwritings *Journal of Forensic Sciences* **10** 441

6

Typewriting and typescripts

INTRODUCTION

Typewriters have now been in existence well over a hundred years. After initial experimentation in manufacture, a standard form of typebar machine evolved and is still being made today. Alongside these basic models, different and more advanced designs have been introduced and some have become obsolete.

Electric typebar machines, those using interchangeable single elements in the shape of spheres or wheels, electronic typewriters, word processors, and computer controlled printers have given variety to the means of printing characters on paper in the home or office.

They can be used in circumstances of criminal activity or those of interest to civil courts, and the typed document can provide, over and above the content of what is typed, evidence of value to the investigator or court. Knowledge of the make of machine suspected of preparing a document may assist a police officer in locating the actual typewriter. A court may find that the fact that two documents were made by the same machine, or that a particular typewriter was used to type a letter is very significant.

The document examiner, using the scientific principles of observation and deduction, applying the appropriate tests, and comparing the results with the background corpus of knowledge on the subject, can provide answers to many of the questions asked by his clients.

The most significant features of typewritings of interest to the examiner are those which can be adduced from the document itself, the style and shape of the individual characters, and the spacing between them. These and other factors are considered in this chapter together with the methods used to examine them.

Typeface

The most familiar style found in typewritings is that used for many years by most manufacturers. Within this standard form there are differences in size and in design. Some differences found between the products of different makers are fairly large, and others more subtle. Typical of the larger variations are numerals which can include figure 2's with or without straight bases, 3's with flat or curved tops, and 4's which are either open or contain an enclosed triangle. Capital letters M and W can be made with the centre extending to the whole or to half of the height of the letter. Smaller differences found in lower case letters include the shape of the bottom of a letter ɑ and the length and position of the cross bar over the letter t.

There are other styles, which differ more radically. Typical of these are 'shaded' characters, which have differences in the width of the lines making up the letter, 'cubic' designs with rectangular shapes with rounded corners rather than circles, and designs resembling cursive handwriting.

All these designs can be mounted on typebars, moved manually or electrically, or on single elements, colloquially called 'golf balls' or 'daisy wheels' because of their appearance. These are easily removed from a machine and can be replaced by another using a different style.

Originally, the typeface was designed and made by the manufacturer of the typewriter. Now it may be supplied by a specialist producer for the manufacturer of the machine. Similarly, type wheels are often not made by the makers of the machines.

Letter spacing

Typewriters require a mechanism to ensure that the letters are properly spaced. The most common spacings are those where there are ten or twelve letters in an inch of typewriting. It is common practice for document examiners to refer to spacing not in characters per inch but as the length occupied by 100 characters. Thus typewriters which print ten characters to the inch, often known as 'pica' machines, have a spacing of 254 millimetres per 100 characters. Those with twelve characters to the inch, referred to as 'elite' typewriters, have a spacing of 212 millimetres per 100 characters. Similarly, other machines use spacings of 185, 200, 210, 220, 225, 230, 236, 250, and 260 millimetres. These can be found in manual and electric typebar machines as well as in single element typewriters.

Proportional spacing machines are based on units of spacing where letters occupy two, three, four, or five units, depending on their width. The units are typically 1/32 or 1/36 of an inch, producing results approximately equivalent to pica and elite spacings. More recently, word processors and electronic typewriters have brought right-hand justification to typewriting. This practice, normal in printing, varies the spacing so that each line begins and ends exactly below the one above. This is achieved by adding the required number of extra spaces between words in the line or adding a fraction of a space, spreading the added spacing evenly between the words on the line.

TYPEFACE COLLECTIONS

It may be of value to an investigator, when he is faced with a document bearing typewriting, to have some indication of its source. If he knows the make of the machine which made the typewriting he may be helped, particularly when confronted with a large number of machines in one building or room. It is therefore useful for the document examiner to have a collection of the typefaces of many different machines together with a system of classification which enables him to find the style in his collection which corresponds to that of the typewriting on the questioned document. The collection will also be of value as background information when a comparison of typewritings is made between questioned material and that of known origin.

A further advantage in ascertaining the make and model of the machine is that dating of a disputed piece of typewriting might be possible. If the date when a particular style or combination of style and spacing was introduced can be obtained from the manufacturer it can be shown whether or not a document could have been typed at a particular time. A number of systems, all based on differences in typeface and spacing, are used throughout the world, mostly by police forces or government agencies working in the investigation of crime. One operating in the United Kingdom employs a computer-based sorting method which can be operated from several terminals in different locations. The final comparison is made with hard copy of the typestyles in the collection [25]. Another system was produced by the International Criminal Police Organisation (Interpol). Cards containing the typestyles are sorted in order of letter spacing and features found in certain letters and numerals.

These systems enable the manufacturer and perhaps the model of the machine which typed the questioned document to be identified. However, as was discussed earlier, not every typewriter maker produces his own typeface. Some use that produced by a specialist manufacturer, such as Ransmeyer in Germany, and so there is a possibility that more than one company will use the same pattern. Similarly, printwheels are made by specialist manufacturers, and the same considerations apply. A further complication arises with some typeball machines which can use elements made by another typewriter company. This interchangeability of single elements will confuse an investigator who is looking for a particular brand name on all the typewriters which are possible sources of the typewriting in question.

Confusion can also be caused by the practice of mergers of companies in the office machinery business. Although the typestyle of a particular manufacturer may be unique to the company, the machines may be issued under different names. Olivetti and Underwood are two firms which combined, so much of the typeface found under one name is also found under the other. Similarly, the names Adler, Triumph, Royal, and Imperial are part of the same multinational group, and the same machines using the same range of typefaces and spacings will be found under all these names. In previous years these companies were independent, and their styles could be distinguished. It is therefore possible that the typewriter responsible for the material in question could be overlooked if the investigator is concentrating on one or two names and excludes those which he has not been given. Care must therefore be exercised to avoid the rejection of the machine which was responsible because it bears the wrong name.

IDENTIFICATION OF TYPEWRITING WITH A MACHINE

The most important evidence which can be deduced from the typescript on a document, apart from the information it conveys, is the identification of the actual machine which typed it. Clearly, this is of great significance in the investigation of a series of events or in a trial in a civil or criminal court. Any comparison made is normally of like with like, typewriting with typewriting. This is not always the case; a quick comparison can be made with the typeface on the machine. If clear differences are found, say a flat-topped 3 on the machine and one with a round top on the document, the typewriter or type element can be eliminated before any sample is taken. If no such difference is found, typewritings must be made to enable a more detailed comparison to be carried out.

When considering the comparison of typewritings, important points have to be borne in mind. In the typebar machine the typeface and the typewriter are to be regarded as one. In single element models, whether typeball or typewheel forms, there is both a machine and an element component in the typed material, so that what is found is a combination of the two. If all typewriters were made to a standard of absolute perfection and this were maintained as long as the machine was in operation, the results from the comparison of their products would be of limited value. A style could be identified, and the typewriting could be attributed to any one of a large number of machines. This is not found in practice. Variations from perfection are present in typebar machines, in the type elements, and in the mechanism of typewriters using those elements.

Although every manufacturer maintains a quality control over his machines, there will be tolerances within which there will be discernible differences. These may be too small to be of forensic significance. In many comparisons made in forensic science one source will produce variability. If this variation is as great as the differences found between sources, no significance can be placed on a comparison. Many of the small variations found between typewritings from different machines are no greater than those found within the product of one machine. Of greater significance are those features which develop during the lifetime of a typewriter — faults which occur from wear or damage. It is because these occur for the most part randomly that they are different for different typewriters.

Typewriter faults

There are a number of ways in which imperfections occur which will be apparent in the typescript. The first is damage to individual characters. The metal type can be chipped or bent in use, especially when two keys of a typebar machine are depressed together. The resultant collision between the two components can cause damage to one or both of them, and this will show on subsequent printed impressions. Damage is less prevalent in typeball machines, but small moulding defects can occur in manufacture, and these can appear on a typewritten page. Printwheel characters are also prone to damage, but, unlike distortions of the metal type of typebar machines which, once made, can remain unchanged indefinitely, the plastic material of typewheel elements deteriorates rapidly once its hard surface coating has been broken.

A second fault found in typewriters is misalignment of certain characters. When a typebar machine is manufactured the type metal pieces bearing the characters are soldered on to the ends of the bars. The consistency with which they are affixed is not perfect, and this results in small differences in the positioning of the printed characters relative to each other. Later, if a typebar is twisted or bent the impressions made by the characters on that bar will be misplaced. The divergence from the ideal position can be upwards, downwards, to the left or right, or at an angle, or a combination of two or more of these. Also, twisting will produce an uneven image. The character may be more heavily printed on one side than on the other, or heavier at the top or the bottom, depending on the distortion of the typebar. Looseness of the mechanism can produce variable results on the paper, with characters sometimes properly aligned and at other times out of position. In some machines there is considerable variation in the positions of all the keys, so that no consistent misalignment of a single character can be discovered.

In typeball machines, the movement of the ball in both a horizontal and a vertical direction will determine which character is printed. The mechanism which rotates the ball in either plane can be out of adjustment because of wear or damage. This will result in either a horizontal row or a vertical column being out of position at the time of printing. When this happens, all the characters on the row or column are misplaced to the same extent. This feature is produced by the machine and will still be found if another typeball is put in. On the other hand, damage to one of the teeth on the base of the element, the function of which is to position it properly with the mechanism of the machine, will also misplace a vertical row of characters. If the element is changed, the misalignment will disappear; if it is used on another machine the same defect will occur again.

With printwheel machines misalignments also occur. The spokes of the wheel may become distorted, giving displacement of the character. Unlike the conventional typebar machine, only one character will be out of position when this happens; only one is present on each spoke or 'petal'. Preliminary examination of some electronic 'daisywheel' machines suggests that their spacing is very consistent within machines and varies somewhat more between machines. The causes of the differences appear to be in the machine as well as in the element.

Other faults

There are other ways in which less than perfect results are obtained from typewriters. The characters may be dirty, so that what should be an uninked circle in a letter is printed as a solid one. This is clearly a temporary condition which can be easily corrected by cleaning. The shift key mechanism can move too far or not far enough, resulting in capital letters and other characters being higher or lower than they should. The mechanism holding the paper may be loose so that the lines of typescript are unevenly separated. The platen may be out of position, making all the characters print heavily at the top or bottom. The mechanism which moves the platen to space the letters can 'misfire' occasionally, giving either a gap between characters or two letters crowding on each other. In electric machines using typebars the adjustment for pressure of one or more characters may be different from that of the rest, so that they print consistently more heavily or more lightly. The alignment of the ribbon in the typewriter might be defective, giving either a cutting off of the top or bottom of all the characters, as opposed to damage of certain individual typefaces, or a mixture of black and red typescript if dual colour ribbon is used.

COMPARISON OF TYPESCRIPT

To reach a conclusion on typewritten material depends on careful and accurate comparison of the known and questioned typescript. The terms 'known' and 'questioned' refer, as in handwriting comparisons, to the origins of the material being compared. Known typewritings are those whose source is established either by other evidence or by the fact that they have been made by the investigator or the document examiner using the typewriter which is the subject of the enquiry, perhaps the property of the defendant in a criminal trial. The questioned document is the one of disputed origin.

Methods

Comparison of typescript can be performed in two ways. The first, as in the comparison of handwriting, is simply to observe the two documents side by side, noting each letter, figure, comma, question mark, pound or dollar sign, and all the other characters present to see if they match. At the same time, imperfections caused by damage are noted and compared. Observation is made of any clear misalignments present, and their consistency and the results noted. The whole picture, of similarities, significant features, differences and variables, is assessed and a conclusion reached. This is in many cases an adequate procedure for the purpose. In many comparisons the within-sample variation is quite considerable, caused by looseness in the mechanism of the typewriter, variation in the quality of the ribbon, and factors introduced by the typist. The features of significance noted in a side by side comparison are often sufficiently large to be compared accurately and noted so that properly arrived at conclusions can be reached. A more finely tuned examination would not necessarily reveal any more information other than the 'noise' of variable factors of no significance.

Grids

Frequently, however, more sensitive methods are needed. Small but significant differences in alignment may not be apparent by such methods, but they can be detected by the use of specially designed grids. These are glass plates or transparent plastic sheets marked with regularly spaced parallel vertical lines. The spacing of the lines on the grids is specially designed to fit the spacing chosen by typewriter manufacturers, 2.12 mm, 2.54 mm, 2.60 mm, and others. For proportional spacing machines the vertical lines are spaced in units where each represents between a half and a fifth of the space of the character, depending on its width. In addition, horizontal lines spaced at 4.25 mm, the normal single spacing for lines of typescript, are added. This produces a grid of small boxes each designed to be occupied by a character when the appropriate grid is placed over the typescript. The position of the character within the box gives a clear indication of the correctness or otherwise of its alignment.

When defects in alignment are present in typescript they are not always immediately apparent. It can be assumed that those characters not perfectly in position will be in the minority, and that the majority in the typed passage will be the normal from which some deviate. It is possible, however, that several characters will deviate in the same direction, so if they are all present in one word there will be no appearance of misalignment. If they form most of a word, the minority of properly spaced letters will appear to be out of position. Conversely, when two adjacent characters are misplaced in opposite directions their defective alignments will be accentuated. The apparently smaller differences from normal shown by those letters elsewhere in the passage could give the erroneous impression that the misalignment was inconsistent or variable. The use of a grid obviates this difficulty. Once the grid is placed so that the majority of the characters are properly in place, those which deviate can be discovered. Quite small misalignments can be detected and the consistency of the printing established.

The comparison projector

In some cases the use of a comparison projector can be of great value. This apparatus, which projects magnified images of two documents on to a screen, either simultaneously so that they are superimposed or alternately so they are viewed in quick succession in the same place, gives a very sensitive method of discovering similarities and differences. When the alternating image method is used, places where documents are identical appear still, as if only one sample is present. Differences are shown as an off-on variation where a feature is present on only one of the two documents or as an oscillating character where it is present on both documents but in a slightly different position. Differences in design or in damage to a character are easily detected even when they are small, and, if the same words are compared, variation in alignment of their letters shows up as an oscillation of those which are not perfectly in alignment with each other.

The sensitivity of the instrument is in some cases too great to be of value. Differences which are apparent can be those referred to earlier which are caused by variations in the mechanism or in the ribbon. If, however, the typewriter produces consistent results with little variation, images of the same word typed twice will appear steady, as if only one document were being observed. By contrast, if the same word typed on another machine is compared there is likely to be a clear difference noticed, with several letters oscillating to varying degrees.

Before any conclusions are reached from this examination, sufficient samples from the machine in question must be obtained to establish that it operates in a consistent way. If it does not, its own variations may well be as great as those between its products and those of another machine. When the outputs of consistently operating machines are examined, results superior to those of side by side observation or by the use of grids are obtained. In these cases, differences in alignment which are too small to be regarded as caused by wear or damage, because they are present on new machines and are therefore acceptable by the manufacturer and his customers, can be detected (see p. 164).

The significance of differences

The first task of the document examiner is to discover whether or not the two or more pieces of typescript are similar or whether they have any clear differences. If differences in spacing, in letter or figure design, or in other characters are found, if there is damage or misalignment on one sample and not in the other, or if a character, a figure 1 perhaps, is present on a document but is not available on the machine, there is an indication that the two samples do not have a common source. Before completely eliminating the possibility some care is needed; for one machine can produce different results for various reasons.

Obviously, if a single element machine is involved, a change of the typeball or printwheel will give very different results. In some typeball machines, the IBM 72 for instance, there is a facility to print at either ten or twelve letters to the inch. Similarly, many electronic typewriters using typewheels can produce typescript at more than two different spacings. Another spacing property is that of justification, giving an even right hand edge to a page of typescript, like that found in printing. Many electronic typewriters are equipped for both this and conventional typewriting.

If faults are found in one sample and not in that being compared with it, a single source is not necessarily ruled out. These differences could have developed over a period, so, if the later sample of typescript has a number of damaged or misplaced characters while the earlier one does not, it is possible that these features have developed between the typing of the two documents. If the reverse is true it is possible that the machine has been serviced and its alignment defects corrected.

All these points must be considered before any conclusion that two documents were not typed on one machine is reached. If the machine itself is available the task will not be difficult. It will be clear if it is a single element typewriter or not, and any dual or variable spacing capability it has will be apparent. Any replaced type is usually clearly recognisable by a different appearance of the shape of the block or in its soldering to the typebar. If the machine is not available, reference to a typeface collection will indicate whether or not the style is found on single element machines. Despite these considerations, in most cases differences of style, spacing, and damage are found to be due to a different machine having been used. The same applies if there are clear consistent differences in alignment of characters.

The significance of similarities

When two typescripts are found to match, that is when all the characters are found to be similar and when the letter spacings, both overall and individually, are the same, there is no evidence that more than one machine is involved. Although both could have been made by one typewriter, there may be other machines which could produce indistinguishable results. This possibility can be ruled out if there are sufficient features present which would not be expected to occur in exactly the same way in other machines. These features are the faults referred to earlier, both damaged characters and misalignments. Although any one fault could be found in more than one typewriter by coincidence, when a number occur together the chances of this becomes negligible. It is not reasonable to expect that damage and misalignment will occur in the same places in other machines. There are more than forty keys on a typewriter, each producing two characters and any one of these can be chipped or bent in a number of different ways. The odds against the same damage occurring by chance on the same character in two different machines are high, and higher still for two or more such faults. Not every piece of damage or misalignment is evenly probable; some are likely to occur more frequently than others, but study of faults found in a number of different typewriters has indicated that this basis of identification is sound.

Special considerations have to be taken into account in typeball machines. Here, with characters in rows and columns on the single element, misalignments do not occur randomly. While in typebar machines a fault in one letter would not make one in another more likely, with a 'golf ball' machine a single feature can affect a number of different characters. If a tooth, part of the mechanism for fixing the element to the machine, is broken away from the base of the ball, there will be a displacement of the four characters of one of the columns on it. These misalignments must be regarded as one fault, not four, and they indicate that any similar ball, similarly damaged, could have been used to make the typewriting.

The mechanism which rotates and tilts the ball to select the appropriate character can produce slightly different results in different machines. The distance travelled is not always exactly the same between different machines. This results in misalignment of a whole row or column of characters. Again, a misplacement of a row or column represents one fault not several, and is therefore less significant than it might at first appear [17].

Similarities with differences

The significance of differences has been discussed earlier. If they are present in style, or damage, or alignment between two samples of typescript, there may be reasons why they do not exclude the possibility of common origin. If two typewritings are similar and have faults, such as damage, in common which could not be explained except by the attribution of both to a common source, and if there are in addition certain differences present, the inference is that something must have happened which has caused these to occur in the time between the typing of the documents. Such an explanation is the only logical one if all the observations and comparisons are properly carried out. Greater confidence in the conclusion is gained if the typewriter can be examined to see if reasons for such variation are present or if they could have occurred because of the design of the machine. Another way of establishing that this is the explanation is to obtain typewritings which were made at the same time as the questioned document.

Dating of typewritings

Features which are present in one sample but not in another can be used to date the preparation of a typed document. If samples of the output of a machine made at regular intervals over a period are examined, the first occurrence of examples of damaged characters can be discovered. If new damage occurs fairly regularly, and in some machines this happens, there will be a changing pattern of faults. There may be occasions on which it is required to establish when a certain document was typed. If it is found that a fault is present on a certain document but not another, the period during which the situation existed can be discovered from the examination of the series of dated documents. Also, if repairs have been carried out, information about the date of typing can be obtained [14].

DOT MATRIX MACHINES

So far consideration has been given of machines using typefaces which leave their impressions on the document. Recently, the development of an entirely new method of typewriting has complicated the situation. Instead of producing a complete image of a letter or other character in one stroke, the shape is built up of individual dots. The matrix used to produce a character creates rows of columns, a rectangular pattern not unlike a miniature chess board. Instead of alternate black and white squares the areas are made black or white in the shape of the character to be printed.

In fact the areas are not squares but dots which are produced in a number of different ways.

The simplest method is to use a vertical column of pins mounted in a head which moves horizontally a space at a time. As it progresses, different combinations of pins project to strike the ribbon so that it marks the paper. If a letter L is being printed the first space employs all the pins and the next few use the bottom one only. This is a simplified description, because, depending on the complexity of the letter and the number of pins available, many different styles of lettering can be produced.

The same dot matrix principle is employed by ink jet printers which deliver a drop of ink to each appropriate point of the matrix. The positioning of the individual drops is controlled by variation in an electrostatic field. In another form of printing the pins on the matrix are either heated or not. A head containing the matrix is pressed on to a special ribbon which deposits a dot when a point of the matrix is heated, but does not do so when it is cold.

Dot matrix printers are used in association with computers to record, for instance, the data displayed on a video screen. They are, however, increasingly used for typewriters and word processing equipment. They are faster in operation than normal typewriters and are far more flexible in output because they can also print diagrams and graphs. Their operation is generated by electrical signals to the dot-producing areas of the head. The signals are controlled by computers which have in their memory a variety of styles in different sizes. The quality of the printing is determined by the number of points the head is capable of printing in a vertical line. The more of these there are, the greater the quality. In some heads there is a double column of pins which has the effect of filling in the gaps to produce better-looking lettering.

The examination of dot matrix printed documents
The appearance of lettering produced by dot matrix machines varies, depending on the number of positions in the matrix. In those which do not claim to be of high quality the dots are clearly visible, separate from each other. This does not necessarily mean that such a printer has been used; some conventional printers and word processors use a typeface made up of separate dots. When machines containing a larger number of dots are used these are less obvious but can be identified under the microscope especially on diagonal lines where the dots are more clearly seen.

The appearance of the material making up the dots is indicative of the method used to form them. Normal fabric ribbon is used for mechanically operated pins, while ink jet printers use a liquid ink which penetrates the paper surface. In contrast, heat-sensitive ribbon produces a deposit, not unlike the appearance of photocopy toner, which seems to be raised from the surface of the paper.

The shape of the characters and their spacing can be compared with that produced by the printer suspected of making them. If they do not match they could not come from that source, but if they do, that machine or a similar one could have been used. Some individualisation of a machine may be possible by examination of the alignment of the dots, their width, and their intensity, but these are characteristic of the head which can be replaced when defective. At the time of writing too little work has been done to establish whether or not there are other features which can be used to distinguish between similar machines.

Other methods of printing include a dot matrix printer which employs electrical sparks from points on the matrix which affects a metallic paper surface. These are mainly used in cash registers or similar machines; the special paper would be unsatisfactory for normal documents. The misalignment of the dots in an adding machine has provided useful evidence in one reported case [16].

A different principle is used in other computer controlled machines. A battery of four small roller ball pens each containing a different coloured ink is mounted in front of the platen holding the paper. Any one of the pens can be made to make contact with the paper while it is moved to 'draw' the appropriate character. Different styles and sizes can be selected and graphics produced. The method of production of machine writing is very flexible and inexpensive, and may increase in popularity. Microscopical examination of the products of this type of machine shows a characteristic pattern of continuous lines or elongated dots.

Large computer printers

Other and earlier forms of computer printers include those using conventional typeface. Instead of a machine containing one die for each character, these contain many. They are mounted either round a drum or on a chain. While the printer is operating the chain or drum rotates rapidly and the characters are printed by the type being struck on to the ribbon. Because the type is moving horizontally or vertically the printed characters are slightly smeared in a horizontal or vertical direction, depending on the type of printer.

Laser printers

The latest method of printing out 'typewritten' material is the laser printer. Whether or not a dot is printed is determined by whether or not a scanning laser beam is off or on at the appropriate point.

As in other matrix methods a variety of styles can be produced on the same document, and headed paper including the company's logo can be printed at the same time. As yet no clear method of identifying the particular printer which produced a document has been developed.

Laser printers have narrowed the distinction between typewriting and printing methods, and are also referred to in Chapter 8.

THE COLLECTION OF SAMPLES

The role of the investigator in cases involving the comparison of typescripts is important. The case may require either the identification of the source of the document with a particular machine or the connection of two or more typewritten documents with each other.

In most cases the acquisition of the typewriter itself is of advantage to the examiner, and, ultimately, to those for whom his conclusion is directed. There are a number of reasons for this. In the first place it is possible to discover all the characters which are present on the machine. A figure 1 appearing on the letter but not in the typeface on the typewriter will be sufficient to rule it out as a possible source of the typescript, unless a replacement of the key has been made, and this will show on examination of the machine. If a character is damaged it will be apparent when the typeface itself is examined, eliminating the possibility that an unusual design could be mistaken for a fault. Other faults, imperfect operation of various mechanisms, broken parts, misalignments, and wear can be detected at source and reasons for their effects on documents determined. The consistency of operation of the type-writer can be tested to discover whether or not variations are within the range produced by the machine or outside it. Other evidence provided by the ribbon, correcting tape, electronic memories, or other factors apart from the comparison of typescript can be deduced from the machine. These will be dealt with later, but they emphasise the desirability of the access of the examiner to the typewriter rather than merely samples from it.

If a single element machine is in question, any extra elements will need to be taken with the machine itself. However, when the machine cannot be removed, samples from it should be taken either using the ribbon, if it is in good condition, or a piece of carbon paper with the ribbon control in the stencil position. Provided that the carbon paper is new, this gives better results and does not destroy any evidence which the ribbon may yield. Another method is to replace the ribbon with a new one and take the samples with that. This can be unwise if a heavily inked fabric ribbon is substituted, because it can produce lines which are so thick that they obscure detail, but is a satisfactory method for 'carbon' ribbons which give a much clearer outline of the characters.

The samples taken should be of the entire keyboard, both with and without the operation of the shift key, so that upper and lower case letters, all the figures, punctuation marks, and other characters are recorded. As far as is possible the passage in question should be typed in the same layout as that being compared. This should be done four or five times so that the consistency of the output can be tested. It is important to identify the machine from which the samples have been taken, so the make, model, and serial number should be typed on each. Other material, known to have been typed on the machine, could provide possible valuable evidence if there has been a change over a period. Letters typed on or around the date of the document in question as well as others typed before and after this date are essential if it is necessary to show when the typescript was made. Variable factors such as dirty typeface and the condition of the ribbon, in addition to the combination of faults which have developed over a period, are important in these cases.

When many machines are possible sources of a typewritten document, the investigator may find that he can save both his time and that of the document examiner by looking for obvious features like the length of the centre of capital M's and W's, the top of the 3, and the shape of the 4. Provided that he is aware of the danger of missing the right element in single element machines, he can safely ignore those where these characters are clearly different.

CONNECTING FACTORS OTHER THAN TYPESCRIPT

Evidence to connect a piece of typescript with a typewriter can be provided by means other than by comparison of the typescript. The most important of these is by the examination of the ribbon, of which there are various types in use. The first and still the commonest, especially in cheaper machines, is the fabric ribbon. A strip of ink-soaked cotton or man-made material is struck by the typeface, the image of which is thereby printed on to the paper. The effect on the ribbon is to remove some of its ink, but the letter shape is not, or is rarely, permanently impressed upon it. Instead, the ink flows from around the impression to restore an even distribution. The effect on the typeface is to cover its surface with a layer of ink.

Some typewriters are provided with a mechanism to alter the position of the ribbon so that either the top and bottom half is struck by the typeface. This enables a two-coloured, usually red and black, ribbon to be used so that both colours can be employed on the typed document, When the change from a normal black typescript to a red one is made the back of the red half of the ribbon is struck with a typeface covered with black ink. So, as well as marking the paper with a red image of the characters, the typeface leaves its shape on the back of the red part of the ribbon. The words typed in red on the document are therefore left on the ribbon. This will apply only for a few strokes of each character, after which the black ink will have been removed from the typeface. The ribbon is designed to move both from right to left and from left to right, so, depending on that movement, the words may be reversed or the right way round.

'Carbon' film ribbons, those made of plastic material, depend on the shape of the letter being punched out by the typeface and pressed on to the paper. The effect is to give a sharp black clear typescript on the document and to leave a gap in the ribbon for each character typed, that gap exactly reproducing the shape of the letter. As the ribbon moves after each character the whole passage is recorded on the ribbon. Errors which have been typed and then corrected are also present, and underlining is found after the words which have been underlined. The ribbon which made the passage can therefore be identified. The value of this is, of course, great, but because the ribbon has a limited life and is thrown away the machine has to be discovered before this has happened. There can be another reason for the examination of the punched out letters. If the element has been removed deliberately to destroy evidence of its existence, the plastic ribbon can show the style of type which it possessed.

Carbon ribbons are packed in various ways, depending on the model for which they are designed. Originally, a single strip wide enough to take one row of letters was provided. This type is easy to read; the only problem is to discover where each word ends, because the ribbon is not moved when the space bar is depressed, so there is no gap between separate groups of characters. Cassettes are now the normal method of containing this type of ribbon because they provide a much easier method of replacement. These are often wider, with each bearing either two or three rows of characters along its length. Reading information from them entails examination of each column of two or three characters across the ribbon, followed by the next. This is a slow and tedious method, but in many cases it is of great value. The discovery of the contents of a questioned letter on the ribbon provides proof of its use.

It is not only on the black or red ribbon used to print typescript that evidence can be left. Some machines are fitted with correcting devices which work by substituting another ribbon which will either remove or cover the typed character. The first type employs an adhesive tape which will remove the letter-shaped piece of plastic which has just been typed. The second punches a piece of white plastic on top of the black character already there. In both cases the evidence is left on the ribbon, on one as black characters caught on the sticky tape like flies on fly paper, and on the other as character-shaped holes in the white plastic correcting ribbon. Only one or two characters are insufficient to indicate with certainty that the letter has been corrected by the ribbon, but a number in the correct order would be difficult or impossible to find by coincidence.

A similar method of correcting is provided by strips of paper prepared specially for the purpose. These are placed between the paper and the typeface, and the incorrect character typed over the error. The character is thus retyped in white (or other colour designed to match that of the paper) so that it covers the mistake, and the correction can be typed over it. As with the similar built-in correction ribbon the letter is punched out of the paper. If a number of alterations have been made on a single piece of correcting paper and they also occur in the questioned document, significant evidence is provided. In one case twelve such characters were found in a letter in dispute and also on a piece of correcting paper found with the suspected machine. The typeface match was without characteristic features, but the correcting paper provided the linking evidence. The odds against the same twelve letters occurring by chance are astronomical.

Ribbon composition
Typewriter ribbons are temporary fixtures and do not need to be substituted by identical replacements. This means that the fact that the ink of a ribbon in a machine differs from that on the paper does not exclude the machine from having typed a letter. Conversely, because ribbons are made in large numbers to carefully controlled standards there is little significance in a match. There is therefore little point in comparing the ink or plastic material on the paper with that on another document or in a ribbon on a typewriter. However, there may be occasions where this is of value, usually to find out if there are differences between two pieces of typescript which should have been typed at approximately the same time on the same machine.

As indicated earlier, there are two basic types of typewriter ribbon, one using ink and the other a carbon film. The two are clearly distinguishable under low-power magnification. To compare different types of ink the normal methods of examination of inks described in Chapter 7 can be employed. There is, however, a smaller range of variation in the products in general use than there is for inks found in pens.

A number of different manufacturers produce 'carbon' ribbons, and these can be distinguished on paper by microscopical means. The clearest separation of different types is obtained by using the scanning electron microscope (see p. 164).

ERASURE OF TYPEWRITING

Typewritten documents, like any others, are subject to alteration. One of the standard methods of correcting typing mistakes is to apply a special correcting fluid which when dried on the surface covers it with a layer of white or coloured material on which the correct characters can be added. Alterations to a document can be made with the material, and can be detected by a number of different methods.

As the paper of the document is likely to be thinner than the layer of dried correcting fluid, the best approach is from the back of the page. Strong lighting either through the page or directly on it is necessary. The materials can be made more transparent with the use of freon, 1,1,2-trichlorotrifluoroethane, an inert, volatile liquid which soaks into the paper and correcting fluid, making it translucent, and does not affect the typewriting. Examination of the soaked area must be made quickly because freon evaporates rapidly. There is, however, normally time for a photograph to be made, and the process can be repeated if necessary. The document is not permanently affected by this process.

Infrared or visible light luminescence can be effective in determining what has been obliterated by correcting fluid. Some inks may fluoresce and therefore be more easily visible. The laser provides an invaluable source of illumination for this. This method is particularly useful for ball-point pen and other writings obliterated with correcting fluid (see Chapter 7).

Typewritings are also erased by mechanical means, scraping the surface with a sharp blade or using a specially hard rubber eraser, for instance. Their indentations, examined under oblique light, or traces of ink remaining, or a combination of both, may be sufficient to identify what was erased.

In some cases the erased typewriting may fluoresce in the infrared or far red region of the spectrum. This appears to be because an invisible component of the ink has penetrated more deeply into the paper than have the visible pigments.

Typewritings made with carbon ribbons adhere to the surface of the paper and do not penetrate further. They can be removed with less abrasion than that required for typewritings made with inked fabric ribbons. This is especially true for those designed to be corrected by being lifted off with an in-built adhesive tape. The indentations remaining after characters from carbon ribbon have been erased are rather deeper than those found after erasure of typewritings made with inked ribbons, and they provide a means of identification of what was erased.

OTHER EXAMINATIONS OF TYPEWRITTEN DOCUMENTS

Besides the need to identify the make of machine or the particular machine which made a questioned document there are other questions to which the investigating officer or a court may require answers. The date when the typewriting was made, whether part of it was typed later than the rest, and who typed it are all subjects of enquiries directed to the document examiner.

Dating of typewritten documents

As with most dating problems in document examination there are great difficulties in giving an answer. Apart from general considerations such as that the typestyle or ribbon had not been produced before a certain date, little can be done. As discussed earlier, progressive damage to different characters can be of assistance, but the typescript itself on the paper does not change in any detectable way over a period unless it is subjected to some form of damage.

The best methods of timing are those where some reference is made to marks elsewhere on the paper. Folds, holes, or writings made before the typing will affect the printing of the characters in a way different from those when the typewriting is already on the paper. Typewriting made over a crease will not give an even coating on the rough edge of the broken fibres, but may, when examined under a micros-cope, appear broader and more deeply ingrained into the paper. Such differences are not very marked, in contrast to written strokes, and it is advisable to make test examples of typewriting before and after creasing to ensure that it is possible to distinguish between them. The sequencing of typewriting made over writing in 'wet' or ball-point ink can often be achieved with certainty. This is dealt with in Chapter 9.

Added typescript
Another method of determining the timing of two pieces of typewriting on the same document is in testing the consistency of alignment. It is sometimes alleged that a piece of typewriting was not present on a document when it was first seen, perhaps when it was signed. The suggestion is that it was added later for the purposes of deceit. To add extra typewriting to that already there, the paper has to be replaced in the machine and accurately aligned both vertically and horizontally. This is not so easy as it sounds. Although care will be taken to make the added portion appear in the correct position it will be difficult to ensure that it is exactly aligned. The apparatus of the document examiner, grids, methods of accurate measurement, and magnification, together with the greater ease of examination of a document in laboratory conditions compared with estimation of alignment in a typewriter, means that the task of correctly lining up the paper to leave no evidence that this has happened is very difficult.

To examine typewritten documents for this, the grids used for testing of the alignment of individual characters are invaluable. The main body of typescript is covered with the grid so that each character on a line is in position in its box with most of them centrally placed. Other lines will fall into place, or, if half spacing is employed, only alternate lines will be accurately positioned. Examination of the questioned passage will show whether or not its characters fall into the correct places in the grid.

Problems can arise if the document is creased. A fold can reduce the length of a sheet of paper and give the appearance that typewriting below it is out of alignment. This must be allowed for before any conclusions are arrived at.

Identification of a typist
There are a number of different methods of office practice taught in business schools to students of typing. These change with fashion or because of technical developments, and, like styles of handwriting, those taught will apply individuality to the basic pattern. There will therefore be a wide variation in the way a letter is typed. The spacing of lines, the size of the margins, the depth of indentation at the beginning of paragraphs, the number of spaces after full stops or commas, the use of capitals, are all variable and might be consistent in one typist. The touch of the typist can give an indication that he or she made the typewriting in question. This is particularly of value in those exceptional cases where a very heavy pressure has been used, sometimes to the extent that full stops and letters 'o' are punched out of the page.

All these factors will not be unique, even considered in combination, and will be related to how the operator was taught. They may, nevertheless, give some indication of who may have made the typewriting, or, conversely, who is unlikely to have done so. A person with no training in the proper methods of laying out a letter is unlikely to be able to type a well produced piece of typescript. Indications that a professional typist or one well practised has prepared a document may also be given if there is an absence of mistakes, or by the use of a small 'l' for figure '1' when that figure is present on the keyboard.

It is from the errors which are made that some indication of common authorship of two pieces of typewriting may be given. The figure '1' may cause problems for the unfamiliar typist who is quite likely to use a capital I. A similar frequency of errors, forgetting of spacing or of capitals, and other unusual factors may be found in two pieces of typewriting. There would need to be a number of such features before any conclusion that the two documents were typed by one person was stated. Many mistakes made by the amateur typist are shared by those of similar lack of skill. Some errors are particularly common, so the possibility of coincidental match cannot be ruled out.

However, in a limited population the evidence may be sufficient to pinpoint only one or two people who are likely to use a particular style of production. Of course it would be possible for another person to disguise his ability or to copy the errors of another person, so, as in any other investigation, all the possibilities have to be considered.

Comparisons between known and questioned typewritings to determine the identity of the typist are best made by using previously typed material which can be shown to have been made by the person suspected. It is difficult to take samples of typewriting on request.

Spelling mistakes, frequent use of certain words, unconventional punctuation, and similar features of the style of composition which may indicate a particular writer are also of value. The dividing line between these and the characteristics of text analysis is not clear. The latter is an area not normally considered, as within the expertise of the forensic document examiner. In any case such analyses require far larger passages than those usually encountered in the comparison of typescript. This is dealt with more fully in Chapter 2. The document examiner acting as an expert in court must keep to those factors about which his experience and background knowledge enable him to comment. As in all his work, it is by reference to his background corpus of knowledge that he is able to make decisions on the findings in any particular case.

FURTHER READING

[1] Allen, M. J. (1987) Dot-matrix printers *Forensic Science International* **38** 283
[2] Anthony, A. T. (1988) Letter quality impact printer hammer impressions *Journal of Forensic Sciences* **33** 779
[3] Behrendt, J. E. (1988) Class defects in print wheel typescript *Journal of Forensic Sciences* **33** 328
[4] Behrendt, J. E. & Meuhlberger, R. J. (1987) Printwheel typescript variations caused by the manufacturing process *Journal of Forensic Sciences* **32** 629
[5] Brunelle, R. L., Negri, J. R., Cantu, A. A. & Lyter, A. H. (1977) Comparison of typewriter ribbon and inks by thin layer chromatography *Journal of Forensic*

Sciences **22** 807

[6] Casey, M. A. & Purtell, D. J. (1975) IBM correcting Selectric typewriter. An analysis of the use of the correctable film ribbon in altering typewritten documents *Journal of Forensic Sciences* **21** 208

[7] Crown, D. A. (1968) Class characteristics of foreign typewriters and typefaces *Journal of Criminal Law, Criminology and Police Science* **59** 298

[8] Dawson, G. (1982) Identifying the typist of anonymous letters *Canadian Society of Forensic Science Journal* **15** 42

[9] Del Picchia, C. M. R. (1980) The mathematical determination of the number of copies of a typewritten document *Forensic Science International* **15** 141

[10] Estabrooks, C. B. (1983) Differentiation of printwheel and conventional typescript *Canadian Society of Forensic Science Journal* **16** 19

[11] Estabrooks, C. B. (1986) IBM Quietwriter *Canadian Society of Forensic Science Journal* **19** 251

[12] Fryd, C. F. M. (1974) The forensic examination of typewriting today *Medicine, Science and the Law* **14** 237

[13] Gayet, J. (1950, 1951) The individual identification of typewriting machines (3 parts) *International Criminal Police Review* **42** 301; **43** 340; **44** 21

[14] Hardcastle, R. A. (1986) Progressive damage to plastic printwheel typing elements *Forensic Science International* **30** 267

[15] Hilton, O. (1986) Problems in identifying work from printwheel typewriters *Forensic Science International* **30** 53

[16] Jones, D. G. (1981) A case involving the identification of an adding machine *Journal of the Forensic Science Society* **21** 351

[17] Leslie, A. G. (1977) Identification of the single element typewriter and type element *Canadian Society of Forensic Science Journal* **10** 87

[18] Leslie, A. G. & Stimpson, T. A. (1982) Identification of printout devices *Forensic Science International* **19** 11

[19] Levinson, J. (1979) Single element typewriters *Forensic Science International* **13** 15

[20] Mathyer, J. & Pfister, R. (1984) The examination of typewriter correctable carbon film ribbons *Forensic Science International* **25** 71

[21] Miller, A. L. (1984) An analysis of the identification value of defects in IBM Selectric typewriters *Journal of Forensic Sciences* **29** 624

[22] Noblett, M. G. (1987) Image processing and statistical analysis as an aid in the comparison of typewritten impressions *Journal of Forensic Sciences* **32** 963

[23] Nolan, P. J., England, M. & Davies, C. (1982) The examination of documents by scanning electron microscopy and X-ray spectrometry *Scanning Electron Microscopy* **II** 599

[24] Thornton, D., Totty, R. N., Hall, M. G., Harris, B. R. G. & Harris, J. A. (1980) A technique for the decipherment of entries obliterated by typewriter correction fluids *Journal of the Forensic Science Society* **20** 230

[25] Totty, R. N., Hall, M. G. & Hardcastle, R. A. (1982) A computer based system for the identification of unknown typestyles *Journal of the Forensic Science Society* **22** 65

[26] Waggoner, L. R. (1987) Examination of correction fluid obliterations *Journal of Forensic Sciences* **32** 539

[27] Winchester, J. M. (1980) Use of Projectina Universal Comparison Projector in comparing typewriting, photocopies and computer-printed and mechanically produced documents *Journal of Forensic Sciences* **25** 390

[28] Winchester, J. M. (1981) Computer-printed documents as part of a computer crime investigation *Journal of Forensic Sciences* **26** 730

7

The materials of handwritten documents — substances and techniques

In this chapter the substances from which documents are prepared and the techniques which are used to test these materials are considered. It is possible only to describe in outline the make-up of paper, inks, and other materials; discussion of the principles of the methods of their examination is also brief, but special processes and the apparatus required for their application are dealt with in Chapter 8.

Photocopy toners and printing inks are covered in Chapter 8, and typewriter ribbons are referred to in Chapter 6.

Paper

Most documents are based on paper, and those which are not are too rare to be considered here. Electronically stored information is likely to play an increasingly important part in administrative and financial activities, destined perhaps largely to replace conventional paper-based documents. The examination of this type of stored information, whether on tape or disc or in any other form, is not dealt with in this book. These areas are not regarded as the province of the forensic document examiner.

Manufacture of paper

Paper is made from pulped fibres which originate from wood, linen or cotton rag, esparto, hemp, or straw. To enable wood fibres to be used — and wood is the most common fibre constituent — it is first treated to break it down to a suitably fine pulp. This is done by mechanical or chemical means, a variety of chemicals being used for the process. The fibre pulp is mixed with a large quantity of water and other materials. These include size, which is made from gelatin, resins, or similarly effective materials which assist in binding the fibres, minerals such as kaolin to add weight, and dyes and 'whiteners' to achieve the right colour. The mixture is then passed over a frame where it loses much of its water and becomes a wet matted fibre mass spread evenly over the surface. The frame, which itself gives a characteristic wire pattern to the paper, may incorporate a 'dandy roll', or other devices to reduce the fibre content in an area with a recognisable shape. This produces a watermark, which will be more transparent than the rest of the paper.

The fibre mat is finally pressed and heated until it is dried. Some papers are specially coated to produce a surface suitable for the proposed use of the final product. After collection on a large roll the paper is cut to the required dimensions.

Testing of paper
The methods of manufacture described above give rise to differences in the end product which can be tested in the laboratory. Invaluable information can be obtained which allows different samples of paper to be compared and dated. In addition, it may be possible for the country of origin of a piece of paper to be discovered. Other techniques can determine what has happened to the paper after its manufacture, and thus provide useful guidance in the investigation of crime.

Some of the tests which are employed can be performed without damage to the specimen being tested, but others require the removal and destruction of a small part of the piece of paper.

Non-destructive tests
Most of the operations in the manufacture of paper provide features which can distinguish one type from another either by direct observation or by more elaborate techniques. Colour, shape, size, and thickness of the sheets, the watermark and 'laid' marks from the dandy roll and patterns produced by the frame, the appearance of the surface, which may be evenly coloured or mottled, can all be examined by simple observation and measurement. The 'feel' of the paper, how smooth it is or how stiff, can be ascertained by handling, and by the noise it makes when shaken. These apparently crude tests nevertheless have value in comparing two pieces of paper. They detect difference in make-up with a certainty as great as more sophisticated methods, and have the advantage that nothing is damaged or destroyed.

Fluorescence
When light falls on certain compounds and is absorbed it excites radiation at a higher wavelength. This is described as luminescence, which term embraces both fluorescence and phosphorescence; the former term referring to an immediate effect and the latter to one where the emitted light is delayed.

Fluorescence can also be tested without change to the paper. This phenomenon, of interest in many areas of document examination and other branches of forensic science, depends on the absorption of light and its simultaneous emission at a different wavelength. The eye is sensitive to a range of wavelengths, from about 400 nanometres (nm), which it sees as violet, to about 700 nm, which it sees as red. The wavelengths in between are seen as the other colours of the spectrum, and a combination of all is seen as white light. Ultraviolet radiation (UV), which as its name suggests is radiation beyond the violet end of the visible spectrum, has a wavelength between about 200 and 400 nm and will produce fluorescence in the visible part of the spectrum. Different substances fluoresce with different wavelengths and intensities. Under the ultraviolet lamp, some papers emit a strong luminescence, while in others it is weak or not present at all. There is a wide variety in the colours of the fluorescences excited by ultraviolet radiation by different papers, and subtle differences in shade can be easily detected. Similarly, fluorescence also occurs in the infrared region when papers are excited by radiation of shorter wavelength in the visible region. This can also be used to differentiate papers. Infrared is radiation with a wavelength greater than about 700 nm and is, like ultraviolet, out of the range to which the eye is sensitive. This type of fluorescence therefore cannot be seen by the eye, but can be detected by photographic and electronic means described later (see p. 106).

Destructive tests

Further tests can be carried out if a small amount of the paper can be removed. This may not be allowed if it is necessary for the document to remain undamaged, but the possible advantage of gaining extra information has to be weighed against the value of the document remaining intact. Usually, only small areas of paper need to be removed to determine the fibre type, the method of pulping, the dyes present, and the inorganic elements in the paper.

The first examination, known as 'fibre furnish', involves the breakdown of a portion of paper, using water or on occasions dilute acid or alkali, into a pulp in which the individual fibres can be examined microscopically. This enables the determination of the original method of pulp preparation (whether mechanical or chemical) to be determined, and different varieties of fibres to be identified. These can be materials such as cotton, grasses, and straw, and many varieties of fibres from different species of wood. Tests can also be performed to determine the chemicals used during manufacture to prepare the pulp from shredded wood.

Other tests determine the elemental composition of the paper, or identify the materials used for the surface coating. The scanning electron microscope in its analytical mode (see Chapter 10) can be used for the former, the X-ray diffraction for the latter. X-ray diffraction uses X-rays to indicate the crystalline structure of the material, which is characteristic of the compound.

Further techniques can be used on coloured paper. Thin layer chromatography and absorption spectroscopy can be applied to the dyes in paper. Because these tests are more commonly used on inks they are considered later (pp. 115 and 104).

Comparison of paper

In forensic science the tests previously outlined are usually carried out for one purpose, the comparison of one piece of paper with another. The significance of this is to show whether or not two pieces have a common origin, or to indicate the genuineness or otherwise of a possibly counterfeit document by comparing its paper with that of the genuine article. In the latter the examination may be assisted by the introduction of small pieces of paper (planchettes) or coloured coarse fibres into special security papers as a safeguard.

When two papers are found to be different they can normally be assigned different origins. However, there may be another reason for this. The source of a piece of paper may be a writing pad or a similar block of different sheets. Although it might be assumed that all the paper in one such pad might be the same, this is not always so. Machines which make up blocks of sheets of paper may use multiple reels.

Paper from several reels is fed into the machine so that each reel provides parts of the block. The resultant pad will contain paper from each reel in sequence.

When papers are found to be the same, consideration has to be given to all the possible reasons for this. Clearly, they could be from the same source and the same batch, but care must be taken not to overestimate the significance of the similarity. A large batch or carefully controlled manufacture leading to a very consistent product means that a considerable quantity of paper would also be similar, allowing for the very real possibility of a chance match between two samples.

Mechanical fits

A more certain indication of a common source of two pieces of paper is the possibility of a mechanical fit between two or more pieces which were once one piece and have been torn apart. Often the fit is obvious, hardly requiring close examination, but this is not always so. Confusion can arise when two identical sheets are placed together and then torn in two in one action. One piece of one will nearly fit the other because the general shape of both tears is the same. Erroneous conclusions may also be drawn from a torn edge which appears to have overlapping areas, the apparently extra paper suggesting that the two pieces could not have been one. This occurs because the tear is not always perpendicular through the thickness of the paper but can be at an acute angle, resulting in surfaces, which were exactly opposite each other, ending on different parts of the divided sheet. In other cases, fibres can be pulled out of the tears and can modify the shape of the resulting edges.

In most cases when two torn edges are fitted together, it can be proved that the pieces did or did not form one piece. The irregular tear pattern normally found could not be deliberately or accidentally reproduced in another specimen. The problem is often made easier when ink lines, folds, or watermarks cross the torn edge. The chance that these would be exactly in the same position in another piece of paper must be very low, and the presence of such artefacts adds another parameter to the accumulation of evidence against a coincidental match.

Sheets of paper designed to be torn apart have perforations which are usually circular but can be elliptical. Other perforations are made with short cuts separated by narrow strips of uncut paper. When the page is torn apart the breaks which occur in the paper between the holes will not normally be even. Instead, the tongues of paper which remain on either side of the torn perforation will be of varying lengths, the longer tongues on one side corresponding to shorter ones on the other. It is therefore often possible to show that two parts of a perforated document were at one time joined.

Although book matches can hardly be regarded as documents, they too can provide invaluable evidence by the same processes of mechanical fits of paper. Matches left at the scene of a crime have been shown to originate from a book in the possession of a suspect [18].

Watermarks

Watermarks are produced in the manufacture of paper by a thinning out of the fibres in the required shape and area. When the paper is finally completed there is little reduction in the dimensional thickness, but there are fewer fibres present. This makes the watermark more translucent than the surrounding area and so creates the familiar effect of the appearance of an image when the paper is held up to the light.

When printing, typewriting, writing, or other marks are made on the paper the watermark is more difficult to examine. To overcome this problem it is necessary to employ methods which are sensitive to the difference in mass of paper but which do not detect the extraneous information on the paper. If the writing or printing is not visible in infrared it can be 'removed' by photography or electronic means, using light transmitted through the paper and a filter which allows only infrared to pass through the lens. This method is more commonly employed for the comparison of inks or the apparent removal of obliterating inks, and is dealt with elsewhere (p. 107).

A more elegant method of displaying watermarks so that their details are clear is the use of soft X-rays or beta particles emitted by a radioactive source. This can be achieved by using a sheet of polystyrene containing carbon-14, a radioactive isotope which emits a steady stream of beta particles of low activity. The handling of the material is therefore not hazardous. However, as the radiation is of low power, long exposure to photographic film is needed. To reproduce an image of the watermark the paper is placed between the sheet of radioactive polystyrene and a piece of light-sensitive photographic paper. After several hours' exposure — it is usually conve-nient to leave it overnight — the latent image of the watermark will be present on the photographic paper. The radiation has passed through the document attenuated to varying degrees dependent on the mass of the fibres present in the paper. The thinner paper of the watermark allows more radiation to pass than does the rest of the paper, and so its shape is reproduced as a photograph. Any printing or writing will have little mass compared with that of the paper in either its thicker or thinner areas, and will therefore not be detected.

The watermark can give clear information as to the origin of the paper. From it the manufacturer can be identified, and, if the design is periodically changed and records of these changes kept, the period in which the paper was made can be discovered. The value of a watermark as a means of security is very high. Although it is possible to imitate one by printing or drawing, the results are rarely convincing. It is particularly difficult to copy the complicated multi-tone watermarks produced in high quality security papers.

Dating of paper
The methods of production of paper have changed over the centuries. New materials have been introduced into the manufacturing process which can then be found in the final product. Antique documents counterfeited with modern paper can be shown not to be authentic because certain materials are present which could not have been used at the purported date of the document.

The Vinland map, for many years considered to be centuries old, was proved to be a fake by the discovery of titanium dioxide in its paper. This was not used until modern times. Two sets of diaries, by Mussolini and Hitler, were shown to be spurious by the discovery of straw fibres and optical brighteners respectively [23, 38]. The inclusion of these components in the paper could not have occurred at the professed date of the writings, as they were introduced considerably later. In the case of fake paintings purporting to be by the nineteenth century painter Samuel Palmer, part of the paper used in a picture was shown to be of modern origin.

In most criminal investigations smaller time scales are of significance. A document may purport to have been produced a year before the actual date of manufacture. In such cases, only if a change of practice in the manufacture has occurred between the two possible dates of production can any evidence be adduced to show which is the actual date. Changes in practices occur when different types of pulp are used, incorporating different varieties of wood for instance, and records of these may be kept by the paper mills. Some manufacturers regularly change the dandy roll which produces the watermark because it is in their interest to know when the paper was made if there are complaints about its quality. This is of evidential value if the date of a document is in dispute.

To adduce such evidence the cooperation of the producer of the paper is required, either by providing information from records or by supplying samples of each different batch when changes are made.

Envelopes

Evidence of the manufacturer may be also provided by the design of envelopes. The size and shape of the envelope, the shape of the flaps, the type of glue, and the pattern it forms, all vary between manufacturers, and, in some cases, batches. These can therefore be usefully compared. Some self-seal envelopes bear printed codes which may indicate the date of manufacture and provide another parameter for comparison.

WRITING MATERIALS

The materials used to produce a line of writing on paper can provide considerable information over and above that obtained from whatever can be read. Evidence of considerable value may be supplied to the court from comparison of different inks, detection of ink which has been erased, and occasionally, determination of the date inks were placed on the document. Techniques for these investigations need to deal with very small amounts of material; the quantity of pencil lead or ink deposited on paper is far less than its appearance suggests. Although a complete analysis is not possible, many tests, often non-destructive, can be used and are described below. These tests cannot identify the particular instrument used, but the type of ink or other material can be compared. Matching inks indicate that they could have come from the same source, but also from different sources of similar ink. Differences in inks found on one document are usually more significant.

Pencils

Pencils are rarely the subject of forensic investigation, as most documents are completed in ink. In any examination of the mark made by a dry instrument the amount of substance left on the paper is very small, and the variation between different products is not great. Ordinary 'lead' pencils are made with graphite mixed with varying amounts of clay or other fillers, a greater proportion of which increases the hardness of the product. Softer leads have a higher percentage of graphite. Coloured pencils or crayons are made of wax and coloured pigments; different waxes provide a range of hardness to the core of the pencil.

The use of pencils and crayons depends on the friction caused when they are applied to the writing surface. Finely divided residue breaks from the solid core and is embedded in the irregularities of the paper surface. The particles remain on the surface and do not penetrate into the fibres, enabling them to be removed by pressure from a rubber eraser.

Analysis of the small amounts of graphite or wax present on paper requires sensitive techniques. Scanning electron microscopy in its analytical mode can give a quantitative assessment of the elemental composition of the written line. There is a high proportion of inorganic material in the composition of pencil and crayon leads, and, although the quantity present is small, it is adequate to distinguish between different products.

Erased pencil lines may contain a few traces of graphite which can be detected by increasing the contrast between their absorption of light and that of the paper or whatever substrate on which they occur. Photography using appropriate filters allowing infrared to pass, electronic means of detection, or computer-based image enhancement methods, described elsewhere (pp. 149, 159 and 162), sometimes assist and allow what was erased to be detected.

Inks

The application of a coloured liquid or paste to paper as a vehicle for printed or written information is the basis of the vast majority of documents.

Inks used in printing differ considerably from those employed for writing. They are conveniently considered in Chapter 8 where printing techniques are discussed. Similarly, in that chapter photocopy toners, now of considerable and increasing importance, are dealt with. The present chapter considers the manufacture and examination of inks used in hand-held writing instruments.

Liquid inks

Inks were first developed thousands of years ago in China, and for centuries were based on carbon particles suspended in an aqueous dilute solution of glue. Today's so-called Indian inks, made in much the same way, produce a jet black permanent writing line.

Subsequently, iron-tannin inks, mixtures of salts of iron and tannin with some glue, were developed, and they continued in use in a modified form until recent times. The most important modification made in the nineteenth century was the addition of the dye indigo. This gave a blue colour to the line of writing which after a time turned black as the iron-tannin components oxidised. The mixture was therefore known as blue-black.

The use of dyes was extended firstly to replace part of the iron-tannin component and then to replace all of it. The advent of the fountain pen which, unlike the earlier quill and iron nib pens, carried its own supply of ink, hastened this development. The use of dyes increased the range of colours available and enabled washable inks, with entirely water-soluble colouring materials which could easily be removed, to be developed. Other changes, including the addition of alcohols, were made to make the ink dry faster.

Ball-point inks

The invention of the rolling ball pen has introduced a new concept to placing ink on paper. A ball at the end of a tube picks up ink from the reservoir above it and transfers it to the paper surface. Because the ball rotates so long as the pen is in motion across the paper, the flow of the ink is continuous and applies the required amount to the written line.

Ball-point inks are not based on an aqueous solvent but on a quick-drying paste. Mixtures of dyes provide the colouring matter, and an important constituent is the resinous material which remains after the solvent has evaporated and serves to bind the ink to the paper. The convenience of the ball-point pen has given it pride of place amongst all other forms of writing instrument. By far the majority of handwritten documents are now completed with one, and it appears that it will remain the most popular form of pen for years to come.

Fibre tipped and roller ball pens
After the development of the ball-point pen, felt tipped and fibre tipped markers were produced. These depend on a compressed fibre stylus transferring ink from the reservoir to the paper by capillary action through the gaps between the fibres. In felt tip markers the fibres are less densely packed, and the writing tip is wider. In a fibre pen a more compressed fibre bundle can be made sufficiently narrow to produce a line similar to that of a fountain pen. The inks used in these instruments are water-based, with alcohols and other solvents added to induce quick drying, and for colour use dyes similar to those of other aqueous inks.

A further development in pen design produced rolling ball pens, employing the same principle of ink delivery as that of the ball-point pen, but using an aqueous-based ink. The inks used in these pens, like those in felt tipped pens, depend on water-soluble dyes for their colour.

The examination of inks
It is sometimes necessary to show whether or not a particular pen was used to write certain material. More often it is necessary to show whether or not two inks on one document are the same. By adding extra writing the meaning of the wording or the amount of money can be greatly changed. Additions range from long passages to a single digit as simple as a figure '1' which can increase the apparent value of a document many times.

During the manufacture and development of pens and inks tests are performed with the aim of improvement of quality, reduction of cost, and other factors of importance to the maker. Ample quantities are available and complications, such as the presence of paper, can be removed or controlled. In contrast, the examination by the forensic document examiner is made on a small amount of ink already dried on the paper. There are extra problems in that the document is preferably not damaged. The first techniques employed, therefore, are those designed to obtain as much information as possible from the ink by visual or other non-destructive means. After this, those requiring samples to be taken from the paper are used. The methods are described in this order.

Visual examination
The eye is in itself a powerful scientific instrument, capable of discovering much information from an examination of ink on paper. With the aid of a microscope, using low power, giving a magnification of up to one hundred times, the appearance

of a line written on paper may give invaluable information. The appearance of ball-point ink under a magnification of around twenty to fifty times provides clear evidence of its origin. As ball-point inks are only partly absorbed into the paper, they have a characteristic glossy appearance, and their pasty texture is unmistakable. In many cases striations caused by imperfect or dirty ball housings are apparent, and there is a tendency, just after the pen has turned a corner, for an extra amount of ink to be deposited in the line. The extra pressure required when writing with a ball-point pen will frequently produce indentations in the paper.

In contrast, a water-based, or 'wet' ink, will colour the paper by being absorbed into it, in effect by dyeing it in a narrow line. The ink itself will not be visible as a layer of added material but rather as a coloured area of an evenly textured surface. Whether the line is made with a modern fountain pen with a tipped nib giving an even width, or with a fibre tipped or rolling ball pen, will not normally be apparent from the appearance, even under magnification. The depth of indentation will be small or non-existent, but a faulty instrument may leave some indication; the housing of a rolling ball pen when it is held at an oblique angle to the paper may leave an indentation parallel to the line. However, the use of a wide pen nib will be shown by the variable width of the line.

Other non-ink writing instruments will leave characteristic traces. Pencils and crayons smear solid deposits on the paper, and these can be seen as such under the microscope. The shiny appearance of graphite and the waxy look of crayon on the surface of the paper are unlikely to be confused with other materials. Carbon paper impressions can sometimes cause problems, but their most distinctive feature is the gradual shading of the edges of the line. This, produced by the lower pressure of the depressed paper away from the centre of the writing instrument, contrasts with the sharp cut-off of the edges of writing made directly on the paper.

Apart from the distinction between different types of ink, variations can be detected between inks of the same type. The texture may vary considerably, especially within ball-point inks, and the width of line will depend on the size of the ball or stylus used. The presence of striations in a ball-point line can also distinguish between different pens. Erasable ball-point inks have a characteristic appearance under magnification of about 100×. Because they use a rubber-based vehicle which shows fine strings of ink, they can be distinguished from normal ball-point inks.

As well as differences in appearance, colour is very significant in the comparison of inks. Shades and depth of colour vary considerably, and under the microscope differences between inks can be detected visually. Care has to be taken because a line made at one time by a single instrument can vary in intensity.

Examination of colour

Reasons for the colour of an ink are conveniently discussed at this point. Light is essentially electromagnetic radiation of certain wavelengths or frequencies which can be detected by the eye. Not only can the eye detect this radiation, but it can distinguish between the wavelengths present. Thus, if light with a wavelength of 550 nm strikes the eye it is recognised as yellow light, whereas if the radiation has a wavelength of 450 nm it appears blue. The eye is sensitive to radiation ranging in wavelength from about 400 to 700 nm and sees this spectrum in colours ranging from violet to red, as in a rainbow.

Sources of light are rarely monochromatic, that is, of one wavelength. Sunlight and the radiation from an incandescent electric light bulb contain wavelengths in the whole range, and their combined effect on the eye causes it to see white light. If a mixture of two wavelengths impinge on the eye a third colour will be seen. A mixture of red and green light will be seen as yellow, a colour also seen when monochromatic light at a wavelength between those of red and green light is detected. A demonstration of the range of colours available from only three sources, red, green, and blue light is daily seen in the natural hues appearing on a television screen. Even white light can be created from these three colours.

However, most colour detected by the eye is not from mixtures of different lights but from light reflected by coloured materials. Certain compounds absorb light at particular wavelengths. They do this because they have in their structure combinations of atoms, called chromophors, which have this property, and these absorb not single wavelengths but a range or ranges of wavelengths. If white light falls on compounds which appear coloured, part of it is absorbed at the appropriate wavelengths and the rest is reflected. It is the reflected light, that part of the spectrum which is not absorbed, which is detected by the eye. Because it contains some of the wavelengths but not the whole spectrum it will appear not white but coloured. Thus if the blue, green, and yellow components of white light are absorbed, the remaining red will be reflected, giving the object a red colour. If all the wavelengths of the incident white light are absorbed the object will appear black. Illumination by a single wavelength or a narrow band automatically eliminates other colours; a red jumper is not seen as red under a sodium street lamp.

Absorption spectra and the examination of inks

When wavelengths or colours of light are referred to above it must be understood that this is a range rather than an individual value. Any substance which absorbs some colours and reflects others does so in a way which can be recorded on a graph. If the absorption at a particular wavelength is, say, 50% and at another is 75% and at a third is 100%, these can be plotted as points on a graph on which one axis represents the wavelength and the other the percentage absorption. If the points are connected with a line, which continues for all the wavelengths measured the absorption spectrum of that substance will be produced. Typically, for an ink this will consist of a curved line with peaks and troughs. The peaks will indicate those wavelength ranges which are strongly absorbed and the troughs those at which the light is reflected, at least in part.

Inks are made up of mixtures of dyes which, in combination, absorb the appropriate wavelengths to give the required colour. The dyes used are not common to all inks, so there is considerable variation both in the colour and the absorption spectrum of the combinations. Sources of reflected light with two different absorption spectra can appear identical because the eye mixes the combination of wavelengths reflected. The emitted colours of red and green, which are together seen as yellow, is an example of the same phenomenon. Therefore because two very similar colours can be produced with different dyes with different absorption spectra the fact that two inks look the same is not an indication that they are. Methods have therefore been devised to detect these differences.

The simplest method is to use light of a colour other than white and observe both inks under it. This will detect differences if those parts of the coloured incident light which are reflected from the inks appear different to the eye. This separation does not occur very frequently.

Another method of detecting differences in the spectrum is to use a dichroic filter. This is a combination of two coloured glass or gelatin filters bound together so that light passing through one must pass through the other. A useful combination is that using a red and green filter. Light passing through both filters will be partly absorbed, dependent on the absorption spectrum of the combination of the two filters. The light which is thus transmitted will consist of small 'windows' at certain wavelengths. If a small quantity of a particular colour is reflected and is of the same wavelength as a window, that colour will be visible. A difference in absorption at that wavelength in two inks which appear similar will therefore be detected.

A more sophisticated method of determining the absorption curve is to measure it with special equipment. The problem of only a small amount of material being available in the width of a line has been to some extent overcome by a refinement in technique. The apparatus used for this is the microspectrophotometer. Because of the complexity and expense of this method it is not in common use.

Ultraviolet and infrared radiation

From about 200 nm to 400 nm where violet light begins the visible wavelengths, the radiation is described as ultraviolet. Similarly, in the range from about 700 nm upwards infrared radiation can be generated. Although not detected by the eye ultraviolet and infrared radiation are absorbed like visible light.

Most blue and black inks absorb ultraviolet, so that little is gained by examining its absorption and reflectance. In contrast, while visible light is absorbed by different inks of a similar colour in ways which are only slightly different, there is a very big contrast between certain inks in their infrared absorption (see Fig. 7). Whether or not an ink absorbs infrared also depends on the chromophors in the molecules of the dyes present. Some will absorb a range of frequencies which extends well into the infrared range, while in others the absorption will be confined to the visible or near infrared. This variation will not affect the colour of the ink because the eye will not detect the presence or absence of infrared radiation.

Therefore the absorption spectrum of an ink may show that it continues to absorb radiation from the red through to the infrared, or the absorption may fall to nothing near the end of the red end of the spectrum. In the first case the ink when radiated with infrared will absorb it, but in the second case it will not. In the latter event the radiation will pass through it or be reflected through it as if it were invisible or transparent.

Infrared radiation is not of a single wavelength but a range of wavelengths. For convenience of detection in document examination it can be regarded as having wavelengths between 700 nm and 1000 nm, although it extends far beyond this into the range where it is used as a means of identification of chemical compounds. As it is not visible it must be detected by other means. These are by photography, using emulsions which are suitably sensitive, and by electronic means whereby a photoelectric cell picks up an image and makes it visible on a visual display unit.

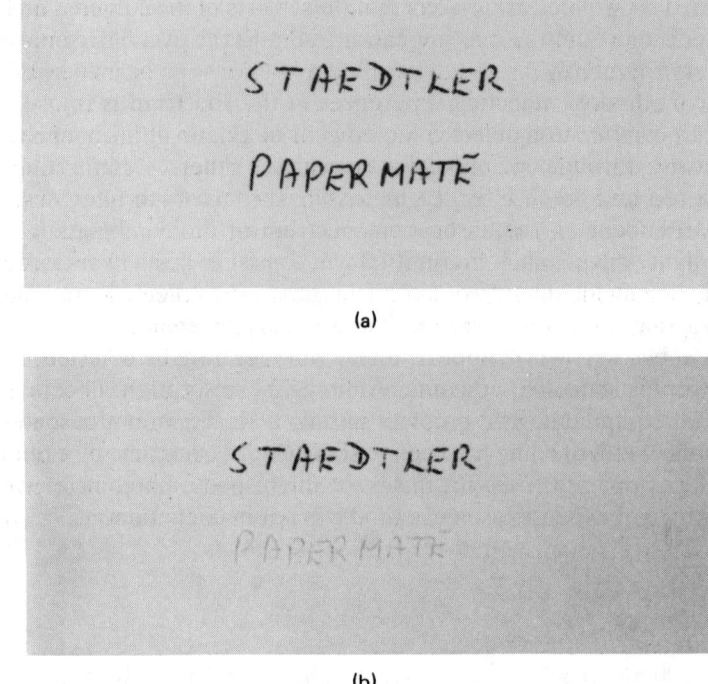

(a)

(b)

Fig. 7 — Two black inks of different manufacture photographed in (a) normal light and (b) infrared radiation, showing the difference of absorption in the infrared region.

Infrared photography

Photography was the first method of detecting infrared radiation to be employed, and it is still of considerable value because it requires no special equipment and produces the clearest and sharpest images. To photograph the infrared image of a document it is necessary to have a source of illumination and a filter which will allow only infrared to pass. The filter is necessary because all convenient sources of infrared also emit visible light. In fact the normal tungsten filament lamp provides a useful source of infrared. There are a number of filters available which remove all or most visible light but transmit parts of the infrared range. These fall into two classes, the standard optical filter depending on dyes to absorb the wavelengths, and interference filters which allow only a narrow band of wavelengths to pass.

The filter is placed over the lens, either inside or outside the camera. The document is illuminated with normal tungsten light, and only that part of the infrared spectrum which passes through the filter will have any effect on the emulsion. The resultant photograph is therefore of what the eye would see if it were able to observe only infrared radiation. An adjustment in focus has to be made when infrared radiation is photographed.

Electronic detection of infrared radiation

The weakness of the photographic method of detection of infrared radiation is that in order to test the absorption of different inks at different wavelengths it is necessary to take several photographs, using different filters. The electronic means of detection is much more convenient in that the eye can actually observe on a screen what it would see were it sensitive to infrared radiation. Examinations can be made while different documents or parts of a document are moved in front of the camera.

The first means of using electronic forms of detection of infrared radiation was the image converter which was developed as a low light detector for military use. This incorporated a small fluorescent tube which was observed through a lens, rather like that of a microscope. This was later adapted by increasing the gain of the signal electronically to give a much brighter image, although this still required a narrow aperture through which it was viewed. This apparatus, known as an image intensifier, gives a greater sensitivity than that of the image converter.

The next development was to use a closed circuit television system fitted with a tube which is very sensitive in the infrared [44]. The image of the document is shown on a monitor screen, giving the advantages of a degree of magnification and the ability for two observers to discuss what is seen. The screen can also be photographed to provide a record of the observation, but direct photography will give a clearer picture. A number of filters each passing a different range of infrared radiation can be used successively by placing them in front of the lens of the camera. This method

(a)

(b)

Fig. 8 — (a) An obliteration of one black ink with another, photographed in normal light. (b) The same photographed using infrared radiation.

provides a fine adjustment of wavelengths and a sensitive method of detecting differences between inks. Some inks contain components which absorb into the far infrared and so are detectable throughout the range. Others contain dyes which absorb only in the visible part of the spectrum and are therefore invisible when viewed in the near infrared, around 730 nm. Others absorb further into the infrared region, becoming 'invisible' at around 800 nm. It is therefore possible to test the similarity of inks by determining at what wavelength they cease to absorb infrared radiation and become 'invisible'. In some cases it is possible to discover a clear difference between two inks on a document, one disappearing at a certain wavelength while the other remains visible. When comparing two ink lines by this method care must be taken to allow for the fact that a thicker, more intense line will show up more clearly than a weaker one of the same ink in the same conditions. The difference can be mistaken for that between two inks, one absorbing more strongly than the other.

A second effect of the varying absorbencies of different inks is in cases where an entry has been heavily obliterated with another ink. If the added ink is invisible in infrared and the original entry is in an ink which absorbs infrared, the original will be detected as if the obliteration were not there (see Fig. 8).

Apart from comparison of two inks, the technique of examining documents in infrared conditions has other uses. Firstly pencil lead, which is made largely of graphite, absorbs throughout the infrared range as well as in the visible spectrum. If a simulated signature is made by writing over pencil lines in an ink which is transparent in any part of infrared radiation, the graphite can easily be detected. Even when the pencil line is removed by an eraser, traces may still remain, and without the overwriting ink can be clearly identified.

Secondly it aids in the interpretation of postmarks which are made less clear by the pattern of the postage stamp beneath them. The ink of most cancellation marks is based on carbon black which strongly absorbs infrared wavelengths while the pigments of the printing ink may not. The contrast is therefore improved, and in many cases the postmark can be read.

A similar increase in contrast can enable a faint trace of largely erased pencil writing to be identified. Such lines are often much clearer when examined in the infrared range than when they are observed in normal light. The same method can be used to detect traces of other infrared-absorbing material including some printing inks, which remain after removal of most of the material. In rare cases erased writing inks may be also revealed.

Ultraviolet fluorescence

Ultraviolet fluorescence produced by paper varies greatly, and, as has been discussed earlier in this chapter, can be used as a means for testing whether two or more pieces are similar or different. Other materials such as glues, adhesive tapes, and sealing waxes can also be distinguished by their fluorescences. The application of solvents or chemicals to paper can cause the fluorescence to change, so that when they have dried and apparently have left no trace, an area of different fluorescence will be found when the document is examined under infrared.

Red inks may fluoresce under radiation from an ultraviolet lamp, and this may give a means of distinguishing one ink from another if they are both of similar appearance. Fluorescence in the higher wavelength range of the ultraviolet region can be produced by ultraviolet radiation of lower wavelength, and some differences between inks in this respect have been reported [54]. As the fluorescence is not in the visible region and cannot be observed, special equipment is needed to detect it. This, in addition to the likelihood that differences which can be detected by these means can also be found by other techniques, has resulted in little use being made of this phenomenon.

Inks affected by chemical action rendering them invisible may leave traces in the paper. These inks, if they are not diffused by the solution, may be detected by their fluorescence emitted when ultraviolet radiation falls on them; ultraviolet examination may therefore reveal the writing which has been erased. This method was more useful in the past, as the older formulations of ink were more likely to leave evidence enabling their detection by this means. Infrared luminescence, described below, is more successful for the dye-based inks of today.

Some modern inks, however, are intended to be visible only in ultraviolet radiation. These are special preparations used to mark items to enable their identification if they are recovered after a theft. There are also those inks used to write signatures on various documents which for security reasons are visible only when viewed under ultraviolet. It is rare for any of these 'invisible' inks to be involved in any laboratory examination.

Infrared luminescence

A confusion of terms exists when fluorescence is referred to in document examination. In discussing fluorescence excited by ultraviolet radiation the term ultraviolet fluorescence is used. In contrast, by infrared luminescence, document examiners mean that luminescence emitted in the infrared region, excited by visible light. The inconsistency of these terms is now too widely accepted to change except for reasons of pedantry. The term luminescence rather than fluorescence is usually applied to those emissions in the infrared range, again without a completely logical reason. Similarly those who argue that great precision in the use of terms should be applied may feel that the term light should not be applied to infrared and ultraviolet radiation, because they cannot be perceived by the eye. However, as with the other terms, provided that no misunderstanding occurs, the terms most commonly employed and understood can be used.

Infrared luminescence together with luminescence in the red region of the spectrum is emitted by inks, papers, and the remains of erased inks when radiation of appropriate wavelength falls on the document (see Fig. 9). In the same way that fluorescence excited by ultraviolet radiation is of a higher wavelength and normally occurs in the visible range, so visible light excites fluorescence only in the longer wavelength regions in the visible spectrum or in the infrared region. The efficiency of the excitation of luminescence is not great, so a high intensity is required to produce a detectable result. With infrared luminescence there is also the problem that, in contrast to that excited by ultraviolet radiation, little or nothing can be seen by direct vision. It is therefore necessary to use either photographic or electronic means. Suitable sources for the excitation of infrared luminescence are provided by intense tungsten filament or quartz iodine or xenon arc lamps, with appropriate glass or gelatin filters or with a saturated solution of copper sulphate. These allow the green-blue exciting radiation to pass, but prevent infrared or red light from the source from

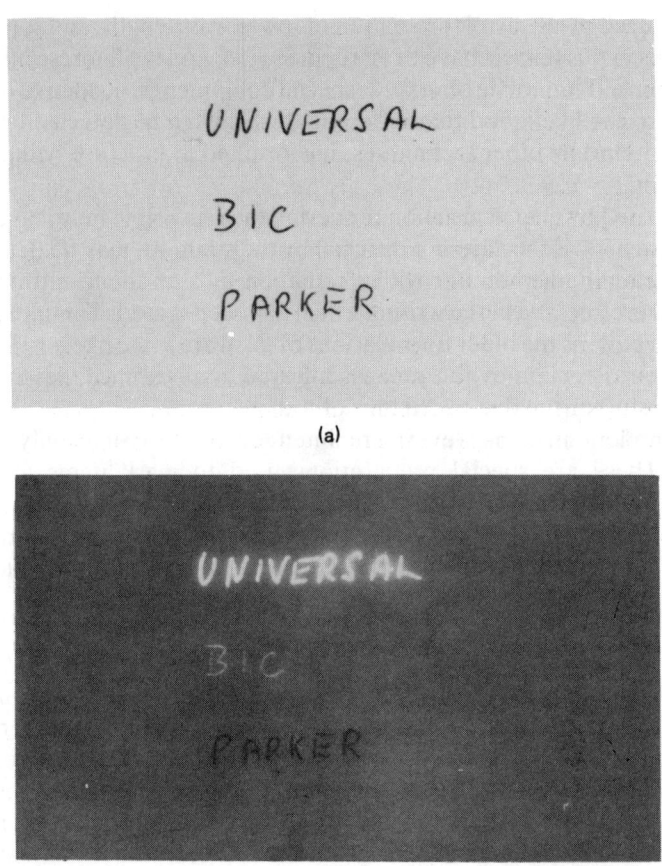

Fig. 9 — Three blue inks of different manufacture photographed in (a) normal light and (b) conditions suitable for the excitation and detection of infrared luminescence.

falling on to the document thus illuminated. Further protection from adventitious strong light must also be provided, as this too can swamp the weak luminescence.

With this illumination the document will reflect green-blue light as well as emitting infrared or red luminescence from those areas which will generate it. A further filter is therefore needed to eliminate the exciting light from the means of detecting the luminescence.

The detector can be either a photographic film or a light-sensitive cell such as an image converter, image intensifier, or video camera. The second filter can be one which allows a wide range of red light and infrared to pass, or one of narrower range which will allow some but not all of the emitted luminescence to reach the detector. The advantage of the latter is that differences in the wavelengths of luminescence from different inks can be detected by using a range of filters.

An extension of the use of green-blue light to excite luminescence is to use the light from a laser. The advantage of this is that the light is intense and monochromatic, so the need to filter out unwanted radiation does not arise. This means that visible luminescence much closer in wavelength to the exciting light can be detected. Observation of visible luminescence is made through filters which are specially made to cut out the laser wavelengths. These are normally incorporated into goggles which are in any case necessary to protect the eyes. Alternatively, the luminescence can be recorded either by photoelectric or photographic methods, which are the only ways of detecting radiation emitted in the infrared range.

In many instances the best way to discover what is present is to take a photograph, because the resolution of a photograph is greater than that of the video screen, and, when working with a laser, the ease with which a photograph is studied is preferable to the discomforts of observation through goggles. Laser light can be produced at different wavelengths, expanding the range of potentially detectable luminescence.

Comparison of inks using infrared luminescence

Infrared luminescence has proved to be of immense value in the examination of documents, far exceeding in importance the effects of ultraviolet radiation.

Firstly, although many inks luminesce in the infrared region, some do not (see Fig. 9). Secondly, there is a further variation between different inks both in the wavelength range at which the luminescence appears and in its intensity. Because examination of inks normally takes place on paper which itself may produce fluorescence, that of an ink will appear different on different papers. If the fluorescence of the paper is stronger than that of the ink the latter will appear not to fluoresce. In most cases, however, inks are examined for the purpose of comparison of two writings on one document. The typical case is where an addition or alteration may have been made at a later date.

If it is necessary to compare ink from a pen or a bottle with ink on a document, a mark can be made with the ink on the same page. Comparison under infrared luminescence conditions can then be made.

The distinction between different inks was discussed earlier when absorption or reflection of infrared radiation was considered. Observation of the questioned entries on a document in conditions which will detect infrared luminescence will often distinguish between two inks, whether or not they can be separated by infrared reflection. Again, care must be taken if there appears to be a slight difference between two inks. This could be caused by different quantities of ink on the surface.

The fact that luminescence will be quenched by materials which will absorb its wavelength can also cause complications. An ink absorbing radiation at, say, 750 nm may also contain a component which emits luminescence at this wavelength. This will then not be detectable, because it is self-absorbed, but if the component spreads away from the quenching constituent its fluorescence will be observable. This can occur when the surface is moistened, the water or other solvent removing the fluorescing component from the body of the ink. If this happens in only a part of the document the luminescence of that part may erroneously be taken to indicate a different ink. Generally, however, infrared luminescence can complement infrared reflectance in distinguishing two different inks in one document.

The complications caused by relative fluorescences are increased because the wavelengths at which they occur may be different. By changing the filters in front of the detector, different effects are observed. An ink will appear brighter than its background at one wavelength and less so at another. The effect of absorption of light at a particular wavelength will also reduce the fluorescence of an ink, so that that from the paper will be greater.

Comparison of inks on the same background, using the luminescence of ink, depends, therefore, on a system which will enable its detection to be made at a number of different wavelengths, from about 650 nm to 900 nm. The same system or apparatus can be used for the detection of erasures and alterations. Photographic methods require a separate exposure to be made at each wavelength, but apparatus using the silicon Vidicon^{TM} tube, such as the Video Spectral Comparator described in Chapter 10, are designed for this purpose. Their flexibility enables examinations under a wide range of different wavelengths and light conditions to be made.

Erasures
While the use of ultraviolet, referred to earlier (p. 109), has been of decreasing value in the detection of erased writings, modern inks have proved to be more productive of luminescence excited by visible light. Inks which have been made invisible by removing the coloured components can be detected by the luminescence of whatever remains on or just below the surface. Erasures are made by three methods, the mechanical removal of the ink by scraping the surface until all the visible ink has been removed, the treatment by bleaching solutions which convert the dye into colourless compounds, and the removal of the soluble dyestuffs by suitable solvents. In all these processes it is possible that traces will remain which will fluoresce or luminesce when illuminated with visible light.

As previously noted, the fluorescence will be weak, so sensitive methods of detection are required. Again, the observation will be affected by the luminescence of the paper which can in some cases be greater than that of the traces of ink residues. It is therefore necessary to observe the erased area in all possible variations of wavelength. Sometimes, too, the exciting light can be varied. The laser is a particularly useful tool for erasures on documents because it provides high intensity illumination and because luminescence which is close in colour to the exciting light can be detected.

It is not always clear what is being observed. When an ink dries on the paper, certain components may penetrate more deeply into the surface than others. If these are not visible there will be no reason to remove them when mechanical erasure is being made. If they are not soluble they will not be taken out when the coloured components are dissolved away. If the dyes are converted to other compounds these may luminesce, even if the original ink did not. The reasons for what has occurred are not so important as the fact that the ink or its remnants can be detected and the erased entry identified.

Infrared luminescence can be of value in detecting erasures of other materials such as typewriter ribbon and stamp pad inks.

In some cases it is not possible by this method to find out what has been erased: not every erased ink will produce a luminescent trace. Usually, however, evidence will be found to show that something has happened to the paper surface, that some action has taken place. A ring of fluorescence, rather like a tide mark, different from that of the rest of the surface is an indication that a liquid has been applied to the paper. This in itself can be of importance to show that the present entry is not necessarily the original one.

When written entries are altered by removing parts of an ink line it may be possible by simple observation to determine what was originally present. Although the more sophisticated methods described above are available, they do not always produce satisfactory results. With or without the aid of a microscope, traces of ink or pencil may be detected and visually pieced together to identify an erased entry. This is best done with a number of lighting facilities available. Oblique lighting, exploiting any indentations of remaining writing which may be present, and different coloured filters, to ensure the greatest contrast between the ink and the paper, will be of assistance. It is not always the brightest of illumination which is most effective; sometimes the best results are obtained in low light levels.

Traces of pencil from an erased entry can be enhanced by photography using high contrast conditions or infrared film. Electronic means of detecting infrared can also be employed to make the traces more visible.

Indirect methods can also be of assistance. Indented impressions on the piece of paper below the erased writing or 'reverse impressions' on the back of the page detected electrostatically (see Chapter 9) have been of value. In one case these, combined with enhanced visibility of traces of a pencil line, were used to identify very significant erased pencil writings.

Obliterations

Obliterations of an entry are sometimes made in a different ink. As has been mentioned earlier it may be possible to decipher the original by examination under infrared radiation if the overlying ink does not absorb infrared radiation and the covered entry does. If both react in the same way in these conditions the technique will be of no value. However, if one luminesces, the problem may be solved (see Fig. 10). A luminescent ink under a non-luminescent one will be visible, provided that the obliterating ink does not absorb the luminescence. On the other hand, if the covering ink is luminescent and the obliterated entry absorbs that fluorescence, a dark area corresponding to the shape of the latter will be apparent. The luminescence of the covering ink is quenched by the ink of the original writing below it. Sometimes careful control of the lighting and filtration conditions is required.

When an ink has been heavily written over and the techniques using infrared reflectance or absorption described above are not effective, microscopic examination may prove able to solve the problem. If the obliterating ink is of a different colour the choice of filters to render it as invisible as possible can help. A photograph taken in conditions which give the greatest contrast for the original ink and its background and the lowest for the obliterating ink, will sometimes 'remove' much of the obliteration.

In some of these cases it is possible to identify an obliterated entry because there is sufficient of it uncovered to provide the evidence. By making an enlarged photograph under the most favourable conditions and then 'whitening out' on it

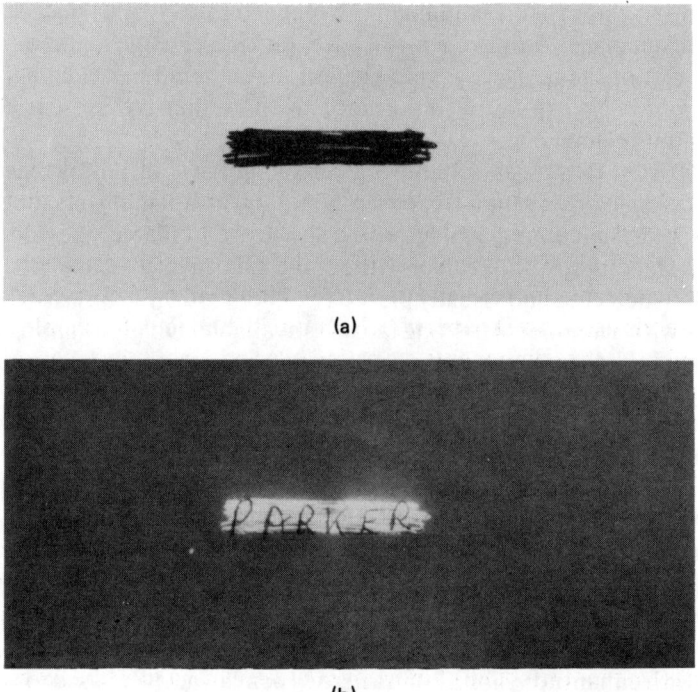

(a)

(b)

Fig. 10 — (a) An obliteration of one blue ink with another, photographed in normal light. (b) The same photographed in conditions suitable for the detection of infrared luminescence. Although the obliterating ink luminesces strongly the non-luminescing ink absorbs the luminescence.

those lines which are clearly in the obliterating ink, the portions of the original entry which remain, even though they are not complete, are more easily read without the distraction of the overwriting.

Obliterations are also made with typewriting correction fluids; these are dealt with in Chapter 6.

Other luminescence effects

Luminescence has been observed under laser radiation when a component of an ink has been off-set from another page with which it has been in contact. It is not clear what part of the ink has been 'printed' on to the adjacent page, but the effect is detectable only under the laser. Many substances luminesce strongly in laser light and may be transferred from one source to another. Transparent plastic tends to absorb traces of ink or paint from credit cards, so wallets specially designed for these will often show an impression of the details from the cards which they once contained.

A case has been reported where a vehicle index number was written on a hand

and later washed off. Traces of the number could be detected by their fluorescence under laser light many hours later. Prints made with fingers contaminated with fluorescent materials can also be detected [13].

Destructive techniques
So far the methods described to examine inks have not included those where there is need for any damage to be made to the document. They have the advantage that the ink, erased or not, the paper, and any other marks on it are not affected in any way. Other tests may be performed which provide additional information but which require portions of ink or other materials to be removed. Earlier, mention has been made of methods used to test paper which require the taking of a sample on which to operate. Similarly, the components of writing inks, whether they are from ball-point pens, fountain pens, or fibre tipped pens and markers, can be further examined by chemical techniques which cannot be performed except away from the paper.

Needless to say, there is no point in causing damage to a document if any information so obtained would not carry the case any further. If, for example, two inks have been shown to be different by non-destructive methods, there is no need to proceed with further work. If it is important to discover whether two inks are similar or different and they cannot be distinguished by visual and other non-destructive means, further work is necessary. Before any damage is made to the document it is important to make a permanent record of the entries to be tested. A high quality photograph is best for this, but a photocopy could provide a substitute if photography is not possible.

The methods used for the further examination of inks, usually for comparison purposes, can exploit the variation found either in the colouring materials or other components of the ink. Dyestuffs provide the best opportunity of discrimination between two different inks. The most sensitive method to detect the components that are dried on the paper is to exploit their strong colour and to use methods which depend on this.

Chromatography
The principle of chromatography is that individual components of a mixture are separated and therefore identified or compared with others. Two methods are employed in the examination of inks, thin layer chromatography and high-performance liquid chromatography. The former is in more general use. The principle depends on a small amount of the material being analysed being introduced on to a 'stationary phase', which will absorb it. The 'moving phase', a fluid, is then passed through the stationary phase and carries the material with it. The speed of travel of the material through the stationary phase is dependent on its composition. Different compounds will travel at different rates, so the method is ideal for separating mixtures and identifying their components by the speed or distance of travel.

Thin layer chromatography
A coating of silica gel spread evenly on a background of plastic or aluminium constitutes the stationary phase in thin layer chromatography. The materials being analysed are introduced to the plate — the name given to the layer and its support — by adding drops of a solution of it, one at a time, to a small area near the bottom edge.

As the solvent dries between each drop the material is concentrated in a small spot of about 2 mm in diameter. This is known as 'spotting' the material. The plate is then dipped into a suitable solvent, the eluate, so that this rises by capillary action through the thin layer. As it does so it takes with it the different components of the mixture which, because they rise at different rates, are separated. When the eluate has nearly reached the top of the plate, the plate is removed and the components of the material being analysed remain in the positions they have reached.

In the analysis of an ink it is necessary firstly to dissolve it in a solvent such as a pyridine–water mixture. To do this a portion of the ink line is removed, either by cutting out small circles with a ground-down hypodermic needle or by slicing a thin sliver from the surface of the paper. A suitable amount of ink is provided by about a centimetre of a normal line or the equivalent number of cut-out discs. This is dissolved, and the solutions of inks which are to be compared are 'spotted' along a line near the bottom edge of the plate. This is then placed in a shallow quantity of eluate which is typically a mixture of solvents such as ethanol, butanol, or ethyl acetate. When the eluate has travelled to near the top of the plate, the plate is removed and the run is complete. The individual dyes present in the inks are each positioned at a fixed place and will not move further. By running two or more inks side by side a comparison of the components can be made by direct observation. A standard ink is run on the plate to check if the system is working properly. Further examination of the plates under different lighting conditions can be made so that fluorescence under ultraviolet and luminescence under visible light provided by a laser or more conventional sources, can be compared. The inks can also be run using other eluates.

Some indication of the relative proportions of each component can be obtained by direct observation, but further examination with a densitometer can provide quantitative information about the proportion of each dye in the formulation.

It is necessary to place extracts of the paper of the documents on the plate. Paper may contain dyes which might be attributed to the ink.

High performance liquid chromatography
Instead of the solution of the ink being evaporated as a spot on a chromatography plate, it can be forced by high pressure through a column of absorbent material which, like that of a thin layer chromatography plate, will slow down the passage of each component to a rate which is dependent on its physical properties. As each component will be retarded to a different degree a separation is again achieved. Instead of leaving the dyes on the column the pressure is continued until they have all passed through the column. They are detected as they emerge by a device which measures their absorption or colour at a particular wavelength or at a number of wavelengths. As the absorption is proportional to the quantity of material present a quantitative assessment of each component is achieved.

The results are obtained as a graph with peaks representing the presence and proportion of each component. The advantage that high performance liquid chromatography has over thin layer chromatography is in its ability to determine more accurately the proportion of the major components of the mixture of dyes. A disadvantage is that the cost of the apparatus is considerably more than that required for thin layer chromatography.

Further chemical tests

In certain cases it is possible to distinguish between two inks by their solubility. When a drop of a solvent is applied to a line of writing the dyes may 'bleed' into the surrounding paper. Generally speaking most ball-point inks are based on similar vehicles which bind them to the paper surface and react in the same ways to whatever solvent is applied. Other inks may or may not be soluble in water, so could be quickly distinguished from each other by the application of a simple test, making a saving in time and avoiding further change to the document.

When an iron-based ink, now rarely found, has been made invisible by chemical agents, the coloured compounds having been converted to colourless ones, it is possible to perform a further chemical reaction to create another coloured iron salt and render the ink visible again. This can be done in two ways. In the first the document is exposed to fumes of thiocyanic acid prepared by mixing potassium thiocyanate and dilute sulphuric acid. Any iron salts in the paper are converted to the red-brown ferric thiocyanate. In the second method a dilute solution of potassium ferrocyanide can be applied to the surface, and the iron-containing ink traces will turn dark blue as they combine to form ferric ferrocyanide.

Other components of inks

Apart from the dyes present in the ink dried on to a piece of paper there are other components. The most important of these is the vehicle which in the case of ball-point inks is a mixture of resins with, in a recently applied ink line, traces of the solvent. In water-based inks there is a much smaller amount of vehicle. The very small amounts which are present on the surface of a written document are insufficient for any practicable comparison to be made. Although the amounts of dyes present are not appreciable greater, their strong absorption of light and other optical properties make their examination easier. One exception is that erasable ball-point inks contain a rubber-based compound which is sufficiently different from conventional vehicles to be distinguished from them.

Relative ageing of ball-point inks

Distinction between vehicles can be made by exploiting the ease of detection of colouring material. The solubility of dried ball-point inks in certain solvents is dependent on the length of time that the ink has been on the paper. It is possible to test how soluble an ink is by dissolving it and measuring the amount of colour which has been extracted in a certain time. By taking samples of solution at intervals, say, one and two minutes after the dried ink has been introduced into the solvent, the rate of dissolution can be determined. If the rate is faster for one sample than for another sample of the same ink on the same document, this indicates that the first sample has dried to a lesser extent and has therefore been on the document for a shorter time. It is important that like is compared with like. A different ink or a different surface would give a result which could be misleading. It is possible for inks aged between a few weeks and about nine months to be usefully tested.

The method is of value, therefore, only when the times of writing of two similar inks on the same document are in dispute. This is likely to occur if an extra sentence is suspected to have been added, so before attempting to test for the relative ageing of inks it is necessary to test them by the methods previously described to determine whether or not they are of the same formulation. If they are, the solubility tests will be of value; if they are not, the problem may have been solved by the difference between the inks, which in itself could provide evidence that all was not quite straightforward. The technique is not yet universally employed.

Dating of inks

The relative ageing of ink cannot put a precise time on the act of writing. This is not possible by any other means of ink analysis, but if an ink can be shown to have been made only after a certain date, any writing made with it cannot have been made before then. The principle has been applied when the dates in question have spanned the introduction of a new type of ink, from ball-point pens for example. With the wide variety of different ink formulations and the many manufacturers at work today, such dating methods require comprehensive records and cooperation with ink producers so that well founded information is made available.

In the United States of America the Laboratory of the Alcohol, Tobacco and Firearms of the U.S. Treasury has built up such a collection of ink formulations, but this appears to be unique. In addition, the same laboratory has arranged with producers of inks in the United States to 'tag' their products with special chemicals, compounds of rare earth metals, to indicate the year of manufacture. These compounds, introduced in very small proportions, can be detected only by sensitive analytical procedures such as cathodoluminescence, X-ray fluorescence, and ion probe spectrometry. Their presence also provides another means of distinguishing between two inks where such a comparison is significant.

FURTHER READING

[1] Allen, M. J. & Rimmer, P. A. (1988) The dating of a will *Journal of the Forensic Science Society* **28** 199
[2] Bertochi, M. P. (1977) Envelope association through manufacturing characteristics *Journal of Forensic Sciences* **22** 815
[3] Blackledge, R. D. & Iwan, M. (1983) Differentiation between inks of the same brand by infrared luminescence photography of their thin layer chromatograms *Forensic Science International* **21** 165
[4] Blacklock, R. E. (1987) The laser. A tool for questioned document examination *Journal of Police Science and Administration* **15** 125
[5] Boyd, P. F. J. (1983) Laser technology. A new concept to challenge the forensic document examiner *Canadian Society of Forensic Science Journal* **16** 7
[6] Brunelle, R. L. & Reed, R. W. (1984) *Forensic examination of ink and paper,* ISBN 0 398 04935 1 Published by Charles C. Thomas, Springfield, Illinois, USA
[7] Brunelle, R. W., Cantu, A. A. & Prough, R. S. (1987,1988) Various papers on dating of ink *Journal of Forensic Sciences* **32** 1151, 1502, 1511, 1522; **33** 744
[8] Cain, S. (1984) Laser and fiber optic photographic analysis of single edge paper striations *Journal of Forensic Sciences* **29** 1105
[9] Cain, S. & Winand, J. E. (1983) Striation evidence in counterfeit cases *Journal of Forensic Sciences* **28** 360
[10] Cantu, A. A. (1986) The Paper-Mate ink in the Howard Hughes 'Mormon Will' *Journal of Forensic Sciences* **31** 360

[11] Cantu, A. A. & Prough, R. S. (1988) Some spectral observations of infrared luminescence *Journal of Forensic Sciences* **33** 638

[12] Chowdry, R., Gupta, S. K. & Bami, H. L. (1976) Detection and decipherment of erasures in documents *Journal of the Forensic Science Society* **16** 139

[13] Creer, K. E. (1982) Some applications of an argon ion laser in forensic science *Forensic Science International* **20** 139

[14] Crown, D. A., Brunelle, R. L. & Cantu, A. A. (1976) Parameters of ballpen ink examination *Journal of Forensic Sciences* **21** 917

[15] Dalrymple, B. D. (1983) Visible and infrared luminescence in documents: excitation by laser *Journal of Forensic Sciences* **28** 692

[16] Day, S. P. (1985) Evaluation of the application of the argon – ion laser to document examination. A review of casework and experimental data *Journal of the Forensic Science Society* **25** 285

[17] Dick, R. M. (1970) A comparative analysis of dichroic filter viewing, reflected IR and IR luminescence applied to ink differentiation *Journal of Forensic Sciences* **15** 357

[18] Dixon, K. C. (1983) Positive identification of torn burned matches with emphasis on crosscut and torn fiber comparisons *Journal of Forensic Sciences* **28** 351

[19] Ellen, D. M. & Creer, K. E. (1970) Infrared luminescence in the examination of documents *Journal of the Forensic Science Society* **10** 159

[20] Fryd, C. F. M. (1974) The examination of inks on documents *Medicine Science and the Law* **14** 87

[21] Godown, L. (1964) New non-destructive document testing methods *Journal of Criminal Law, Criminology and Police Science* **55** 280

[22] Godown, L. (1967) 'Optical contrasters', a new instrumental aid in deciphering faint writings and other low contrast evidence *Journal of Forensic Sciences* **12** 370

[23] Grant, J. (1985) The diaries of Adolf Hitler *Journal of the Forensic Science Society* **25** 189

[24] Gross, E., Sin-David, L. & Almog, J. (1980) Transmitted infrared luminescence in document examination *Journal of Forensic Sciences* **25** 382

[25] Gupta, S. K., Mukhi, S. L. & Bami, H. L. (1978) Differentiation of inks on documents by dequenching of ultraviolet fluorescence. A case report *Forensic Science International* **12** 61.

[26] Hardcastle, R. A. & Hall, M. G. (1977) A technique for the detection of alterations to a document from a carbonless copying system *Journal of the Forensic Science Society* **17** 9

[27] Hardcastle, R. A. & Hall, M. G. (1978) A technique for the enhancement of the infrared luminescence of inks *Journal of the Forensic Science Society* **18** 53

[28] Hilton, O. (1981) New dimensions in infrared luminescence photography *Journal of Forensic Sciences* **26** 319

[29] Hilton, O. (1984) Characteristics of erasable ball-point pens *Forensic Science International* **26** 269

[30] Howes, D. S. (1978) A rapid screening device for infrared luminescence examination of questioned documents *Canadian Society of Forensic Science Journal* **11** 23

[31] Keto, R. V. (1984) Characterisation of alkali blue pigment in counterfeit currency by high performance liquid chromatography *Journal of Forensic Sciences* **29** 198

[32] Kevern, R. M. (1973) Infrared luminescence from thin layer chromatograms of inks *Journal of the Forensic Science Society* **13** 25

[33] Kuhn, R. J. (1954) Infrared examination with the electronic image converter *Journal of Criminal Law, Criminology and Police Science* **45** 486

[34] Laing, D. K. & Isaacs, M. D. J. (1983) The comparison of nanogram quantities of ink using visible microspectrophotometry *Journal of the Forensic Science Society* **23** 147

[35] Lyter III, A. H. (1982) Examination of ball-point ink by high pressure gas chromatography *Journal of Forensic Sciences* **27** 154

[36] Mathyer, J. (1986) Optical methods in the examination of questioned documents *Forensic Science Progress* **2** Published by Springer-Verlag

[37] McKasson, S. C. (1980) Dequenching of infrared luminescence *Forensic Science International* **16** 173

[38] Michel, L. & Baier, P. E. (1985) The diaries of Adolf Hitler. Implication for document examination *Journal of the Forensic Science Society* **25** 167

[39] Noblett, M. G. (1982) The use of a scanning monochromator as a barrier filter in infrared examinations in documents *Journal of Forensic Sciences* **27** 923

[40] Olsen, L. A. (1986) Colour comparison in questioned document examination using microspectrophotometry *Journal of Forensic Sciences* **31** 1330

[41] Ordidge, M. & Totty, R. N. (1984) The examination of ink writing on photographic paper *Journal of the Forensic Science Society* **24** 43

[42] Peace, L. L. (1982) The examination of torn and perforated documents *Canadian Society of Forensic Science Journal* **15** 116

[43] Pfefferli, P. W. (1983) Application of microspectrophotometry in document examination *Forensic Science International* **23** 129

[44] Richards, G. B. (1977) The application of electronic video techniques to infrared and ultraviolet examinations *Journal of Forensic Sciences* **22** 53

[45] Rohilla, D. R., Das Gupta, S. K., Gupta, S. K. & Bami, H. L. (1980) A rapid infrared luminescence method for differentiation of ink writing *Forensic Science International* **15** 153

[46] Sensi, C. A. & Cantu, A. A. (1986) Infrared luminescence: is it a valid method to differentiate among inks? *Journal of Forensic Sciences* **27** 196

[47] Sinor, T. W., Wilde, J. P., Everse, K. E. & Menzel, E. R. (1986) Lasers and optical spectroscopy in questioned document examination *Journal of Forensic Sciences* **31** 825

[48] Stewart, L. F. (1985) Ballpoint ink age determination by volatile component comparison. A preliminary study *Journal of Forensic Sciences* **30** 405

[49] Tappolet, J. A. (1983) The high-performance thin layer chromatography (HPTLC). Its application to the examination of writing inks *Forensic Science International* **22** 99

[50] Tappolet, J. A. (1986) Comparative examination of ink strokes on paper with infrared and visible luminescence *Journal of the Forensic Science Society* **26** 293

[51] Throckmorton, G. J. (1985) Erasable ink: its ease of erasability and its permanence *Journal of Forensic Sciences* **30** 526

[52] Totty, R. N. (1977) Colour in document examination *Journal of the Forensic Science Society* **17** 3

[53] Totty, R. N., Ordridge, M. R. & Onion, L. J. (1985) A comparison of the use of visible microspectrophotometry and high performance thin layer chromatography for the discrimination of aqueous inks used in porous tip and roller ball pens. *Forensic Science International* **28** 137

[54] Von Bremen, U. (1965) Invisible ultraviolet fluorescence *Journal of Forensic Sciences* **10** 368

[55] White, P. C. & Wheals, B. B. (1984) Use of a rotating disc multiwavelength detector operating in the visible region of the spectrum for monitoring ball pen inks separated by high-performance liquid chromatography *Journal of Chromatography* **303** 211

[56] Zimmerman, J. Doherty, P. & Mooney, D. (1988) Erasable felt tip writing instrument detection *Journal of Forensic Sciences* **33** 709

[57] Zimmerman, J. & Mooney, D. (1988) Laser examination as an additional nondestructive method of ink differentiation *Journal of Forensic Sciences* **33** 310

[58] Zoro, J. A. & Totty, R. N. (1980) The application of mass spectrometry to the study of pencil marks *Journal of Forensic Sciences* **25** 675

8

Printed and photocopied document examination

INTRODUCTION

Printed documents are frequently involved in crime, but the printing itself is rarely in dispute. However, where the whole document is suspected of being counterfeit, the forensic document examiner needs to understand how it may have been produced and what other documents must have been required for its production. It is important to identify the method of printing, whether it is by letterpress, lithography, or laser printer, for instance. Many of the examinations involve comparisons of genuine documents with suspected counterfeits, so there is a need to compare methods and quality of printing as well as the inks or toners used. It is sometimes necessary to determine whether or not a number of printed documents all originated from the same source. It may be necessary to show if a document differs from the genuine product, how it has been printed, and from what original it has been copied. In other cases the plate or some other part of the printing press can leave evidence that it was the source of the counterfeit. Photocopies present other problems; the original material copied may need to be established, or the make of copier used, or the individual machine, may require identification.

To enable proper evidence to be deduced from the document in question some knowledge of the printing process is necessary. Certain questions can be answered only by a printing technologist, but in many investigations the document itself and its scientific examination will provide adequate evidence when the observations are interpreted properly. The main methods of printing, and the ways in which the products can be recognised, will be briefly described. Printing inks and their examination are also considered.

Photocopies play an increasingly large role in modern life and also in those areas which are of interest to courts of law. How they are produced, how they are examined and what can be ascertained from their examination is discussed.

LETTERPRESS PRINTING

The most simple method of transferring an image to paper, and the one which for many years was the only method, is known as relief printing or letterpress. The image is raised above the background, is inked, and is then pressed on to the paper. As only the raised area receives ink and touches the paper, the appropriate design is transferred to the paper.

Many forms of relief printing are in use. The traditional method of building a 'forme' from movable type and using a flat-bed press is still employed to make posters, letter headings, and similar documents produced in relatively small numbers. The same method can be used to print counterfeit documents. A wide range of type styles is available, and the correct ones can be found to produce a good copy of an original.

More elementary forms of letterpress printing are those made by rubber stamps, post office cancellation stamps and toy printing sets. These can be of considerable interest in many cases involving questioned documents, and are dealt with later in this chapter.

LITHOGRAPHY

Lithography was invented at the end of the eighteenth century. It originally used a special absorbent stone as a printing plate, hence its name. A water-repelling substance was painted on the stone so that it produced the image in reverse on the surface. The stone was treated with water which moistened the areas only where it was not repelled by the coating. The greasy ink was then applied to the surface but did not adhere to the damp areas, only to those where the water-repellent substance was. By pressing the selectively inked stone on to paper the ink was transferred and the image printed.

Modern lithographic methods use plates made by photographic processes and the image is off-set rather than produced by direct printing. The plates are prepared by projecting an image on to a sensitised plate which reacts to light. After development of the plate and suitable treatment the areas to be printed are made water-repellent, while those that are not to be printed become water-attractive. After the plate is inked the image is transferred first to a blanket and from that to the paper. The flexible rubber blanket allows irregularities in the material being printed to be corrected.

Off-set lithography is now widely used in commercial printing both in black and white and in colour. Because it depends on photography to produce its plates it can be employed to copy other doucments and is a commonly used method of making counterfeits. Colour printing is produced by using separate plates for each colour. Multicoloured or full coloured illustrations are reproduced by photographing the original through coloured filters, so that only the components of that colour are recorded. A plate is made for each colour, using magenta, yellow, and cyan filters. The image recorded through each filter is printed with the same colour, and a good quality reproduction is obtained. It is, of course, necessary for the three coloured images to coincide exactly on the printed page.

Other methods of producing lithographic plates are in use. Off-set duplicators are employed in offices to produce short runs of typewritten or similar material. They operate by first making a master on sensitised paper or by methods using static electricity. The master is then used as a basis for off-set lithography.

GRAVURE

Letterpress printing is produced from a surface raised above its background, and lithography uses a flat plate. In contrast, gravure uses an image carrier where the design to be printed is below the surrounding surface. The plate is inked, the ink on the surface is scraped away with a blade called a doctor blade. The only ink remaining will be in the depressions, and when the plate is pressed on to paper the ink is transferred in the shape of the image. Gravure, or intaglio, printing is commonly used for high quality products, especially for full colour pictures.

The plates are produced by two methods — engraving and photogravure. Engraving is used in bank note and other high grade security printing, and the plates are made by mechanical means, either by hand or with the aid of machines. The method produces designs and lettering in solid lines but is limited in that pictures cannot be reproduced.

Photogravure is much more widely employed. It depends on the image to be printed being projected on to a light-sensitive plate. Where light falls on the surface a chemical reaction takes place. The surface is treated with an appropriate developer so that the areas where no printing image is present are made resistant to acid; then treatment with acid etches depressions in the image areas. The acid-resistant material is removed, and the surface of the plate is then highly polished so that all excess ink can be removed from the non-printing areas.

Because the ink which is to be transferred to the paper has to be held for a short time in the depressions in the plate, large areas cannot be printed without a further operation. A grid is placed between the picture to be printed and the light-sensitive plate so that instead of solid areas a series of small cells is etched on the surface. When the design is printed the ink from the cells overlaps so that a continuous tone is produced. By varying the depth or width of the cells, different densities of colour can be obtained. Full colour printing is achieved by the methods described for lithography (page 123) using three or more colours each on a different plate.

RAISED PRINTING

Embossed printing is raised from the surface of the paper. It is produced by two plates, one with the image to be printed in relief and the other with the image depressed into the surface. The depressions are inked and the paper is forced into them by the relief image. The result is the transfer of a much larger quantity of ink than is normal in other methods of printing.

Thermography is a technique which produces similar effects but by a different process. The image is printed with a slow-drying ink which is then dusted with a resinous powder. This sticks to the wet ink. The paper is then pressed through a heater and the powder fuses and swells, giving a raised effect.

SCREEN PRINTING

Screen printing depends on squeezing ink through a mesh made of nylon, silk, or other materials. The non-printing areas are covered with a stencil so that only the uncovered parts of the screen allow ink to pass through. The method is used for short runs. Its main advantages are that thick coatings of ink can be transferred, and that the surface to be printed can be quite fragile as little pressure is employed.

NON-IMPACT PRINTING METHODS

An entirely new field has been developed with non-impact printers. While the standard methods of printing all require pressure, sometimes very great, between the plate and the paper, these require very little contact or none at all. Xerography, where the image is transferred from a drum to paper by a change in a static electric charge, is closely allied to laser printing; other methods such as ink jet printing fire ink at the right places on the paper, guided by electrostatic forces.

Similar methods are used in devices related to typewriters, such as computer and calculator printers and till roll markers. At one time there was a clear distinction between printing methods which reproduced the same information in identical documents and individually prepared mechanically printed material such as type-writings. There is no longer such a separation because the same techniques, allied to computers, can perform both functions adequately and economically. Before considering laser and other non-impact printers some discussion of photocopying is worthwhile.

Photocopying

Photocopiers are related to photography in that they reproduce an already existing document, and in that they originally required special sensitised paper. A number of different techniques were employed, but methods employing static electricity became the most widely used. The principle is that certain substances which have been charged with static electricity will discharge in those areas on which light falls. If the light is a focused image of a typed page only those parts of the surface where the typewritings appear will remain charged because they remained unilluminated. The surface is sprayed with oppositely charged particles which are attracted to the charged areas and therefore print out the image.

Xerography

Xerography differs in that the image is projected not on to the paper but on to a previously charged drum or belt which has been specially coated so that it too will discharge when illuminated. Charged toner powder then forms the image on the drum, and this is then transferred to normal untreated paper and fused on to the surface. Plain paper copiers are now far more popular than all others, and have largely replaced those requiring coated papers. Transparent film can be used instead of paper, providing another advantage of xerography.

Laser printing

The method used in plain paper copiers — xerography — is the principle of laser printing. In copiers the image on the drum is formed by a projection of the document being copied; in laser printing it is made by many thousands of impulses of laser light.

The area on the drum from which the page is to be printed is divided into a grid with very many extremely small squares. The laser beam scans each row successively, and each square of each row either receives an impulse or not, depending on the signals given to the laser. The minute squares on the matrix are therefore discharged by laser light or remain charged. When toner is applied it is attracted by and adheres only to those areas which retain the charge.

Whether a square receives an impuse or not is controlled by a computer which can be programmed to produce an enormous variety of printed material. The printer is not confined to one style of type but can create as many as the computer can manage. In addition the printers have the capacity to change parts of the printed material so that they are different for each copy while the rest of the text is the same.

Ink jet printing

Another form of non-impact printing is provided by projecting ink on to the document. Ink jet printing also relies on a matrix system where a square either receives a drop of ink or does not; all of the printed material is built up from areas where ink drops have been deposited. As with laser printing the areas are very small, and a wide range of printing styles can be produced. The flight of the ink jets is controlled electrostatically through a computer.

IDENTIFICATION OF PRINTING METHODS

Observation of printed material with, when necessary, the aid of a microscope can give an identification of the method used to produce it because the type of plate, relief, lithographic, or gravure, will produce characteristic effects on the surface of the paper. The type of ink used can also give an indication of the printing process; this is dealt with later.

Letterpress

Letterpress or relief printing depends on raised type transferring ink to the paper. To do this, considerable pressure is required. The ink applied evenly to the typeface is pressed on to the paper where it is partly absorbed and partly retained on the paper surface. The evenness of the ink on the type may not be retained when it is transferred to the paper. The pressure may force it outwards towards the edges of the letter where it escapes and settles. This gives an excess at the outlines of the printed letter which is more apparent when letterpress printing is made on a shiny non-absorbent paper. The effect is known in the printing industry as 'squash'.

The pressure exerted where the typeface touches the paper may cause indentations on the surface, and these may penetrate into the paper so that they are visible
or tactile on the back. Examination with oblique lighting or by touch will reveal that
the paper surface is not smooth but indented by the printing. A combination of
uneven inking or squash with indentation of the printed lettering is indicative of
letterpress or relief printing. Without indentation of the surface, care has to be taken
that printing with squash lines visible have not been made by a photogaphic process
which has reproduced a letterpress original. It is possible in these circumstances that
the uneven inking of the original has been faithfully copied.

Lithography

Lithographic methods depend on the deposition of ink from a flat surface, the plate
carrying in reverse the pattern to be printed. As there is no difference in pressure
between image and the non-image areas no indentations are found. The ink will be
evenly distributed through the printed matter with, normally, no concentration at
the edges.

Because of the dependence on photography for the preparation of plates the
processes used cause the image to lose some of the detail of the original. This is most
apparent when sharp corners and edges of clear printing are copied. These become
rounded and tend to lose their definition, sometimes to the extent that small lettering
will become indistinct. These features are typical of lithography but in well printed
material the lack of sharpness is apparent only under microscopical examination.

Gravure

Gravure is now used to print good quality material and is capable of half tone printing
which will enable shades of colour to be produced. Therefore a variation in the
thickness of the ink on the paper is an indication of this method of printing. The
cellular method of producing areas of tone leaves signs of separation at the edges.

Matrix methods

Laser printing and other matrix methods also produce jagged edges especially on
diagonals. The dots making up the image are arranged in a grid pattern, so only
vertical and horizontal lines appear continuous while diagonals are stepped. The
appearance of toner or ink varies between the different matrix ink. Those using
liquid inks appear much like lithographic printing, but laser printing depends on the
fusing by heat, or pressure, or both, of small particles of solid toner. This results in a
solid black shiny conglomeration together with small black adventitious dots where
there is no image.

Documents produced on plain paper copiers have a similar appearance to those
produced by laser printers. The same methods of indirect electrostatic image
production applies to both, and only the serrated diagonals of laser printing,
detected by close examination, can distinguish between them. Even this does not
provide a certain discrimination because with improved methods of laser printing
using a finer matrix the serrations are less pronounced.

PRINTING INKS

Methods of examination

Printing inks differ from those used in pens in that they are oil-based and have a high inorganic content. For the most part they do not react to the tests described for writing inks in Chapter 7, but the non-destructive tests involving reflectance and fluorescence in different lighting conditions can sometimes differentiate one from another. Although they are mostly not soluble in any of the solvents used as a preliminary to thin layer chromatography, other tests can be used to distinguish one from another. The binding agents can be tested by the techniques pyrolysis mass spectroscopy, or infrared absorption spectroscopy, and the inorganic components can be determined by a variety of methods ranging from emission spectroscopy to microprobe electron microscopy (see Chapter 10). As in other methods of forensic science the first tests to be performed are those which do not cause damage. Only if these do not provide an answer, are those requiring samples of ink to be taken then applied. Modern analytical techniques require only small quantities of material, so little damage is done to the document being tested.

Some inks can be tested by much simpler techniques. Water soluble inks are used for background on security documents because they are removed when attempts are made to erase entries by chemical means. A drop of water applied to the surface will dissolve the security ink in a small area, but will not affect a lithographic ink on a counterfeit. Magnetic inks are commonly used to print numbers on cheques to enable them to be read by machine, a counterfeit is more likely to be printed in a non-magnetic ink. The difference can be detected by using a device containing finely divided iron particles which react to magnetised inks but not to others [20].

Purpose of test

The object of testing the composition of printing inks is two-fold. The first is to determine whether or not the ink of a suspected counterfeit is the same as that used for the genuine document. Often this is not necessary because the appearance, macroscopic or microscopic, of the printing, will show clear differences, and in other cases a different paper may have been used, which proves its spurious nature. Where a lithographic copy has been made of a lithographic original on similar paper the discovery of a difference in ink will be of importance.

The second object of the analysis of inks on printed documents is to compare them either with other counterfeits or with inks found at the suspected source of their production. Comparison of inks can indicate a possible origin, but it cannot identify with certainty the source, because inks, though made in a wide variety, are usually not unique to one printing works.

IDENTIFICATION OF THE SOURCE OF PRINTED MATERIAL

Lithographic printing methods and photocopying processes both use the documents as sources for their images. The discovery of the source of reproduced counterfeit or copy is an important aspect of forensic document examination.

To make a lithographic copy of a document, photographs are made of a particular genuine document. If this is one of many, all of which are identical, there will be no indication of which one was used. However, it other marks have been made, serial numbers, written entries, or rubber stamp impressions, for example, these will either have to be incorporated or will have to be removed at the artwork stage in the plate preparation. If they are left, their presence will provide clear evidence that a particular document has been copied, assuming this copy is still extant and can be compared. Any writing on the original could not be exactly matched to any other, and its position and the position of a stamped impression will not be precisely the same on any other document.

If the identifying marks have been removed during the plate preparation, the background printing occupying the same area will also be removed. It may be impossible to take out all of a signature or other written entries, especially if these are cross printed lines or patterns. The position of these signs of erasure or traces of writing can be adequate to identify the copied document. It is similarly possible to identify parts of serial numbers which have been incompletely removed.

Accidental marks from stains or faults in the paper or deliberately introduced variable features may be reproduced in a counterfeit and will also effect a means of identification of the source of the counterfeit. An example of this occurs when the randomly spaced coloured fibres introduced as a security device are photographed along with the other details of the genuine document.

In some instances, printing plates may be made up from photographs of more than one source. It is therefore possible to print a counterfeit which has some features of one original and others of another. The presence of both sources traced to possession of a suspect would therefore be very significant.

Counterfeit documents can be compared directly with their suspected sources. Such features as signatures or stamped impressions which have been reproduced can be aligned with their originals using transparencies made for the purpose or by examination under a comparison projector (see Chapter 10).

Sometimes plates or other components of printing processes are found and can be compared with printed documents. This is best done by photographing the image as it appears on the component and making a transparency which can be compared with the document. Defects and other characteristics of the printing can link documents together and, with certainty, to the plate which printed them.

THE EXAMINATION OF PHOTOCOPIES

Photocopiers are now widely available and are increasingly used to produce documents illegally or with intent to deceive.

As with the examination of printing inks and printed materials, the examination of photocopier toners, the photocopies themselves, and documents which may have been copied provides invaluable information for an investigator or a court.

Photocopy toners

The printed images of plain paper copiers and laser printed documents are not produced by liquid inks drying on the paper but by resinous particles fusing or compressed on the surface. The effect is therefore very different. Most plain paper copiers use dry toners which are, when forming an image on a photocopy, built up on the surface rather than partly absorbed in it. Unlike conventional printing inks whose appearance under magnification will not vary greatly, especially when one type of printing is considered, different toners can be distinguished by microscopical means.

Ordinary low-power magnification can detect differences in the morphology of the fused or composed toner, but a greater distinction can be made by using the scanning electron microscope. Using magnifications of around one or two thousand times the structure of the toner surface can be examined and distinction can be made between one toner and another.

Further tests can be made to ascertain the chemical composition of the toner. The scanning electron microscope can again be used, this time to determine the elemental composition. Pyrolysis mass spectroscopy and infrared spectroscopy are used to identify or compare the organic resins which are an integral part of all dry toners. Iron-containing toners can be distinguished by their susceptibility to be magnetised. Apart from the latter, which is non-destructive, these tests require a very small quantity of material, less than a square millimetre, and they can show whether or not two toners are similar, or they can identify the manufacturer. It is not possible by these means to identify a particular machine, merely a type of toner, and therefore the probable make of machine. Although it is not impossible for a toner to be used in a machine for which is was not designed, this does not often happen; most toners are packed in special containers made especially for a particular model of photocopier.

Some plain paper copiers use liquid-based toners which leave an image with an appearance not unlike that of lithographic printing. They deposit a smaller quantity of material which is less easy to identify. Other copiers use specially coated papers, but these are becoming less popular and are being replaced by plain paper machines. Specially coated paper copiers depend on a film of zinc oxide on the surface, but different manufacturers use different formulations. Analysis of the inorganic components of the coating can determine the type of paper and therefore, normally, the type of machine.

Machine characteristics

Apart from the analysis of toner which gives an indication of the type of machine which produced it, extraneous marks on a copy can provide additional information. These fall into two classes, those which, like the composition of the toner, can identify the make and model of a photocopier and those which will identify the individual machine which made the copy or was instrumental in its preparation.

A photocopier depends on mechanical means for handling the paper. These can leave characteristic marks on the copies and therefore give an indication of the model which produced them. They range from indentations caused by grippers or rollers to marks made by toners in certain parts of the copy. If the page being copied does not fill the area allowed for it, parts of the cover can be copied; this may give a clear indication of the type of machine used.

Photocopiers do not produce copies of exactly the same size as their originals. There is usually a slight enlargement of around one per cent in the copy, which is not necessarily the same in each dimension. Many copiers are capable of much greater magnification as well as reduction. These properties can also show the type of machine used.

IDENTIFICATION OF THE PHOTOCOPY WITH THE COPIER

Apart from those marks which are characteristic of a model, other marks appear on a copy caused by dirt, damage or malfunction of the machine. These can arise from scratches, dust, or other material on the platen, the glass plate which supports the document being copied, on the lid which covers it, or the drum on which the image is first formed. Other problems can also occur, such as defects in the corona wire which charges the drum or in the mechanism which puts toner on to it.

Marks on the platen, lid, or drum can be permanent or temporary. Even those described as permanent can be removed if the part itself is changed. Those on the platen will occur each time a document is copied; those on the lid only when it is exposed by an incomplete covering of the platen, and those on the drum will occur regularly but not necessarily at the same frequency as copies are produced. This means that such marks on the drum may show at a different place on successive copies or not at all on some, depending on the diameter of the drum.

Defects in charging, application of toner, and transport of paper will show as extra lines down the paper or in poor copying in places in the page. They are normally temporary because the faults that cause them are usually soon rectified.

The most significant marks are those which are randomly formed by dust or damage. These give specks or dots anywhere on the copy and sometimes form groups rather like constellations of stars which are easily recognised on all the copies on which they occur. These 'trash marks', as they are sometimes described, may be produced for a long time, or they may completely or partly be removed or added to. Therefore although all such marks on two photocopies may not match, a reasonable number which can be easily superimposed, either using photographic transparencies or a comparison projector, is clear proof that the same machine has been used in the production of both. Their random nature indicates that chance match is not possible.

In some cases the period during which a copy was made can be established because there is a gradual change in the pattern of the marks. It is also possible to establish that a copy has been recopied on the same machine if the constellation occurs twice on a document.

The presence of characteristic marks on a photocopy does not indicate that it must itself have been made on the particular machine. It may be a copy of another which was made on that machine, the marks having been reproduced along with the rest of the information. Some photocopies exhibit marks from more than one machine, indicating that copying of a copy has taken place, but with clean equipment there may be little to show this. Testing of the paper and toner can then assist in establishing if the copies have different origins.

THE IDENTIFICATION OF THE ORIGINS OF A PHOTOCOPY

The document reproduced by a photocopier is very often clearly identifiable. A handwritten letter is unique, and its photocopy could not have had another source; the same applies to a typewritten document which cannot be retyped in exactly the same form because of the variability found in the output of a typist or a typewriter. Many photocopies are, however, made from copies rather than originals, and it is therefore important to show which copy has been the source.

The methods used to solve this problem are ones of logic and common sense. It is in the differences which can be detected between the possible sources that evidence can be found to associate a copy with an original. Written marks made on a copy will not be identical with those on any other, so if these have been photocopied the document which bears them must be the source. If they are not present on the copy their host document cannot be excluded; they could have been made after the copy was made.

Apart from writings, other marks on a document may be copied. Staple holes, folds, tears, stains, and adventitious inclusions may all be reproduced. Their absence may or may not be proof that the document on which they are found was not the source, depending on when the feature may first have appeared. Faults in the manufacture of the paper are clearly more significant than the staple holes or tears.

When a number of copies of a document are made, by various reproductive methods including photocopying, small differences can be found between individual copies of the batches. Some parts may be imperfectly copied, there may be some smearing of ink or toner, marks on a photocopy originating from its drum may be recognised, or the 'trash' mark pattern may be slightly different within the batch.

When a batch of copies is investigated to determine which of them was the one to have been recopied, the original document must also be regarded as a possible source. It is possible that the document is a first generation copy. The slight magnification produced by the reproductive process can be measured to give an indication of how many stages have been made, but as machines do not enlarge to the same extent care has to be taken in such calculations. Folding and creasing of a document can also be a factor in the size of a copy. Creases will reduce the dimensions of a document and confuse calculations of enlargements caused by photocopying.

When photocopies are made it is possible to blank out certain parts by covering them with paper or correction fluid, the former temporarily and the latter permanently. Absence of features which must have been present on the original does not therefore exclude the possibility that it may have been copied. In some cases the obliterating material, or its edges, will be apparent but this is not always so.

FRAUDULENT PHOTOCOPIES

Unlike conventional printing presses, photocopiers are easy to operate and can be handled by nearly anyone. Their use has grown enormously, and in recent years plain paper copiers have become capable of producing copies of high quality not obviously distinguishable from the original documents. The popularity of the medium has meant that photocopies are accepted without question, and take the place of originals in many transactions.

This has led to the practice of producing a photocopy which appears to be one document but is made up of parts of two or more, perhaps with some parts of the writing or typing deleted. The preparation of such composites is not difficult. Signatures can be cut out of one letter and put on to another. Printed headings can be used by blanking out the rest of a letter. Parts of typewriting can be covered and replaced on a copy with other typed material completely changing the meaning. By recopying the prototype a copy is obtained which appears to be of a single letter.

Edges of covering paper do not always show when the combination is reproduced, and correcting fluids which rapidly dry to give a white coating are often not reproduced on a photocopy.

In some modern photocopiers there is an 'overlay' facility which allows a composite copy to be made without the need to cover part of the document with another.

By these means it is possible to produce a photocopy which shows no evidence that it is other than a reproduction of one original document. Because of this a photocopy should never be accepted as an authentic record of a transaction or agreement without other evidence that it is genuine. This is, however, not always the case. Composite photocopies are produced for fraudulent purposes and have to be examined by document examiners.

Although in some cases it is impossible to say that a copy is other than genuine because it leaves no evidence that it is a composite, in others clear signs can be found to establish its fraudulent composition. These arise because of the difficulty encountered in eliminating all signs of paper edges, correctly aligning added typewriting and headings, and ensuring that all added material is complete.

The evidence that a copy is not of a single document is provided, therefore, by such features as thin lines round, over, or under a signature or other added material, headings and typewritings not in alignment with each other, typewritings different in style from or not correctly positioned in relation to others, and parts of signatures missing or containing the remains of other writing which the original once crossed. In some cases the fact that the final product contains material which has been copied twice is shown by the presence of a double trash mark pattern produced by the copier.

Other clear proof of the fraudulent nature of a composite photocopy can be obtained from the discovery of the source of the components. A signature will never be exactly reproduced when it is written again, so if one on one document precisely matches that on a photocopy the latter must be a copy of that signature and no other. If the original is on a document not the subject of the copy, then the other copied material is not genuinely associated with the signature. Similarly, if part of a typewritten text exactly matches original typewriting, or perhaps a carbon copy of it, but part does not, then the copy cannot be of a single document.

These features are unlikely to be noticed by the recipient of a fraudulent photocopy, which may in any case not provide any of them. It is sometimes necessary for the document examiner to give evidence that although he cannot find any evidence that a photocopy is not genuine, that possibility is very real. There are occasions when it is impossible to conceive how a photocopy could have been made from more than one source. These occur when the writings and typewritings are overlapping to the extent that no division or addition could be made without leaving incomplete parts of letters or words. In the absence of such evidence the assumption must be made that any photocopy could be a composite.

OTHER PRINTING METHODS

Information can be transferred to paper by methods other than handwriting or typewriting or by conventional printing and photocopying. Stamps bearing signatures or many other designs and information, date stamps, machines which stamp numbers consecutively, print prices or times on tickets, and toy printing sets, are all instruments which are used on documents involved in events which interest criminal and civil courts. In addition, dry transfer methods of placing lettering and other designs by transferring them from paper charts are commonly employed in documents of forensic interest. A further method of introducing information to paper or other surfaces is by the use of lettering tape on which the impressions of words are stamped before it is stuck on to the document.

Stamped impressions

Stamps made to transfer inked impressions are made either of metal or rubber compounds. Post Office cancellation stamps are made of metal and contain a movable date section which is changed each day. They use rather crude ink based on carbon black in a glycol-based substrate. It is necessary on occasions to establish where a letter was posted by comparing its post mark with a large number of impressions from all of the cancellation stamps in a large city. Variations are found in the size of the mark, in the style of the lettering, in the relative position of words and figures, and in the quality of the lines, especially at the edges. The pattern of two or more stamps may have been exactly the same because of their production methods, but wear and damage may produce some features which are found in the impressions of only one.

When any hand stamp is used it will leave inked impressions of variable quality because the angle at which the paper is stamped, the amount of ink on the stamp, and pressure exerted can all differ with each action. Care must therefore be exercised when comparing stamped impressions to ensure that this is allowed for.

Post Office cancellation marks can be transferred to other documents for fraudulent purposes, and this can be in a variety of ways. Lithographic printing methods or others which produce a relief plate by photographic means are used, but more commonly carbon black inks are 'lifted' with wax paper and transferred to another document. This leaves a fainter impression, grey in colour rather than black, and a thin layer of wax can be seen on the surface, often with indentations caused by the pressure needed to effect the transfer.

However the stamped impression is transferred, there is normally adequate evidence to show that it is not genuine when it is examined under the microscope. In addition, because of the variability in genuinely made impressions it is usually possible to identify the transferred or copied impression with its source. The comparison microscope can be used for this, or a transparency produced either by photocopying or photography of the transfer can be overlaid on the suspected original to test the fit. The same method is suitable to demonstrate the findings to a court. Gas chromatography (see Chapter 7) can be used to confirm the presence of wax on the surface.

Rubber stamps

Like metal stamps, those made of rubber or materials of similar composition are frequently used on documents and occasionally become the subject of an enquiry. They are related to letterpress printing in that they rely on an image raised from the background. They form two main classes, those which are mass produced and those which are made in ones or twos for a special purpose.

Date stamps made from a continuous strip of rubber are produced in large numbers, and each is not normally distinguishable from others of the same style. However, some faults may occur in manufacture, and damage may arise later so that the stamped impression is not perfect. These may provide evidence that a particular stamp was the one which made a date on a document. The relative position of the components of the stamp is a variable factor. If the day, month and year are not correctly positioned the image will be misaligned and a similar misalignment of the same date may be found on a questioned document.

Rubber stamps made for the use of an individual person or office are produced by first constructing a chase out of moveable type similar to that used in letterpress printing. This is pressed into thermosetting plastic material in which it makes a depression from which the rubber stamp is moulded. Alternatively, stamps are prepared from specially made depressed lettering from which the final product is taken. The rubber mat bearing the image is trimmed and mounted on a block to complete the handstamp. It is possible that more than one stamp can be made from the matrix, so, although only one mould has been produced, it cannot be assumed that only one stamp exists. Handstamps bearing facsimile signatures are also prepared by moulding, so, again, more than one could be made [3].

It follows that a stamped impression made from a rubber handstamp will not necessarily be distinguishable from any other made by a different stamp from the same mould. However, a number of features which can make a rubber stamp unique can arise either in manufacture or in subsequent use. Those which are caused when the stamp is made include bubbles or unevenness in the surface, loose 'fins' of rubber caused by defects in the moulding and the trimmed edges of the rubber base of the stamp. These can show in the impressions made on a document and provide proof of their origin. Similar evidence is provided by cuts, wear, and accumulation of dirt in crevices between the letters of the stamp. These are likely to occur differently on different stamps made from the same matrix.

To test whether or not a particular handstamp has made an impression it is necessary to make another with it. The impressions are compared by using either a comparison microscope or projector or a photographic or photocopied transparency. It is rare to find that two impressions are identical; the variability of inking and in the pressure and angle introduced by the action of stamping will give a lack of uniformity. In addition there may be differences caused by wear or damage made to the stamp in the time between the making of the impressions. Also, the rubber may swell slightly after a period of use with inks which it can absorb. Despite these differences the presence of characteristic features can be detected.

Printing sets

Another form of rubber stamp is provided by printing sets consisting of individual letters with a suitable block in which they can be mounted. These are made as toys or for office use but are sometimes used in documents involved in criminal offences. It is then necessary to determine whether or not a specific set made the printed image.

Printing sets are made in large numbers, so the fact that the style matches is of little significance. There are sometimes small moulding faults present in individual letters, and, rarely, damage, but it is normally only when made up blocks of type are found that a set can be identified with a particular printed impression.

The relative position of the individual characters is determined by the person making the composition and is subject to wide variability. Even if the characters are placed touching each other, the positions of the letters in their holders may give rise to variation. When spaces are left between words or when there are two or more lines of print present, their relative positions are significant because the chance that an identical setting could be achieved by coincidence or design is very small or even negligible. If the edge of the block is reproduced with the impression, another variable parameter it provided.

Stamp pad inks

Handstamps are inked by a soft porous pad containing ink, usually kept separately but sometimes incorporated in the stamp itself. Comparison of the ink therefore provides another possible means of finding a link between a document and the instrument in question. Black stamp inks are generally made from carbon black and a suitable medium in which they are suspended, and afford few distinguishing features once they are dried on the paper. Other black inks and those in the variety of colours available are made of a mixture of dyes dissolved in a quick-drying solvent. They can be compared by means of the non-destructive and chromatographic tests described in Chapter 7.

It is sometimes necessary to compare the ink remaining on the rubber letters themselves. In these cases this must be done before test impressions are made with them; otherwise there will be contamination with the ink used to make the impressions. The presence of ink on certain letters of a printing set but not on others may be an indication of what has been printed with the set. If the printing set or a date stamp has been acquired especially for use on the document in question, there may be ink only on those letters or figures required to make up the stamp printed on the document.

Dry transfer methods

Another method of putting lettering and other designs on to paper is the use of dry transfer materials, sold under trade marks such as Letraset or Blick. The lettering, made of plastic material available in a number of colours, is printed on sheets of specially prepared paper and can be transferred to the document by placing the two in contact and exerting pressure on the back of the sheet of lettering with the point of a ball-point pen.

In fraudulent and other criminal activity dry transfer lettering provides a means to fabricate letter headings, serial numbers, and money amounts as well as to write demand notes and other anonymous communications. The wide variety of styles available, mostly based on those in common use in the printing industry, include some which give the appearance of handwriting. In the investigation of documents using dry transfer lettering it is possible to identify both the make of the material and also, if it is available, the actual sheet from which it came.

When dry transfer lettering is applied to paper it is held there by adhesive which is incorporated in it. Under the microscope it has a characteristic appearance and can be lifted from the surface with a sharp blade. The appearance of the surface of the material can be used to distinguish the product of one maker from another, but the far greater magnification provided by the scanning electron microscope enables further differentiation to be made The analytical function of the same instrument can also be employed to advantage.

If the sheet from which the lettering was transferred is available it can be compared in two ways. Firstly, the missing letters can be related to those present on the document; the significance of an exact match between the two can be very important. If the only letters missing from the sheet correspond exactly with those on the document, the chances that this could be coincidental will depend on the number used. If this is reasonably large the chances will be negligible. If there are insufficient missing characters on the sheet it could not have been used.

Secondly, a more positive link can be established if the indentations on the backing sheet, caused by the pen used to transfer the character, exactly match those round the character on the document. In some cases a part of a letter left behind on the sheet may be fitted to the rest of the character on the document.

Documents bearing dry transfer lettering should be treated with care. The characters may be removed if not handled carefully, and liquids such as those used to detect fingerprints on paper can loosen and dislodge them.

Miscellaneous machine printers

Various appliances are made which produce receipts, tickets, and other documents by different processes. They, or their products, occasionally are of interest to investigators, usually because it is necessary to link a machine with a printed entry. There is rarely any evidence in the more simple devices to prove that a particular appliance made the printing in question, but different styles of numerals may indicate the opposite. The same applies to the ink used for the printing which is usually contained in ribbons or pads in the machine.

More complicated apparatus can provide evidence to identify a printed entry with its source. Cheque writers, which are specially made to imprint sums of money on cheques and other important documents, can develop faults which characterise a particular machine in a way similar to that of typewriters [4,19].

FURTHER READING

[1] Anthony, A. T. (1984) Examination of magnetic ink character recognition impressions *Journal of Forensic Sciences* **29** 303

[2] Carney, B. B. (1984) Fraudulent transposition of original signatures by office machine copiers *Journal of Forensic Sciences* **29** 129

[3] Casey, M. A. (1978) The individuality of rubber stamps *Forensic Science International* **12** 137

[4] Crane, A. (1987) Identification of ridge and groove cheque protectors by platen ridge defects *Canadian Society of Forensic Science Journal* **20** 13

[5] Hilton, O. (1979) Detecting fraudulent photocopies *Forensic Science International* **13** 117

[6] Holland, N. W. (1984) Photocopy classification and identification *Journal of the Forensic Science Society* **24** 23

[7] James, E. L. (1987) The classification of office copy machines from physical characteristics *Journal of Forensic Sciences* **32** 1293

[8] Kelly, J. D. & Haville, P. (1980) Procedure for the characterisation of zinc oxide photocopy papers *Journal of Forensic Sciences* **25** 118

[9] Kemp, G. S. & Totty, R. N. (1983) The differentiation of toners used in photocopy processes by infrared spectroscopy *Forensic Science International* **22** 75

[10] Mason, J. J. & Grose, W. P. (1987) The individuality of toolmarks produced by a label marker used to write extortion notes *Journal of Forensic Sciences* **32** 137

[11] Moon, H. W. (1984) Identification of wrinkled and charred counterfeit currency offset printing plate by infrared examination *Journal of Forensic Sciences* **29** 644.

[12] Moore, D. S. (1982) The identification of an office machine copy of a printed copy of a photographic copy of an original sales receipt *Journal of Forensic Sciences* **27** 169

[13] Morton, S. E. (1984) Counterfeits: three groups, one source *Journal of Forensic Sciences* **29** 310

[14] Osborn, J. P. (1987) Fraudulent photocopy of a promissory note *Journal of Forensic Sciences* **32** 282

[15] Summers, G. G. & Lavell, H. H. (1987) Security in instant lottery tickets *Journal of the Forensic Science Society* **27** 261

[16] Totty, R. N. & Baxendale, D. (1981) Defect marks and the identification of photocopy machines *Journal of the Forensic Science Society* **21** 23

[17] Totty, R. N. & Rimmer, P. A. (1987) Establishing the date of manufacture of a sheet of photocopy paper — a case example *Journal of the Forensic Science Society* **27** 81

[18] Totty, R. N., Dubery, J. M., Evett, I. W. & Renshaw, I. D. (1979) X-ray microprobe analysis of coated papers used in photocopy processes *Forensic Science International* **13** 31

[19] Vastrick, T. W. & Smith, E. J. (1982) Checkwriter identification — individuality *Journal of Forensic Sciences* **27** 161

[20] Welch, J. R. (1985) Magnetic aspects of printing; photocopies and bank-cards *Journal of the Forensic Science Society* **25** 343

[21] Welch, J. R. (1986) The linking of a counterfeit document to individual sheets of dry-transfer lettering through the transfer of fluorescent glue *Journal of the Forensic Science Society* **26** 253

[22] Williams, R. L. (1983) Analysis of photocopying toners by infrared spectroscopy *Forensic Science International* **22** 85

[23] Zimmerman, J., Mooney, D. & Kimmett, M. J. (1986) Preliminary examination of machine copier toners by infrared spectrophotometry and pyrolysis gas chromatography *Journal of Forensic Sciences* **31** 489

9

Incidental marks and other scientific examinations

INTRODUCTION

In other chapters, marks made by pens and other writing instruments, typewriters, and printing processes have been considered. These provide the information carried by the document, the reason for its existence. This chapter covers indented impressions, fingerprints, damage and other marks which are incidental to the document's intended purpose but indicate its history. In addition, other matters of interest to the examiner of questioned documents not dealt with elsewhere are discussed. These are the examination of passports, envelopes suspected of having been opened and resealed, and the sequencing of crossed lines.

INDENTED IMPRESSIONS

When writing is made on a piece of paper resting on another it will leave impressions on the latter. The most obvious site of these is on the next-to-top sheet of the writing pad when the top page is being used, but there are many other situations where impressions of writing are found on an underlying sheet of paper.

The discovery of indented impressions can be of great significance. A letter written on a pad of writing paper may begin with the address of the writer, and the impressions of this will remain on the paper underneath. If that page is subsequently used to write an anonymous letter or a demand note it will carry on it an indication of its origins. Similarly, pieces of paper can be associated if impressions of one are found on the other. Impressions of a demand note may be detected on the pad on which it was written, thus providing proof of its source.

A variety of other information can be obtained from indented impressions. Pages next to those torn out of a diary or address book can reveal what has been removed; in some cases the entries removed are rewritten to leave out an incriminating line. The order in which writings on different pages were made can be established, showing perhaps that all were not made in the correct order; in other cases the relative alignment of indentations of certain particulars may show that different parts of a document were or were not written at one time.

Detection of indented impressions
Oblique lighting
The indentations produced by writing on an overlying page can often be clearly seen; for a long time the only techniques used to detect them depended on methods to enhance their visibility. Despite a number of suggested improvements, the best results by visual examination are obtained by the use of oblique lighting. Illumination from a point source at a shallow angle will produce shadows in the depressions and render them visible. In most cases, some of the impressions are too weak to be read clearly, and some patience is required before all that can be read are identified. The light source is moved so that the angle of incidence is changed to show different parts of the indentations more clearly. The document can be photographed under the best lighting conditions to provide a record of the indentations, but because all the variations in the lighting conditions cannot be used in one exposure a photograph will not reproduce all that can be observed by actual examination. A curious feature of indentations photographed under oblique lighting conditions is that they sometimes appear in the photograph to be raised rather than depressed. Turning the photograph round one hundred and eighty degrees eliminates this optical illusion.

Shading
Other methods suggested to improve the visibility of indented impressions have not been very successful, and some have the disadvantage that the document is damaged by them. One such method is to rub the surface lightly with a soft pencil, so that only the depressions are not blackened, and therefore show up against the surrounding areas. This is reasonably beneficial for deep impressions which will in any case be revealed by oblique lighting, but will not detect shallow ones. The method is likely to render other methods less effective, and should not be used.

Electrostatic detection
An entirely different technique, which does not rely on a visual examination and does not damage the document, is the electrostatic method of detection. Impressions made on paper affect its dielectric properties, so an electric charge applied to the surface produces a potential different where impressions are present from that of the surrounding area. Why this occurs is not clear, but the effect is of considerable value to the document examiner and is exploited by using a piece of apparatus designed especially for the purpose.

The Electrostatic Detection Apparatus (ESDA) made by Foster and Freeman Ltd (25 Swan Lane, Evesham, Worcs., WR11 4PE), comprises a flat bed of sintered bronze, a porous metal, from below which the air is evacuated by a vacuum pump, a holder of a reel of thin Mylar™ film (a transparent plastic), and a thin wire in a suitable holder which can be charged to about 8 kilovolts (Fig. 11). To use the apparatus the document is placed on the bed of sintered bronze, which is electrically earthed, covered with Mylar film, and the vacuum is applied. This causes the Mylar and the document under it to be sucked tightly down on the metal bed. A charge is

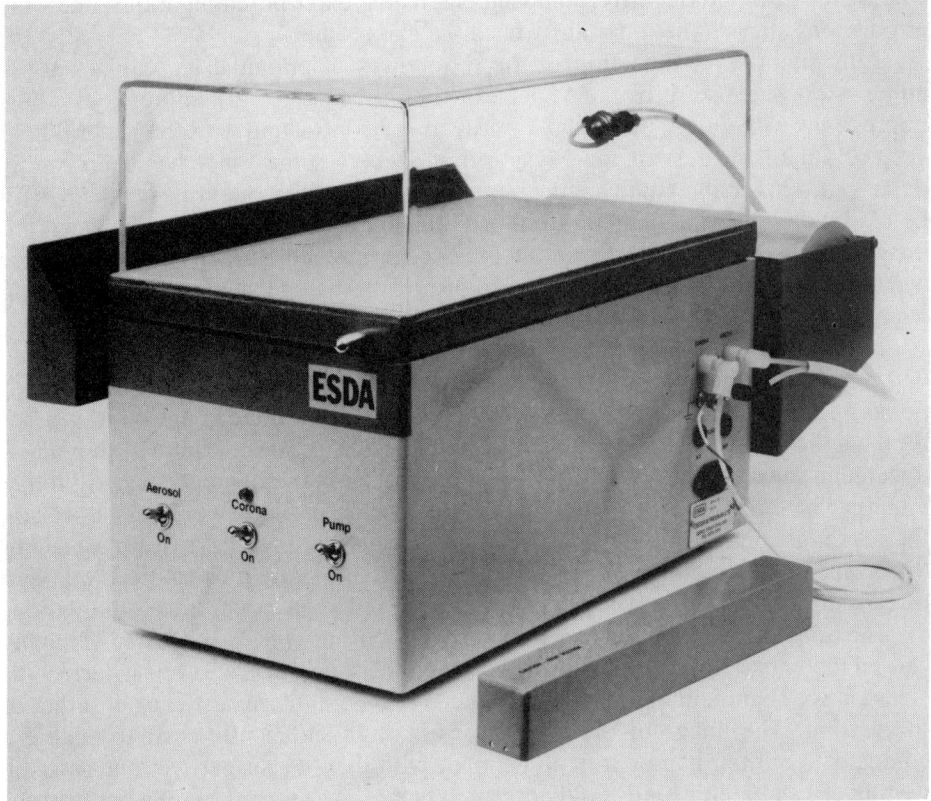

Fig. 11 — The Electrostatic Detection Apparatus (ESDA) made by Foster and Freeman Ltd.

then applied by passing the highly charged wire, called a corona discharge unit, several times just above the surface of the mylar. This produces on the Mylar film an electrostatic charge the potential of which is dependent on the dielectric properties of the paper immediately below it. Because these are different where there are indented impressions, there is a difference of potential on the Mylar film corresponding to the position of the impressions.

The difference in potential between the sites of the impressions is then detected by applying photocopy toner powder to the Mylar surface in one of two ways, or by a combination of both. Included in the apparatus is a pump which forces a cloud of toner powder from a reservoir through a nozzle, charged at the polarity opposite to that of the Mylar surface, which is fixed into the plastic hood. The hood is placed on the flat metal bed so that it covers the document and Mylar film. When the pump is switched on the toner powder cloud is mainly attracted to the impressions as these are the areas of greatest opposite charge. The second way of applying the toner is to pour a developer consisting of toner and glass beads over the surface. The bed is hinged so that it can be tilted, allowing the developer mixture to cascade across the whole area of the Mylar covered document. The greater potential at the site of the impressions attracts the toner away from the glass beads.

Both methods of detection of the differences of potential leave black toner adhering to the surface of the Mylar exactly on the site of the impressions. Most impressions will appear as a black or grey image contrasting with the general light grey colour of the rest of the Mylar surface where some toner has been evenly deposited. This enables many of the impressions to be clearly identified and others to be read with a varying degree of difficulty depending on the contrast between the image and the background. Generally, the deeper the indentations are, the blacker will be the image, but very deep impressions will often be seen in reverse, appearing white against the grey background (see Figs 12 and 13).

The image produced on the Mylar film can be preserved by covering the surface with a sheet of adhesive transparent plastic of the type used as a protective cover for books and other documents. The Mylar film, together with the image on it, is lifted by the adhesive sheet and forms a transparency which can be trimmed to make a document on which the indented impressions are permanently recorded. Although much can be read while the image is still on the apparatus, more can often be seen on the resultant combination of image, Mylar, and plastic sheet. The transparency or 'lift', which has something of the appearance of a photographic negative, although there is no connection between the two, can be used as an exhibit in later litigation.

The transparency can also be used to overlay writing which is suspected of having caused the impressions; if the writing is indeed the source there will be a perfect fit. The relative alignment of the impressions can also be similarly tested against that of the writing. The image of the impressions is often sufficiently clear to enable a comparison of their handwriting to be made with that of a suspect. In one case the writing of a threatening letter did not match that of the suspect, but the impressions of the same wording found on the letter did. On the previous page the suspect had written a draft for an accomplice to copy.

The electrostatic method is very sensitive, detecting impressions too faint to be seen, but is not successful in certain situations. A line of writing, although clearly indented into the paper, will not react in the same way as other indentations, but will usually appear in reverse, as a white line on the grey background. This is an advantage, because writing on the paper on which impressions are found could otherwise be confusing and make the impressions largely indecipherable. As it is, there is sometimes a problem when two or more pages of impressions are found on a page and their superimposition causes difficulties in interpretation.

Electrostatically produced images can be obtained from both sides of a piece of paper, indicating that it is not only the depressions which are detected; it is sometimes found that the back of a page will provide a better result than the front. It appears that dryness of the ambient conditions and in the document are not conducive to good performance, and improvements in weak images can be made if the paper is humidified.

Although it is not always clear why the technique is on some occasions less successful than on others, certain findings indicate that it is likely that what is detected is caused by pressure applied to a paper surface in contact with another piece of paper. An exhausted ball-point pen, for instance, will make indentations but they will not be easily detected by the electrostatic detection apparatus, nor will

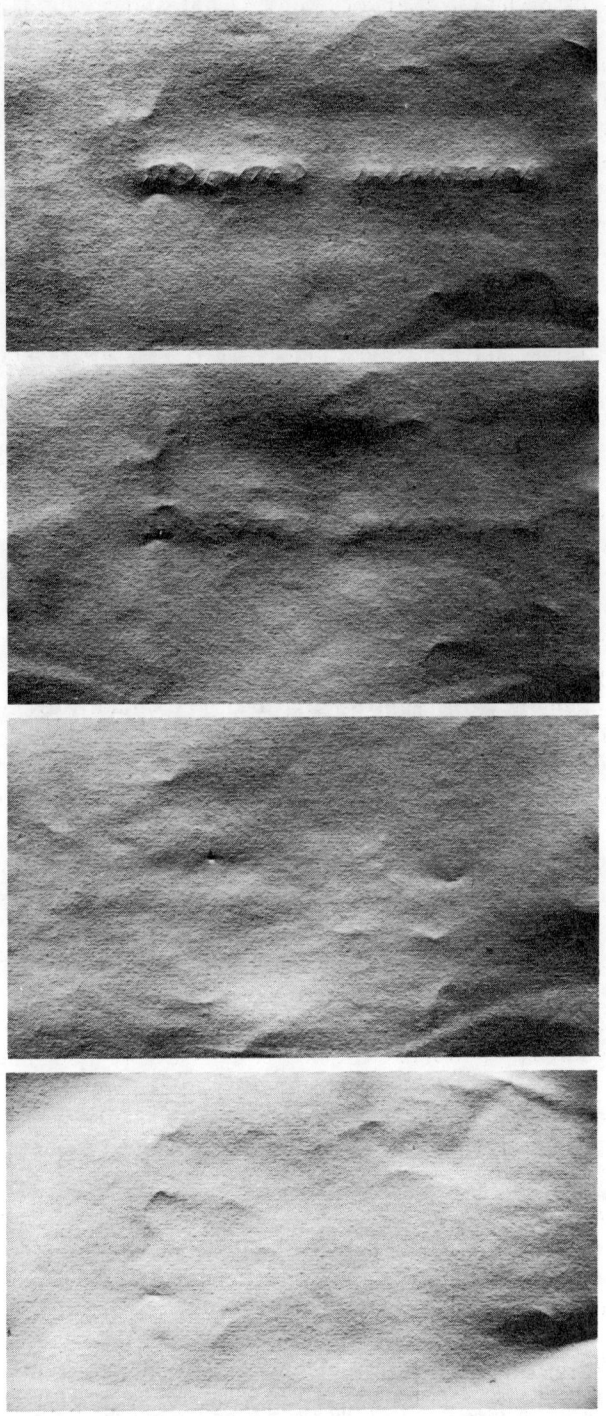

Fig. 12 — Four pieces of paper, which were below another on which the words 'INDENTED IMPRESSIONS' were written, photographed using oblique light.

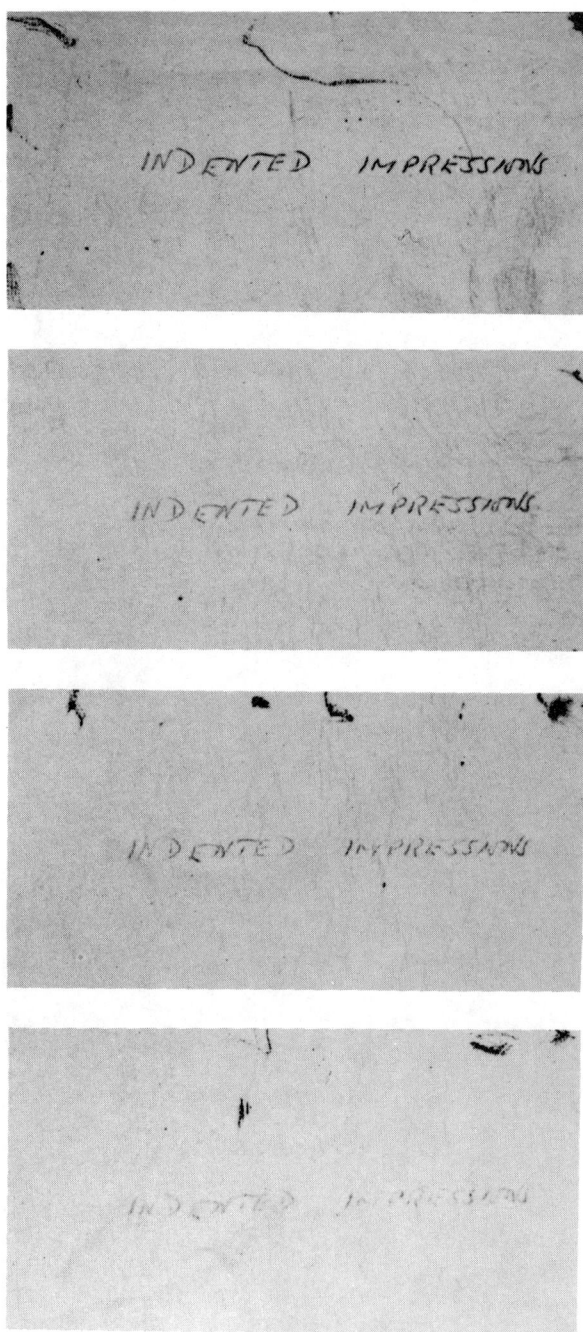

Fig. 13 — The result of the examination by ESDA of the same pieces of paper (shown in Fig. 12). Note that the impressions are easily readable on the first three pieces of paper and detectable on the fourth. In contrast oblique lighting detects impressions only on the first two pieces.

impressions made on paper by writing over plastic where the indentations are made by plastic to paper contact. Although what is detected will remain for years, the method will not work once the document has been treated with a solvent. This makes it important to test for indented impressions before any treatment for fingerprints is carried out.

Indented impressions of typewritings are occasionally found on documents which have been used as a backing between the paper being typed and the platen of the machine. These indentations are best detected by oblique lighting; electrostatic detection is rarely effective for this.

Apart from indented impressions of writing, the electrostatic detection apparatus will reveal other marks on paper. Fingerprints can be found if they are fresh, but it appears that as they dry out they no longer produce any difference in the dielectric properties of the paper. Footprints caused either by the transfer of dust or moisture or pressure can also be detected by this technique.

FINGERPRINTS ON DOCUMENTS

It is not within the purposes of this volume to describe the comparison of finger-prints, but it is common knowledge that a mark sufficiently clear and adequate in size can be identified with its source, a finger, thumb, or palm of a particular person. It is important to note, however, that fingerprints can be found on paper, indicating with certainty that it has been handled by an identifiable individual.

A number of methods are available for the detection of fingermarks on documents; some are destructive, so that any evidence from the document is lost, and others are less so. The most commonly used method, a solution of ninhydrin (indantrione), normally causes little damage to handwriting but destroys any chance of the electrostatic detection of indented impressions. Operational reasons may give priority either to fingerprint development or document examination. In any case where both disciplines are involved there should be cooperation between the experts.

FOLDS AND CREASES

It is often necessary to fold a piece of paper to make it easy to handle or to place it in an envelope. Although such minor damage does not have much significance in most documents, there are occasions on which invaluable evidence can be obtained from it. The effect of a pen moving over a fold or crease is normally noticeable when examined under a microscope. The act of folding a piece of paper breaks the top calendered surface and exposes fibres with different absorbent properties. As the pen passes over the damaged area there is a tendency for more ink to be picked up by the fibres. This is accentuated by the ridge caused by the fold which provides a greater resistance to the pen than does flat paper. The resultant extra ink at the crossing point contrasts with an even coating of that of the rest of the line. When the fold is made after the ink line there is no reason for extra ink to be found, and although there will be some changes in appearance caused by the breaking of the surface at the crossing point they will not show the same effects.

The most important reason for determining whether the fold has been made before the writing line or after it is to show the order in which two writings have been made. It may be important to establish when a fold was made in relation to an ink line, but it is more likely that the relative time of writing of two entries each crossing the same fold will be of significance. Other forms of recording information, such as typewriting, pencil lines, and rubber stamps, will also produce different effects when made over folds or creases, and these can also be used to discover in what order they were made.

Creased carbon paper has provided evidence to show that two carbon copies, each containing different information and with inadequate typewriting for proof of a common source, had been made using the same piece of carbon paper. This had been irregularly creased during its previous use, and the pressure exerted by the machine on the combination of paper and carbon paper resulted in the pattern of the creases being reproduced on both copies. Such an examination is not a routine method in document examination, but it illustrates the occasional unusual finding which can be of great significance.

OFFSET MARKS

When two pieces of paper are pressed together, marks such as writing and printing may be transferred from one to another. The effect is dependent on the dryness of the materials in contact; moist inks obviously are more likely to transfer than those which have completely dried out. The required pressure between the two pages is often provided by a writing instrument. Writing made on one side of a page can cause writing on the back or on a second page to be transferred to the surface with which it is in contact. Such offset marks indicate the order in which writings are made. Clearly, the ink transferred by the pressure of the pen must have been present first.

As well as writing made with ball-point ink or pencil, materials such as printing ink or dirt from the surface on which the paper is resting can be transferred.

STAPLES AND PAPER CLIPS

Although staples are commonly used to keep a bundle of documents together, their presence is rarely of any significance in the investigation of crime or in any other concern of the document examiner. Sometimes, however, it is important to know whether two or more documents have been stapled together, or how many times they have been separated.

The commonly used staple is made of soft metal and is shaped like a rectangle with one side missing. When it is forced into the paper by the stapler its parallel sides are bent round and it makes either two holes or, if it is inserted with greater force, two further marks between the two holes where the bent ends touch the paper. It is possible with care to remove the staple and replace it without leaving evidence that this has been done, but on other occasions the staple will be distorted and therefore show evidence of tampering.

When a staple is inserted the position chosen will vary within certain limits. Although the general position, usually near the top right or top left corner, will be common to many documents, the exact place and angle of the staple will show a considerable variation. This means that once the staple has been removed the position of the two (or four) holes it leaves will not be the same in relation to the edges of the paper as those of another bundle of papers except by a most unlikely coincidence. If the bundle has been separated and restapled leaving further holes, the chances of coincidental match are even smaller. Strong evidence that two or more documents have been stapled together at one or more times is therefore provided. When examining staple marks some account must be taken of the fact that movement of the pages can cause the holes to enlarge. This in itself can provide extra evidence to link two documents if both have similarly wider holes. In other cases the documents may have been torn away, leaving a tear between two holes.

Examination of staple marks can provide evidence that a bundle of documents has or has not been photocopied. The staple or its marks will normally show on the copy, or the turned over corners will be apparent if a bundle has not been separated. The time at which the copies were made may also be ascertained by the presence or absence of copied staples or holes.

The value of occasional or non-routine observations in document examination is illustrated by a case where a woman was attacked and her handbag taken. It had been the practice of the woman's employer to staple all the notes into wage packets so that they could be checked before the staple was removed. A pair of staple holes on a pound note found on the suspect exactly matched the holes on the woman's wages packet when the note was put into it. Comparison with other wages packets showed that there was considerable variation in the position of the staples and that the match was therefore highly significant.

Paper clips leave marks which are obviously less visible than those left by staples, but the impressions which can be found slightly indented into the paper can also provide evidence to link two documents. There is less variation possible in the positions in which a paper clip may be placed, but the chances of an exact match occurring by coincidence are still low.

With both paper clips and staple mark evidence complications can occur when other staples and clips are used after the investigation or trial has begun. These may cause confusion, and it is best to avoid further damage to any document under investigation. There is a need to identify a particular document with a label, but it is important to consider that the act of labelling may damage significant evidence. Labels stuck on to documents also may destroy important evidence.

DAMAGE TO DOCUMENTS

In some respects the marks found on documents and described above represent forms of damage, but in certain cases documents are deliberately damaged or destroyed to avoid the information they contain being discovered. In other cases accidental damage occurs.

It is one of the functions of an examiner of documents to discover what has been lost in such cases. If the page in question has been completely destroyed or lost, the only approach is to examine pages which were previously underlying or adjacent in the hope that indented impressions or offset marks may be found. In instances where the document is completely changed by the action of fire or moisture, chewing for example, it may be possible to discover what was present before the damage was done.

Charred documents

If a piece of paper is completely burned, all the organic material is destroyed and only inorganic ash remains. The appearance of this will depend on its chemical composition which in turn will depend on the filler in the paper and also on the inorganic components of any ink that was present. Ash from inks is more likely to be visible if it derives from printing rather than from writing or typewriting because printing inks have a much higher proportion of inorganic compounds.

Little can be done with documents which are burned down to ash, because they disintegrate almost immediately. Nevertheless, one method suggested for the determination of what was present on incompletely burned or charred paper involves the further charring of what is found until it consists entirely of ash [1].

More usually, documents are examined when they have not been completely burnt but are merely charred, and, although brittle, can be moved with care. In this condition, writing or typewriting or printing contrasts with the background in a number of ways depending on the composition of both the paper and the ink. The information from the document can then be observed. Various methods have been described to improve the contrast between the ink and paper, but most tend not to improve the clarity, or even make it worse. They may also damage or break up the brittle charred fragments. Examination or photography under infrared radiation can, however, be helpful and is non-destructive. This may appear surprising because carbon absorbs infrared as well as all other wavelengths, and the black fragments seem to contain much carbon. In practice, however, the contrast is often improved, presumably because the inks absorb infrared radiation while the charred paper is black because of partly converted resinous material rather than because it has degraded to elemental carbon.

Whether or not photography can enhance the contrast between the writing or printing and the background, it is of great value in recording what is visible. Charred documents can easily disintegrate, so it is important that a permanent record is made.

The preservation of charred paper can be aided by carefully dropping a solution of plastic material on it so that it is absorbed and therefore permanently strengthened when the solvent has evaporated, but this causes the information it contains to be made less clear.

Matted documents

Documents soaked in water are found on unidentified bodies, often in a state of decomposition, or may be recovered from the mouth of a suspect who has attempted to destroy it by eating it. In both cases the effect of the moisture is to cause the paper either to adhere to itself in a screwed up mass or for separate pages to become matted together. The penetration of the water may also cause the ink to run.

To determine what was written on the document it is necessary to separate those areas which are adhering. Careful prising apart of the dried material can be successful (the conglomerated mass is usually dry when it is received); or it can be moistened first and then separated and straightened. Examination under conditions which excite infrared or visible luminescence may enable washed out entries to be identified from the insoluble traces that remain.

Freeze drying has been reported as a successful method of separation. The dried mass of documents is soaked in water and then placed in the chamber of a freeze drier. This results in the water being removed and the substances holding the paper together being broken down so that the pages can be easily separated.

ERASURES AND OBLITERATIONS

In Chapter 7, methods of erasure and obliteration and their detection by examination of inks and traces of inks were discussed. The surface of paper is affected in the process of erasure, either chemical or mechanical, and it is often of importance to show that such action has taken place. Other marks or stains which have been made accidentally or deliberately are found in documents, and these may have some importance in an investigation.

A liquid applied to the surface of a document will leave a mark at the limits of its extent. This may not be visible in normal light but will show when the document is examined under ultraviolet or conditions which produce infrared luminescence. A document completely dipped in a solvent may not show this effect, but the paper may have an irregular or crinkled effect. Tests for the chloride ion, a product of the bleaching agent, can be made but are rarely necessary. Effects of solvents are also found when security papers are altered; these sometimes contain special materials which stain the paper when it is treated with a liquid. Printed security backgrounds also react to such treatment.

Some security papers are made which react to mechanical action, by producing staining, but most altered documents do not. Examination for areas where erasure may have taken place is best made by using oblique light. This shows the loose fibres which result from the breaking down of the surface coating of the paper and the general roughness of the abraded surface. Soft X-rays or a source of beta-radiation, more usually used on documents to record watermarks, will also detect areas where paper has been removed along with the ink which has been erased.

Writing made with pencil or erasable ball-point ink can be removed by a rubber eraser without damaging the paper surface, and if traces of the writing material or indentations cannot be seen, little evidence is left. The action of the eraser, however, leaves on the surface traces of rubber which, although too small to be seen, can be detected with specially stained lycopodium powder. This is composed of very small spores coloured to make them clearly visible. When placed on the erased surface the powder adheres to the rubber particles. The action of gently shaking or tapping the document causes the powder not adhering to rubber particles to fall away and those adhering to remain, thus demonstrating the area over which the eraser has been used. The powder can be brushed off, leaving the document unaffected [9].

ALTERED ENVELOPES

One of the special problems encountered in the examination of questioned documents is the determination of whether or not an envelope has been opened and resealed. There are a number of reasons for this examination. The recipient of a letter may claim that money or some valuable document was not present when it was opened; a sealed safe deposit envelope may have been opened, or the sealed packet containing a sample of blood taken for alcohol determination may have been opened to replace the blood before analysis. In nearly every such case the examiner is given an opened envelope, and he needs to determine from it whether there is evidence for a previous opening and a reclosing of the envelope. In some cases the task is made easier by security measures adopted when the envelope was first sealed. These can include the presence of sealing wax or adhesive tape, or signatures may have been made across the edges of the flaps.

The methods employed to open an envelope with a view to sealing it again are to attack one of the flaps by pulling it gently off, possibly after moistening the glue with water or steam, or to make a clean cut along one edge. To close the opened envelope an attempt may be made to use the original glue or, more often, to add extra adhesive; in the case of a cut edge a very thin line of glue is added to the insides of the cut edges. In some cases an unsuccessful attempt may be made at one site before the task is performed on another.

The detection of such action involves a number of examinations, beginning with those which do not further damage the envelope and continuing to those which require it to be taken apart.

When a flap is opened by moistening with water or steam the surface becomes crinkled, and the action of tearing it away from the main body of the envelope may cause it to become torn. A preliminary examination, therefore, is made to establish whether or not the flaps at the top and bottom and on the sides are smooth and undamaged. The edges should be gently raised to look for extra glue, which may extend beyond the area covered by the flaps. In an unaltered envelope there will be a small gap between the edge of the flaps and the glue, so any adhesive occurring right up to the edge is indicative of abnormality.

Extra glue under the flap can be detected by using a micrometer to measure the thickness of the appropriate areas and comparing them with that of an unaltered similar envelope. A better method to detect extra adhesive is to use soft X-rays. The greater mass of the glue absorbs more X-rays than do the surrounding areas and shows as a lighter area on a negative photographic film. In contrast to glue put on the envelope in manufacture, which is in evenly shaped approximately rectangular areas, added adhesive is irregularly applied with no consistent form.

Signatures written over sealed flaps or seams of an envelope can be reconstructed when the envelope is resealed, but it is not easy to put the flaps back so that both parts of the signature are exactly in alignment. Instead, parts of the writing line may appear under the flap or, if the replacement of the flap is out of line in a horizontal direction, two sections of a continuous line will not connect. Care has to be taken to avoid erroneous conclusions; it is sometimes possible for a pen to slip under a flap when the signature is first made, and the normal action of a pen moving from a higher to a lower surface results in a small gap in the writing line at the edge.

Adhesive tape provides an effective method of sealing an envelope and cannot easily be removed without taking off the surface layer of the paper. Replacement with another piece of tape may disguise the damaged surface, but the appearance will not be exactly the same. Careful observation of the surface through tape will show that the surface has been affected. A signature under the original tape may be partly or wholly removed with the tape and will be almost impossible to replace; its absence will therefore provide clear evidence of tampering.

If a non-destructive examination does not afford conclusive proof of resealing the envelope has to be taken apart. This is best done by cutting the sides where there is no likelihood of destroying any evidence. The inside surface can be examined for excess glue or any resealing of cut edges. The last operation is to pull the flaps or seams gently apart to discover any extra adhesive or any signs of a previous opening. If an envelope has been sealed by using only part of the adhesive it is possible to use the rest to reseal it. In most cases, however, extra glue is needed.

The opening of the flap or seam may also result in tears to the inner surface of the paper; those made at the first opening can be discovered under extra glue. When latex rubber seals are pulled apart, strips of adhesive are produced which break and collapse, leaving coils on the surface. These provide evidence of previous opening.

The examination of adhesives

Although the presence of extra adhesive, detected by soft X-rays or by visual examination on an opened flap, is in itself of significance and may require no further confirmation, chemical analysis of the material may be appropriate in order to show that there are two different materials present. On the small amounts of glue that can be removed for testing only a limited examination can be made, sufficient to identify its type rather than the manufacturer or batch.

There are several main types of adhesive provided for office and domestic use, dextrin or starch-based products, protein glues, latex adhesives and synthetic materials such as solvent-based plastic compounds, epoxy resins, and cyanoacrylic resins. The removal of a few particles of the dried adhesive from the surface and their examination under a low-powered microscope can give an indication of its type. For instance, a latex glue will be pliable, and one based on polyvinyl chloride will appear shiny, while others may crumble easily or remain difficult to break up. Although separate simple tests can be performed to identify the main types of adhesive, pyrolysis mass spectroscopy — which breaks down the sample into small molecular fragments, the combinations of which are characteristic of the adhesive type — provides a single method by which each can be identified. As well as indicating the presence of more than one adhesive the method can be used to compare the added material with any source which may be found in the possession of the suspect.

THE EXAMINATION OF PASSPORTS

Passport examination presents the document examiner with a specific range of problems, some directly involving the techniques employed on other documents and described elsewhere, but others found only with passports or similar articles such as identity cards or driving licences. The task of the examiner is to determine the authenticity and integrity of the document, by testing it for differences from the genuine product and detecting alterations and erasures.

There are essentially three methods of falsifying passports, causing them to give information that is not appropriate to their holders. These are:

(1) The complete counterfeiting of a genuine passport.
(2) Making an alteration to the written or printed information.
(3) Substituting a photograph or a page of the original passport.

The discovery of the evidence for the first two methods is dealt with elsewhere. Counterfeiting requires a copying of the paper, printing, and security features of the original, and its detection depends on comparing genuine documents with those suspected of being spurious. Without adequate authentic examples to compare it is impossible to be sure that a passport is a counterfeit. The quality of some genuine passports is not high, and these can be wrongly suspected to be falsely fabricated.

Alterations to specific written or printed entries in passports are made for a variety of reasons. Names, dates of birth, and other entries are changed by erasure and overwriting, or by simply overwriting or by adding extra letters or words. Entry or exit stamps are also altered, and unwanted endorsements written or stamped in the passport are chemically or mechanically removed. The techniques for the detection of such alterations are described in Chapter 7.

The third method of falsification, by substitution, requires different techniques of examination. A stolen passport is likely to be fraudulently used by another person different in appearance, so it is necessary to change the photograph by removing the original and replacing it with another. Security devices are used to make this difficult. It is very rarely possible for a change of photograph to be sufficiently successful to be undetected by the document examiner, but the earlier more cursory examination at a point of entry may be inadequate to discover evidence of substitution. Similarly, if a page bears an unwanted entry, it may be changed for a page from another passport. This may also be difficult to discover at a glance, but will be detected in the examiner's laboratory.

The techniques of detection of substituted photographs and pages are those of observation. Examination under relatively low magnification can detect the presence of traces of original photographs, evidence of tampering with security devices such as embossed stamps and signatures. Substituted pages are discovered by examination of the binding of the passport and by comparison of the paper. Page numbers are sometimes altered when the appropriately numbered pages are unavailable.

CROSSED LINES

The sequencing of two lines which cross, or the determination of which line was made first, is of considerable value in certain cases. A paragraph or sentence written immediately above a signature may be in dispute, the signatory claiming that it was not present when he signed the document. If part of the writing of the disputed passage crosses the signature and it can be established which of the two was present on the paper before the other, the dispute can be settled.

The problem, however, is not so easily solved as it might appear to be. The concept of a layer of ink over another is easy to imagine but is not found in practice. Instead of forming a film, like a paint layer, ink is absorbed into the paper. A subsequent line drawn across it fills uninked spaces and mingles with the already deposited ink so that direct or magnified observation cannot distinguish the first applied ink from the later one. A darker coloured line or one with a higher proportion of ink, will appear to be on top of a lighter coloured line or a thinner ink whether it is or not. This illusion can be misleading if it is not recognised as such.

Other sequencing problems occur with lines made of a variety of materials, different writing instruments and their inks, typewriting with various types of ribbon, and marks made by rubber stamps.

Liquid ink sequencing

Inks based on aqueous or other mobile solvents soak into the surface of normal paper entirely, and so nothing can be determined from the apparent presence of a top layer. The situation is nearer that of a twice dyed piece of cloth; the darker colour will dominate to the exclusion of the lighter. Evidence of the order of the crossing strokes is provided by the effect of one line on another. In the now largely obsolete iron-based inks the paper in the ink line was affected so that it would take up the ink of the second line and draw some of it away from the crossing by capillary action. This gave a darker appearance to the line along a distance of around one millimetre either side of the crossing, indicating that the partly darkened line was made first.

This phenomenon is now hardly ever found, but if two different inks cross, the second may remove a trace of the first and carry it a short way down its length. Because such a transfer involves only a very small quantity of ink or a component of it, detection is possible usually only when the transferred constituent luminesces or fluoresces strongly and differently from the overwriting ink.

Ball-point inks

Writing with ball-point pens requires heavier pressure than that needed for liquid ink pens. The impressions or grooves which are formed by this pressure can be exploited when considering which of two crossing lines was made first. A pen crossing a groove will be influenced to some extent by it, and this may be detectable. However, heavy pressure of the pen will distort the groove as it crosses it, and, if sufficient, will flatten the paper so that there is no difference in the level of the surface at the crossing.

If a more lightly written stroke crosses a depression, the evenness of the ink line will be affected. A greater quantity of ink will be deposited on the further or uphill side of the groove, with some loss on the side where the paper surface falls into the depression. This effect can sometimes be seen as a narrowing and widening of the ink line, in the shape of an hour glass, as it crosses a previously made stroke. These features are observed under magnification of around ten to thirty times, using a suitable incident-light microscope.

When two inks are similar in colour or if the same ink has been used for both lines, these effects are difficult or impossible to detect. Infrared absorption or luminescence may be used to determine the sequence of writing of two lines if the inks react differently in these conditions. The unevenness of the line at the crossing point may be discovered only when it or the other ink fluoresces or if the crossing is examined in conditions under which the other ink is not visible.

Writing on one side of a page can leave impressions deep enough to affect the surface on the other side. Raised lines caused by depressions on the reverse may influence a line written across them. Provided that the pressure exerted by the pen making the line is not too great to flatten the ridge, a larger deposit of ink will appear on the rising side and a correspondingly smaller amount will be present on the falling side. These effects can be found at a number of points where the writing lines from either side of the paper cross. They may be of value if the order of writing of the two sides is in dispute or if the relative ages of two pieces of writing on one side can be deduced from writing on the reverse.

Depressions made with ball-point pens can affect writing lines made later with liquid inks, but the opposite order of strokes will rarely leave evidence. A liquid ink pen usually leaves the surface of the paper virtually unchanged and flat, so no effects of the shape of the surface will occur.

Various other methods to determine the sequence of crossing ball-point ink lines have been suggested but are not widely used. One of these involves the use of a shiny coated paper, which is pressed on to the crossing with a hot iron so that a partial image of the ink lines is transferred to the paper. This accentuates the edges of the lines, so they appear as narrow parallel 'tramlines'. Continuous tramlines crossing broken ones from the other line provide an indication that the stroke which made their image was made last [7].

Other methods have been described which use a high-powered microscope which combines a light source focused downwards on to the crossing point. These methods rely on a difference in the reflected light from the surface, a continuous line indicating the upper stroke and the different broken reflection the lower one.

Ball-point and liquid ink lines written on glossy paper present few problems of sequencing. Because they are not absorbed into the paper but dry on the surface, they are affected by subsequent lines which cross them. There is a tendency for the ink to concentrate at the edges of the line, rather like squash lines in letterpress printing (Chapter 8); the last-made line is indicated by unbroken parallel edges at the crossing contrasting with the first-made edges which are broken.

Pencil lines

The small amount of material deposited by a 'lead' pencil on paper and the incomplete covering of the whole of the area which it marks, makes any line crossing of two such pencil lines or a pencil line and either liquid or ball-point ink difficult to sequence. It is in fact rarely of any interest to an investigator or to a court; entries of any significance are infrequently made in pencil.

Wax crayon lines

Wax crayon lines are made of thicker deposits of material, and evidence as to whether or not they were made before other lines can be found by using a scanning electron microscope. This instrument will display certain materials at high magnifications so that they can be seen resting on the paper surface. It will not, however, show others, liquid writing ink for instance, because they are in, not on, the paper.

Wax crayon appears as a granular mass, and ball-point ink as having a paste-like consistency. Complications are caused by uneven deposits, but a line made by a pen crossing a wax pencil line will smooth out the granular surface whether or not it deposits ink. A ball-point ink crossing over a wax line or the same lines made in the reverse order can be sequenced by observation of the relative position of the two materials. This is not always entirely clear, and some experience is needed to recognise the appearance of the images of different media.

Sequencing of typewriting

The determination of the order of two typewritten entries made with liquid inks from fabric ribbons is, like those with similar inks from pens, unlikely to be possible. Again, the colouring material is taken up by the paper and does not rest on the surface. Similarly, typewritings made by these ribbons which cross pen lines provide little or no evidence of their order of stroke.

Determination of stroke sequence when carbon ribbons, which operate by depositing a piece of plastic film in the shape of a letter, are used is more successful. Deposits from carbon ribbons are examined by scanning electron microscopy. If they cross lines made with ball-point inks the sequence can be determined by observation of the relative position of each material. Their surface is also affected by pressure from the point of pen, and evidence of this can be found by careful observation of the enlargements.

Scanning electron microscopy of crossed lines may require the crossing to be removed and placed in a small chamber in the instrument. It is therefore partly a destructive method, and if the document must not be damaged it cannot be used. Although the piece of paper removed is not destroyed and could be examined later by another expert, the document cannot be restored to its previous condition.

FURTHER READING

[1] Baier, P. E. (1983) Application of experimental variables to the use of electrostatic detection apparatus *Journal of Forensic Sciences* **28** 901

[2] Bartha, A. (1973) Restoration and preservation of typewriting and printing on charred documents *Canadian Forensic Science Society Journal* **6** 111

[3] Ellen, D. M., Foster, D. J. & Morantz, D. J. (1980) Use of electrostatic imaging in the detection of indented impressions *Forensic Science International* **15** 53

[4] Godown, L. (1982) Recent developments in writing sequence determination *Forensic Science International* **20** 227

[5] Gupta, A. K., Gubshan Rai & Chugh, O. P. (1987) Ball-point determination of writing sequence of strokes of pen versus ball-point pen and other conventional writing instruments *Forensic Science International* **34** 217

[6] Herod, D. W. & Menzel, E. R. (1982) Laser detection of latent fingerprints: ninhydrin followed by zinc chloride *Journal of Forensic Sciences* **27** 513

[7] Igoe, T. J. & Reynolds, B. L. (1982) A lifting process for determining the writing sequence of two intersecting ball-point strokes *Forensic Science International* **20** 201

[8] Jonker, H., Molenaar, A. & Dippel, C. J. (1969) Physical development recording systems 3 Physical Development *Photographic Science and Engineering* **13** 45

[9] Kind, S. S. & Dabbs, M. D. G. (1979) The use of lycode powders for the detection of erasures *Journal of the Forensic Science Society* **19** 175

[10] Kobus, H. J., Stoilovic, M. & Warrender, R. N. (1983) A simple luminescent post ninhydrin treatment for the improved visualisation of fingerprints on documents in cases when ninhydrin alone gives poor results *Forensic Science International* **22** 161

[11] Levinson, J. (1984) Passport examination *Journal of Forensic Sciences* **29** 628

[12] Menzel, E. R. (1980) *Fingerprint Detection with Lasers* Marcel Dekker Inc. New York, ISBN 0-8247-6974-0

[13] Moore, D. S. (1981) Evaluation of a method using powder to detect the site of rubber erasures *Journal of Forensic Sciences* **26** 724

[14] Moore, D. S. (1988) The electrostatic detection apparatus (ESDA) and its effects on latent prints on paper *Journal of Forensic Sciences* **33** 357

[15] Noblett, M. G. & James, E. L. (1983) Optimum conditions for examination of documents using an electrostatic detection apparatus (ESDA) device to visualise indented writings *Journal of Forensic Sciences* **28** 697

[16] Oden, S. & von Hofsten, B. (1954) Detection of fingerprints by the ninhydrin reaction *Nature* **173** 449

[17] Oron, M. & Tamir, W. (1974) Development of SEM methods for forensic problems encountered in handwritten and printed documents *Scanning Electron Microscopy* p. 207

[18] Radley, R. W. (1982) Determination of sequence of ball-point writing utilising infrared luminescence techniques *Journal of the Forensic Science Society* **22** 373

[19] Riker, M. R. & Lewis, G. W. (1988) Methylene blue revisited: the search for a trouble-free erasure sensitive powder *Journal of Forensic Sciences* **33** 773

[20] Schuetzner, E. M. (1988) Examination of sequence of strokes with an image enhancement system *Journal of Forensic Sciences* **33** 244

[21] Spedding, D. J. (1971) Detection of latent fingerprints with $^{35}SO_2$ *Nature* **229** 1

[22] Spencer, R., J. & Giles, A. (1986) Multiple-processing of Visa vouchers *Journal of the Forensic Science Society* **26** 401

[23] Tappolet, J. A. (1985) Use of lycode powders for the examination of documents partially written with erasable ball-point pen inks *Forensic Science International* **28** 115

[24] Taylor, L. R. (1986) The restoration and identification of water-soaked documents: A case study *Journal of Forensic Sciences* **31** 1113

[25] Waeschle, P. A. (1979) Examination of line crossings by scanning electron microscopy *Journal of Forensic Sciences* **24** 569

[26] Welch, J. R. (1982) Lycode powders in a case of erasure *Journal of the Forensic Science Society* **22** 43

[27] Wanxiang, Luo & Xiaoling, Cai (1988) A study of the principle of the electrostatic imaging technique *Journal of the Forensic Society* **28** 237

10

The functions of photography in document examination and other special techniques

PHOTOGRAPHY

There are three main functions of photography in document examination: to make a permanent record of the document before it is damaged in the course of certain examinations, to detect certain features which are not visible and for which other methods are unavailable or less convenient, and to prepare material from which demonstration charts for use in courts are prepared.

Record photography

Although the document examiner will avoid any damage until all other methods have failed to give adequate information, there are tests for inks and other materials which appear on a document as well as for the paper itself which require a small quantity to be removed. Other tests such as those for fingerprint detection stain the whole document, and, rarely, may damage the writing. Dry transfer lettering or newspaper cut-outs may become separated from the paper on which they are placed when this is treated for fingerprints.

A properly prepared photograph of a document is capable of displaying most of the information visible on the original and can therefore be used as a substitute for it in a court or in preliminary investigation. The preparation of a high quality photograph made for a record in such cases requires considerable expertise. Without proper care there may be lack of sharpness due to poor focusing, or too much or too little contrast caused by using the wrong exposure, developers, or materials. Inadequate or uneven lighting also produces poor results. To counter these problems proper equipment is required, and more importantly, a skilled photographer able to adapt his expertise to the varying problems posed by different documents.

A document being photographed needs to be flat, and, in order to achieve this, a suction back, a porous plate with a vacuum behind it, can be used. Alternatively, the page can be covered with a glass plate which keeps it in place. Lighting is provided from two or more sources; one would produce an uneven result. The most suitable cameras for record photography are those using 5×4 film. 35 mm cameras use a far smaller negative so the resolution of a suitably sized enlargement is reduced. The grain of the emulsion is a limiting factor in this format, and important detail can be lost if too large an area is photographed. A scale should be included in the photograph to enable the final print to be made equal in size to the original. As a short exposure time is not required, a slow film producing good resolution is generally best.

The variety of available film is very wide. Colour photographs have considerable advantage in that they show differences in the colour of inks, but are more expensive and have limitations in that the dyes available can result in failure to reproduce the true colours. High-resolution black and white emulsions produce photographs of excellent clarity, and in most cases show everything required.

A photograph taken as a record, although of good quality, will not always be an adequate substitute for the original document for scientific examination. Without the right lighting conditions it may not be possible to detect evidence of tracing, and without adequate magnification the method of the construction of the handwriting may not be visible. In many cases, however, it is possible to find on a photograph adequate material on which to base a firm conclusion if the document is no longer available or is not in a suitable condition for direct examination.

Recording invisible radiations

Photography is capable not only of reproducing what can be seen but, in certain conditions, of recording what the eye cannot detect. Photographic emulsions can be made sensitive to both ultraviolet and infrared radiation and also to X-rays, none of which are seen by the eye. Techniques which employ those invisible radiations to differentiate between inks or to reveal erasures or watermarks can therefore use photography as a primary method of detection as well as to provide a permanent record of the findings.

The significance of infrared absorption, ultraviolet and infrared luminescence, and X-ray absorption has been dealt with elsewhere. The detection of the latter in document examination is exclusively achieved photographically, but, as described in Chapter 7, in ways which differ from those of conventional photography.

Fluorescence in the visible range of the spectrum excited by ultraviolet radiation can be photographed by using a filter which prevents the exciting radiation from falling on the film. Infrared radiation can now be recorded by image converters or by sensitive tubes in video units, but originally was detectable only by photography. There is still an advantage in infrared photography in that the resolution of a photograph is greater than that achieved on a video screen: finer detail can therefore be detected.

Infrared photography requires suitably sensitive emulsions, found only on films or plates made for the purpose. Focusing of the image requires an adjustment to allow for the difference in refraction of infrared and that of visible light. Some camera bellows and plastic processing tanks transmit infrared, so these have to be avoided.

Illumination of the document being photographed is provided either from a tungsten lamp or from a source suitable for the excitation of luminescence (see

Chapter 7), but to ensure that only the appropriate wavelengths of infrared are recorded, filters are required. Without the aid of a video system this is rather a hit-and-miss process. It is necessary to test different wavelengths in the infrared region by placing different filters successively over the camera lens.

If a video system is available, the choice of the appropriate filter is made easy. The best conditions are found by selecting the most effective filter, and this, or one of the same type, is used for the photograph. The alternative method of simply taking a picture of the screen is simpler, but the resolution is much poorer. In some cases the exact conditions of lighting and filtration of a successful detection of an erasure may be difficult to reproduce away from the video apparatus, so it may be necessary to photograph the screen and accept a lower level of resolution.

The use of filters

Apart from the separation of infrared reflection or luminescence from a background of visible light as described above, filters can be used to increase the contrast between two parts of a document. A filter which allows light of only a certain colour to pass will cause writing or marks of that colour to react in the same way as a white background. Only the colour of the filter will pass through, whether the object is entirely of that colour or is a mixture of some or all wavelengths. A partial obliteration of a black ink with a blue ink which cannot be interpreted by other means can be photographed through a deep blue filter. This has the effect of reducing the intensity of the blue obliteration without affecting the black entry, and may provide sufficient contrast to answer the problem. The reverse situation, the identification of an obliteration with black ink, cannot be helped in this way because no coloured filter can allow black areas, caused by a total absorption of all wavelengths, to appear lighter.

The examination of some partial obliterations, therefore, even when photographed through filters, will not be aided by attempts to increase contrast in the image of the two inks. However, photography can assist in these cases. An enlarged print of the obliteration can be made, and those parts which are clearly from the obliterating ink can be visually removed by covering them with white correcting fluid, leaving only those traces which appear to be from the obliterated entry. The interpretation of these is much less difficult when they stand apart from the obliteration.

In some cases where the overwriting ink cannot be rendered invisible by filters, but where that which is required to be identified can be, an ingenious method can be employed. A negative photograph is made of the document, using a filter which makes the required entries invisible, and a second photograph of the same area is made under conditions which make these entries as contrasting to their background as possible. A positive transparency is made of the second photograph, and it and the first negative are bound together so that their images are exactly superimposed. The negative image will tend to cancel out the positive overwriting and the background, and leave the image of the required entry unaffected. Some adjustment of the intensity of the images is necessary to achieve the right balance and a print is made from the combined transparencies. In certain cases the technique can be very effective.

Photography for demonstration charts
Much of what is needed to prepare charts for the demonstration of the conclusions of a document examiner in court has already been covered. The most common need is for photographs of writing to be made to demonstrate the similarities and differences apparent between the known and questioned writings. In such cases the writing rather than the whole document is photographed to provide maximum resolution when the negative is printed to give a magnification of between 1.5 and 2 times the original. Because the photographs are cut up to prepare a chart it is necessary on occasions to print two copies so that writings which overlap can be separately shown complete.

In contrast to record photography where every detail of the document should be reproduced, it is sometimes an advantage to remove from the picture those extraneous features which have no bearing on what is to be demonstrated. The coloured security background on cheques, or the marks made by a bank cashier across the signature, are often of a different colour from that of the questioned writing and can therefore be removed from the photograph by the use of an appropriate filter.

It is not necessary to print each example of writing with the same magnification. In some cases large writing has to be compared with small, and it is clearly advantageous for the images of both to be approximately similar in size when their detail is being demonstrated. Size is not an important factor in many comparisons, and because the documents themselves or photocopies of them will clearly show that there is a dimensional difference, any confusion should be minimal. The more important similarities or differences in detail are more clearly appreciated if both known and questioned writings are shown similar in size.

Differences in inks or restored obliterations or erasures detected by photography of infrared radiation or fluorescence excited by ultraviolet are often clearly shown in the resultant photographic print. This is therefore ideally suitable in itself as a method of demonstrating the findings. In many cases where documents are examined by electronic methods, photography is used only as a means of producing demonstration charts. Where such photographs are made it is helpful to those to whom the findings are to be demonstrated if normal light photographs are also included. This enables a 'before and after' comparison to be made.

Photography of indented impressions is often useful to show guide lines from which a signature has been traced or to demonstrate the impressions themselves if electrostatic methods are not available or do not work for the particular case. Illumination of the document from a source nearly parallel and close to the paper casts shadows in the impressions and makes them visible in a photograph. However, to achieve satisfactory results considerable practice and skill are needed. Again, a normal light photograph contrasting with that taken in oblique lighting will be of assistance.

Examination of photographs as questioned documents
Photographs themselves are on occasions questioned documents. It may be necessary to identify the camera in which the negative was made. The masking frame in the camera may have irregular edges, caused by damage or dirt, which leave their images on the film exposed in the camera. Because the irregularities are normally suffi-

ciently random to allow for no practical chance of coincidental match, the negative, and perhaps prints made from it, can be positively associated with the camera.

Polaroid films have throw-away masking frames, and the camera cannot therefore be linked to a photograph. In some cases the discarded backing sheet will bear a faint image of the photograph which can be enhanced by treatment with fluorisol and careful photography. Damaged photographic prints can sometimes be restored by specialist treatment.

Photographs can be faked by adding parts of other pictures and rephotographing. Edges of cut-out parts of another print may be detected, and inconsistencies in shadows or focus may provide clear proof that the photograph is a composite. Examinations of this type require expertise in both the theory of photography and its practice, and are not normally regarded as within the province of the document examiner.

VIDEO TECHNIQUES

Infrared and ultraviolet radiation are invisible because they are outside the range of wavelengths which the eye can detect. The sensitivities of photographic film and the compounds used in photoelectric cells used to convert radiation to electrical energy is unrelated to that of the eye, although both are also dependent on wavelength. The photoelectric tubes which detect light in television cameras can be made to react to infrared, and the silicon diode Vidicon^{TM} tube is ideal for this purpose. Similarly, other tubes are made which detect ultraviolet radiation, but these find little use in document examination.

Apparatus specially designed for document examination is the Video Spectral Comparator made by Foster and Freeman Ltd (see Fig. 14). The apparatus consists of a video camera fitted with a silicon diode Vidicon tube operating at 625 lines, a zoom lens of 18–108 mm focal length, and a 9 inch video monitor. Four light sources are provided. These are two 25 W tungsten filament lamps, controlled by a power regulator giving unfiltered light of a variable intensity of illumination, two long-wave ultraviolet lamps, and a 500 W fan-cooled tungsten halogen source which is focused and filtered to give an intense blue-green illumination for infrared luminescence. The filters of this light source can be easily removed and changed to give a variation in the exciting wavelength. A base providing transmitted tungsten lighting is also provided.

Provision is made to accommodate a sliding filter holder in front of the camera tube, and filter slides are provided. These consist of a series of eight filters in a holder allowing radiation from 630 mm to 1000 mm to pass, a similar holder with filters transmitting different wavelengths of visible light for the examination of ultraviolet fluorescence, and a red/infrared continuously variable interference filter which passes a different wavelength at each point along its length. A similar filter covering the visible range is also available.

These components are combined into a piece of apparatus measuring about 75 cm long, 50 cm deep, and 40 cm high. Controls at the front allow switching of the light sources, adjustment of the magnification, focus, and aperture of the lens, (these adjustments are either manual or electrical, depending on the model), and manipulation of the filter slide. Between 1× and 5× magnification is obtained on the screen.

With this apparatus the whole range of infrared aborption and luminescence

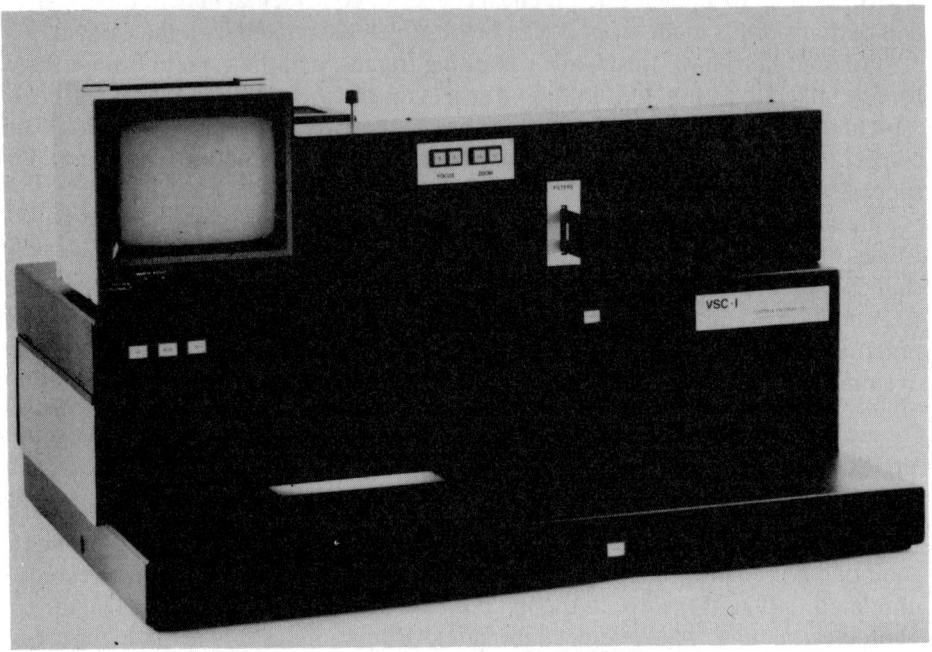

Fig. 14 — The Video Spectral comparator made by Foster and Freeman Ltd (25 Swan Lane, Evesham, Worcs, WR11 4PE). This instrument enables examination of documents in infrared luminescent and absorption conditions to be carried out. A document placed inside the cabinet is viewed on the video screen. A wide variety of lighting conditions is available for the observation of the document.

effects can be obtained. The resolution is good because of the relatively large number of lines on the screen and the magnification available. The results are comparable to those produced by photography, and can be produced almost immediately. It is possible to photograph the screen.

The main advantage in infrared absorption is obtained from the magnification and clarity of the image and the very fine adjustment possible in wavelength by using the continuously variable filter. The value of the ultraviolet facility is in the ease of operation and in the magnification obtained. It is, however, in the detection of luminescence in the infrared and visible regions of the spectrum that the apparatus has its greatest advantage. The sensitivity of the tube enables this to be easily and clearly detected.

IMAGE PROCESSING

When a picture is produced on a video screen it consists of a large number of points of light of different intensities and colours, called pixels (picture elements). By adjustments of certain electrical signals these pixels can be varied so that the overall picture is changed; such changes can be exploited to enhance the clarity of what is being viewed. The process by which this is achieved is very complicated and depends on the storage and subsequent manipulation of the information by the use of appropriate computers.

The processing of the picture can require relatively simple operations such as edge enhancement and increase in contrast, or more complex tasks such as the deblurring of an indistinct image.

The process is not yet universally employed, and only limited success has been reported. The methods of increased contrast tend to make clearer those features which can already be identified without making visible those which cannot. Deblurring methods work well on photographic images taken with faulty techniques where poor focus or movement of a camera or subject has made the image unclear, but have not achieved outstanding success in identifying erasures or obliterations. It is, however, too early to say that, given time and considerably more research effort, these methods will not one day be considered essential in document examination.

A different form of manipulation of stored visual data does, however, appear to be of value in document examination. By recording an image of a document in normal or special lighting conditions and displaying it or part of it on a screen, the document can be compared, wholly or in part, with another document shown on the same screen. The image of two documents can be divided vertically or horizontally, or can be 'windowed', showing only a small part of one in the middle of another. By this means two documents or their significant entries can be compared.

An extension of this technique is the facility to place parts of two documents conveniently close together so that they can be easily compared. For instance, each example of a particular word could be called up from both documents and placed side by side, or images of two or more signatures could be superimposed to test for tracing.

Another function which can be used is that of the reversal of the colour of the image so that black areas become white and white black. By these methods and with superimposing of two images, parts of documents can be apparently removed, leaving those that are important but not clearly readable as pronounced as possible. Some commercially produced apparatus is available, aimed to simplify what can be a highly technical operation. An example of this is the Digital Image Processing System produced by Messrs Foster and Freeman Ltd.

OPTICAL MICROSCOPES

Magnification is an important feature of document examination. Some enlargement can be produced by the use of photography and video methods, and also by a magnifying glass, but the optical microscope is the most used tool of the examiner. There are many arrangements of lenses and lighting systems which are described as microscopes, but the stereo microscope, which gives a magnification of around 10−50× with a relatively wide focal range, is the most suitable for document examination. Lighting can be provided from any direction, but for most examinations illumination from above is most convenient. Most commercially available stereo microscopes provide a range of magnifications, using either a series of different lenses on a turret or a zoom lens which gives a continuously variable range.

The mounting of the microscope head is important. For the examination of documents the most suitable way is on a long arm, rather than on a compact stand. The arm allows the document to be positioned on the bench and provides adequate room for a large document and for its easy movement. It also gives the operator freedom to vary the direction of the light falling on the field under examination.

Smaller magnifiers can be obtained which do not have the power, flexibility, or ease of operation of the stereo microscope but are more portable. Instruments which are hand-held and have a built-in light source can give magnifications up to about 10×. These may be satisfactory for the examination of handwritings, because they enable the method of construction of certain letters to be determined when this is not possible by direct vision. Other hand lenses or magnifying glasses provide enlargement of two or three times and are usually of value to examiners of middle age whose visual accommodation has declined and who find close observation difficult. They enable little extra to be seen by those capable of examining a document from a distance of a few inches, but assist those who are unable to do so. Similar instruments, such as large lenses with a surrounding light source, fulfil the same function.

Comparison microscopes
Comparison microscopes have a system of optics which display images from two objects through one lens so that they can be observed together. In some instruments the observed field is divided into two at a vertical line, each object occupying one side. Close comparison is therefore possible, but no provision is made for superimposition of two areas. The method is more suitable for the examination of fibres or bullets where a continuous similarity or difference along the length of an object can be observed. If the dividing line can be moved, some comparison of area is possible, but generally this is less satisfactory in document examination than full field comparison methods, those where the images of two documents can be superimposed. By optical means it is possible to show both documents together, apparently occupying exactly the same area, but in these circumstances it is not always possible to be sure on which document a particular feature occurs. This can be overcome by the provision of an oscillation facility, so that first one, then the other document is observed in the same position. The advantage of this is that any difference between the two images is shown either by the flickering off and on of a feature present on only one document or an apparent movement of a feature which varies in position between the two documents. An example of apparatus of this type, specially designed for document examination, is the Projectina Universal Comparison Projector (Fig. 15). The images are projected on to a screen rather than being observed through an eyepiece, and this makes comparison more convenient. The apparatus also incorporates an infrared image converter.

SCANNING ELECTRON MICROSCOPY

The final limit to greater magnification with the optical microscope is the wavelength of light; detail smaller than the wavelength of the incident radiation is not resolved. Higher resolution, and therefore, higher useful magnification, can be achieved by 'illuminating' the sample with electrons, which have very short wavelengths. However, just as information can be obtained from the chemical as well as the physical

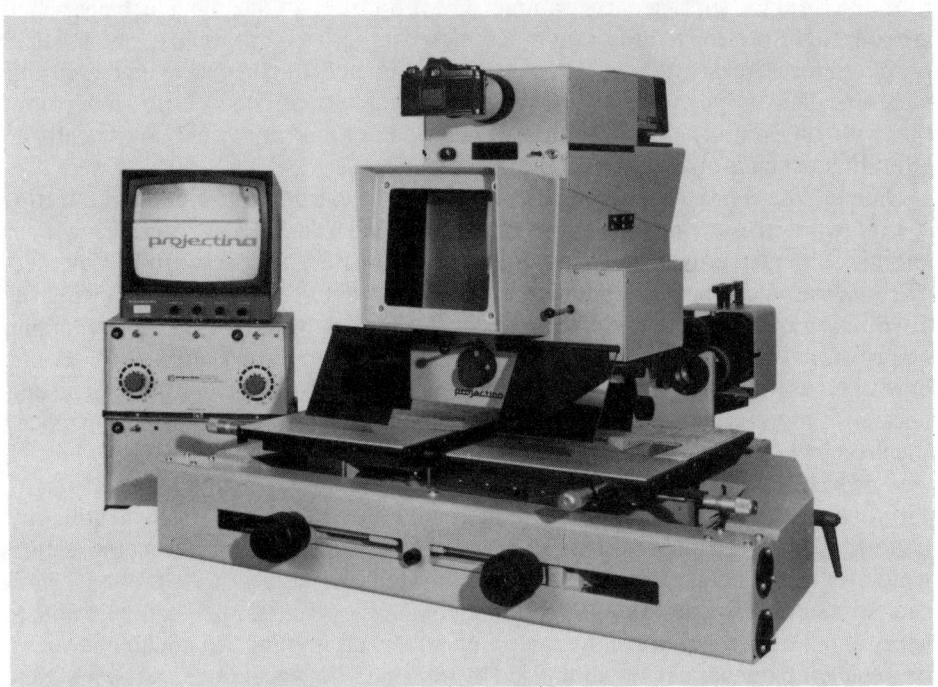

Fig. 15 — The Projectina Universal Comparison Projector UCP-8032, made by Projectina Ltd, of Heerbrugg, Switzerland. This comprehensive instrument enables a close comparison of two documents to be made and also incorporates an infrared image converter and a 35-mm camera. Documents to be compared are placed on the two stages and their images viewed on the screen above or on an separate video monitor.

interactions of infrared, visible, and ultraviolet radiation with the sample, so the use of electrons provides more than a high resolution image.

The scanning electron microscope is an instrument for observing the various phenomena which occur when a finely focused beam of electrons is scanned in a line and frame raster across the surface of a sample. The most important of these are secondary electrons, backscattered electrons, and X-rays.

Secondary electrons are emitted by the sample itself; they are collected and processed to form a topographic image which is displayed on a video monitor. Magnifications of 100 000 times or more can be obtained, although the upper limit of useful magnification is usually determined by the nature of the sample, rather than by the wavelength of the electrons in the primary beam. The image has great depth of field, typically 300–400 times that of an optical microscope, and it is this property, rather than high magnification, which is more important for the examination of documents. In fact the instrument is often used for such problems as determining sequence of writing and identifying dry transfer lettering and photocopying materials at magnifications well within the range of the optical microscope, because of the greater depth of field which can be obtained.

Backscattered electrons are electrons from the primary beam which have been reflected from the surface of the sample. The proportion of incident electrons which are reflected is related to atomic number; elements such as chromium, iron, and lead produce more backscattered electrons than carbon because they have higher atomic numbers. This property is useful for distinguishing between inks of the same colour but with different chemical compositions, and for imaging what is beneath an alteration which is opaque to infrared.

Finally, the elemental composition of the sample can be determined by collecting X-rays emitted as a result of the electron bombardment and measuring their energies. All elements from sodium upwards in the periodic table can be detected. The analysis is displayed either as an X-ray spectrum or as an image showing the distribution of a particular element across the surface of the sample. Printing and security inks and the various mineral components of paper can be analysed, though little or no useful information is obtained from many ball-point and water-based inks because they contain chemical elements which cannot be detected by X-ray spectrometry.

For best results the area of interest on a document is coated with a thin layer of carbon or gold by vacuum evaporation to render the surface electrically conductive, although this can be dispensed with in certain cases by carefully masking those parts which are not to be examined with metal foil. Items as large as a sheet of newsprint can be examined without sampling, provided that they can be folded and are able to withstand the high vacuum of the sample chamber. If sampling of a document cannot be avoided, damage may be minimised by punching out small discs with a modified hypodermic needle. The resulting holes are often visible only when the paper is held up to the light.

FURTHER READING

[1] Baier, P. E. (1983) Technical improvements of scanning electron microscope methods in document examination *Forensic Science International* **22** 265

[2] Beattie, J. A., Denton, S. & Morgan, B. (1983) Visualisation of obliterated features on Polaroid SX70 photographs *Journal of the Forensic Science Society* **23** 103

[3] Creer, K. E. (1976) Unusual photographic techniques in document examination *Forensic Science International* **7** 23

[4] Creer, K. E. (1984) The forensic examination of photographic equipment and materials *Forensic Science International* **29** 263

[5] Gupta, S. K., Rohilla, D. R., & Das Gupta S. K. (1981) Photographic negatives as evidence — a case report *Journal of the Forensic Science Society* **21** 355

[6] Nolan, P. J., England, M. & Davies, C. (1982) The examination of documents by scanning electron miscroscopy and X-ray spectrometry *Scanning Electron Microscopy* **II** 599

[7] Roberts, B. R. G., Totty, R. N. & Merchant, J. J. (1979) Enhancement of latent images on backing sheets of Polaroid photographs *Journal of the Forensic Science Society* **19** 219

[8] Waggoner, L. R. & Spradlin, W. B. (1983) Obliterated writing — an unconventional approach *Journal of Forensic Sciences* **28** 686

11

Document examination in court

The conclusion which a forensic scientist expresses in his report will be directed to his client. It may be favourable to the client's interests or it may not; it may be too inconclusive to be of any use either way. In many cases the final outcome is a hearing in a court of law. Often, this is avoided by a settlement beforehand or a plea of guilty or a decision not to prosecute in a criminal enquiry, but most reports and statements of a document examiner are liable to be the basis of an eventual testimony from the witness box.

There are different proceedings in the two branches of courts, civil and criminal. In each, however, it is necessary to present to the judge or jury, or magistrates in a lower court, the conclusions, their strengths and weaknesses, and the reasons for them. Usually, evidence which is not disputed can be read, without the attendance of the expert. This means that the original report or statement must be sufficiently clear and unambiguous to be properly understood. Nevertheless, if the examiner is present in person to explain his findings and to interpret points which may be of particular interest to one or both parties, there may be a considerable advantage to the judge or jury.

THE CONDUCT OF THE WITNESS

The technique of giving evidence is of considerable importance in the work of the document examiner. Without the ability to convince the court of his conclusions, all the work he has done previously will be wasted. A correct conclusion reached perfectly may be lost in the confusion of a situation in which the examiner is not able to present his findings adequately. In contrast, a properly prepared performance, clearly presented and, if required, well illustrated, will convince the court of the validity of the conclusion. The aim should be not to proclaim the opinion as if it could not be challenged, giving no grounds for it other than the status of its originator. Rather, the witness should argue the reasons in a logical, precise, and convincing manner so that the hearers will be persuaded by the evidence and appreciate for themselves that the conclusion is justified.

Dress

The bearing of the witness is of importance. The judge or jury will be impressed by what he says, depending on its clarity and logic, but other factors such as appearance and dress may not be ignored. A survey in the United States showed that most people expected the expert witness to be smartly and soberly dressed. Although there is now less formality in dress, and more attention is likely to be paid to what is said than to the more superficial personal appearance, a lack of courtesy may be inferred from unsuitable attire.

Manner of giving evidence

The evidence is essentially for the judge and jury and not for the counsel calling it, so the questions are best answered not to counsel, but to the jury or to the judge. As the latter will be writing down much of what is being said, glances in his direction will indicate the speed at which the evidence should be given. The expert will be more appreciated by the jury if he directs his evidence to them, and, by observing their reception of his words, he will notice if he is making himself clear.

Technical evidence

Evidence on technical subjects needs to be appreciated by the jury. They will have previously heard evidence of fact from lay witnesses which is for the most part within their experience, but expert evidence differs in that the subject is not familiar. The witness must therefore make allowances for this and use language that is clear to the layman. Those areas where technical terms have to be used present a particular difficulty. Clearly, the use of words not likely to be understood by those hearing them is undesirable; care needs to be taken to avoid expressions which are so familiar to the specialist that he forgets that they will not be comprehended by others.

The best policy is to explain the technical features of the evidence in language simple enough for the non-specialist to understand, but at the same time avoid oversimplification if this diminishes the truth. Generally, when a term is first used it should be described briefly, after which it may be used without further explanation or perhaps with brief reminders. More complicated methods such as infrared absorption or scanning electron microscopy in its analytical mode are very difficult to explain to a jury. This is, however, rarely necessary because conclusions based on such techniques are infrequently challenged. In contrast, handwriting comparisons and their conclusions are more easily understood and are more frequently disputed; these and other examinations are discussed in more detail later.

If the evidence is not fully understood and appreciated by the judge, magistrates, or jury at an early state, the cross-examination will be able to increase any unwarranted doubts that may already be there. In an adversarial situation it is not for the opposing counsel to clarify what his opponent has left uncertain unless it is to his advantage. In this situation even the most experienced and able witness may not be able to convince his hearers of the validity of his evidence.

THE ROLE OF COUNSEL

To present the evidence to its best advantage in the adversarial context of the courts, the expert requires the cooperation of the counsel introducing the evidence. It is his job to maximise its effect for his own case, but if he knows that it is already accepted by the other side he may simply ask what the conclusions are and leave it at that. Unfortunately, this practice may extend to those cases where there is a contest and the evidence-in-chief is not adequately presented. The attitude that it is up to the expert merely to express his findings, and if the opposition wish to challenge them they may, is not the ideal way of presenting technical evidence, especially on handwriting.

Conferences

In order that the counsel introducing the testimony should do so in the most effective way, a conference with the expert is often very helpful. There are many reasons for this. On the one side the counsel can make it clear in a complicated case what parts of the evidence he will be referring to and in what order he will introduce them. On the other side the expert can make clear the reasons for his conclusions and their strengths and weaknesses. He can indicate what he might reply to certain questions if they occur in cross-examination; it is advantageous if his later answers do not surprise the counsel calling him. A general discussion, both of the principles involved in the particular examination and its specific significant details, should ensure that both parties are on the same wavelength. Normally, even in criminal trials, the expert witness is able to be present in court to listen to any evidence which bears on his own and to the evidence of opposing experts. Whether and when the expert is to attend is one point that can usefully be cleared up in conference.

CROSS-EXAMINATION

The purpose of cross-examination will vary from case to case. In some the whole of the evidence of the document examiner is contrary to the interests of the opposite side, and in others only part of the evidence is in dispute. In other cases the only point to be clarified is one which may have been of marginal interest to the expert at the time of his examination. It is sometimes of value to the cross-examiner to emphasise a point already made in evidence-in-chief to make sure that it is appreciated by the judge or jury. Occasionally, further examinations on the same or different documents are required, and these are requested in cross-examination.

The difference most noticeable to the witness is that the questions put in cross-examination are usually not so predictable as those in evidence-in-chief. While the former will follow a statement or report prepared by the expert, perhaps in a way agreed at a conference, those put by the opposing counsel will not be entirely anticipated. Although the purpose may be merely to clarify some points or to emphasise an uncertainty already expressed, it may be to discredit the witness or, at least, his conclusions.

In a debate or argument in a meeting or in a social exchange, a view may be expressed which is hotly contested. In the court room, however, the expert witness is in a public place, perhaps with the glare of media coverage. What he says will be noted by more than a handful of people, perhaps reported at length. In these circumstances he is placed in a far more vulnerable position than another scientist presenting a paper at a meeting or symposium, and any mistake he makes will be of greater significance to his reputation. Such a mistake may be over a small detail rather than an important conclusion, but in the adversarial system it may be magnified out of all proportion by the cross-examining counsel.

It is therefore of vital importance that the expert in the witness box be fully aware of all the aspects of his evidence and its background. Apart from answering questions truthfully and accurately he may need to foresee what the next question will be. Too much conceded in one reply may lead to a further answer which reduces the strength of the evidence to a degree which does not represent the proper conclusion. It is not the sole object of counsel cross-examining to elicit the truth, but to reduce the evidence to a position most favourable to the case of his client. The witness, however, must keep to the truth, conceding a point if that gives greater accuracy than an earlier answer, but not bending to pressure if it does not.

In normal argument or debate outside of a court of law the bearing of the opponents will be of less importance than the points they make. In the witness box, however, the expert will be to a large extent judged by his demeanour. This is tested by the pressure of cross-examination. His attitude must be dignified, courteous, and polite, and he must be fair but firm in his answers. Little is gained by trying to score points off his opponent, even if the temptation to do so is sometimes very great. In the long run a far better impression is given by a patient but authoritative dignity than by an argumentative display.

There are, however, occasions when a firmness is necessary. A tactic employed by some counsel is to interrupt an answer if it appears to be going the wrong way. If this is not stopped by the judge, the witness should make it clear that he will not be deflected from finishing his reply. A lack of respect or courteousness on the part of counsel is best treated with disdain, but there are times when it is better to make it clear that it is not appropriate. The most important point for the witness to remember is that in such situations a loss of temper is very damaging to his bearing.

In most cases, however, the cross-examination of an expert witness is carried out along far more civilised lines, and the evidence is tested by logical questioning about the methods employed in the examination and about the validity of the conclusions reached. From the point of view of the cross-examiner, there is a need to reduce the evidential value of the testimony to a point where the judge or jury will regard it as unsound, unreliable, or even mistaken. If the conclusion is soundly based the cross-examination is likely to fail, but if it arises from inaccurate observation or reasoning, effective questioning will expose this.

From the point of view of the expert witness, cross-examination can be testing or merely time-wasting. If the observations and conclusions are correct, the questions will cover ground already considered. A properly based conclusion will have already taken into account all the points which may have indicated an opposite result or an expression of uncertainty. Clearly, if there are reasons for reconsideration they must be accepted; pride or stubbornness cannot be allowed to take precedence over an admission of an error.

The task of the cross-examining counsel is not easy in that he as a layman needs to understand the methods of working of the expert, his techniques, his findings, and his deductions. He may be assisted by an expert of his own who may or may not agree with the findings of the witness. Little is gained by a personal attack, which rarely impresses, or even by an appearance of uncomprehendingness which may not be shared by the hearers. A better and more effective attack is by careful consideration of the qualifications of the expert and the observations and deliberations which led to the conclusions. An erroneous opinion will be difficult to maintain if the questions are properly directed to these issues, but can be left unscathed if the only challenge is one based on the integrity of the witness.

FURTHER OBSERVATIONS

Giving expert evidence on document examination is not always a straightforward procedure; although the basic pattern of testimony is the normal practice, complications sometimes occur. One of these is that other documents, not previously seen by the examiner, are presented for comment. This practice should be resisted because it is not possible to form a properly considered conclusion in such a short time without adequate resources. Although it is possible to use a small magnifier in the witness box, there may be a need for higher enlargement; sometimes the use of infrared radiation or similar more elaborate techniques may be required. It is, however, not so much the lack of equipment that is likely to be a problem but that the time and conditions required for proper consideration of the observations are not available. It is not unreasonable for the witness to make observations about the document he is examining in these circumstances, but it is unwise to make any deduction from these observations unless it is very cautiously expressed. A desire to assist the court may be commendable, but the chance that it may be misled by a hastily arrived at opinion has to be considered. It also has to be appreciated that the request for a conclusion may not be a need for information but a trap. The right answer may already be known, and if the wrong deduction is made the rest of the evidence will be discredited. The fact that this had been properly arrived at in contrast to the instant opinion on the new material may well be lost.

A better solution is to offer to take the new document away and return later with a fully considered answer. It may be possible to do this after a short time by examination of the items in the court precincts; or it may be necessary for a proper examination to be made in laboratory conditions. Either way is preferable to expressing a conclusion from a witness box examination, which should always be refused.

OPPOSING EXPERTS

The theory that it is always possible to find another expert who will say the opposite of the first does not apply to document examination. Although there are many examinations carried out by both sides in legal disputes both in the criminal and civil fields, the appearance of two experts giving different conclusions is relatively rare. It is, however, a situation which occurs on occasions, essentially for one of two reasons; it is either a genuine disagreement by two competent and honest examiners or it is due to the lack of ability or integrity of one of the two participants.

The first circumstance is unusual, especially those when there is a radical disagreement. More often a difference in the strength of a conclusion is encountered; one expert may consider the evidence is more strong than does the other. In such cases both the examination-in-chief and the cross-examination should clarify what each person is saying, because the difference may be no more than the way in which the conclusions are expressed. The problem of making technical evidence clear is not always solved in a statement or affidavit, and can continue into evidence; but the appropriate questions may clarify the position and show that the conclusions of the two experts are not so far apart. Another reason for disparity in conclusions in handwriting comparisons may be that the known writings are different, and each examiner has worked from a different basis.

However, if there is a clear disagreement both points of view will be put before the court, which must then decide between the two, taking other evidence into consideration, and reach a verdict by whichever standard of proof applies.

Incompetent examiners

The second occurrence, that of an incompetent practitioner, is a different matter. The methods used to examine handwriting and to draw conclusions from the examination are not impossible to understand by the layman. The logic of the approach and the accuracy of the observations can be tested by cross-examination, and this should show up incompetence. This is not always achieved because the counsel cross-examining may not be sufficiently aware of the proper methods, and so finds himself baffled by the apparent credibility of a complicated explanation of erroneous findings. Even if the credibility appears to be lacking he may discover that it is difficult to break down the certainty of the conclusion and the confidence with which it is given.

The assistance of the expert whom he will later call or has previously called will be of value, but this is not always possible. If notice has been given, its detail may not be as full as that given from the witness box, so decisions on the line of cross-examination and on the individual questions have to be made quickly. The best question, like the most appropriate answer, may not be formulated until it is too late. It is the experience of many involved in litigation both as counsel and expert witness that the best questions or answers are thought of on the way home from court.

It is necessary, therefore, in countering erroneous conclusions that the cross-examiner be aware of the correct approach to the subject and to the details of the particular case. A conference before the opposing expert gives evidence is advisable so that counsel is aware of these. In addition, the presence of his expert behind him is advantageous. Although the communication between the two is not easy, with counsel on his feet and the seated expert whispering advice or passing hurridly written notes, points which may be profitably put to the witness can be communicated to the cross-examiner. Most judges are willing to give time for a short consultation in court between counsel and his expert while the witness awaiting cross-examination is still in the box.

PRESENTATION OF HANDWRITING EVIDENCE

When giving evidence on handwriting, it is best that the expert describes his findings and the reasons for them at some length, so that the judge and jury will see for themselves why the conclusions have been reached. From this position the cross-examination will not be so effective in reducing the impact of the testimony.

The desired results can be achieved either directly from a consideration of the writings in question or, preferably, by a short outline of the principles of the method employed followed by a demonstration of the application of those principles to the handwritings before the court. The general principles can be described verbally with appropriate clarifying questions from counsel if it appears to him that they are not fully understood, but the details of letter construction and proportions are best shown by photographic enlargements specially arranged to show the features of interest.

Demonstration charts

The usual method of preparing such photographs for court is to prepare charts showing the known and questioned writings in juxtaposition so that the comparison between them can best be demonstrated. An example of such a chart is shown in Fig. 16. This is typical of many similar charts used regularly by document examiners at the Metropolitan Police Forensic Science Laboratory to demonstrate their conclusions. Other laboratories in the United Kingdom employ charts which are either very similar or slightly different. Alternative methods such as slides projected on to a screen are used in other countries.

To prepare a chart similar to that shown in Fig. 16 black and white photographs of the documents, both the known and questioned writings, are made usually about one and a half times to twice the size of the original. If the writing is large, little enlargement will be needed, and in some cases a reduction in size is appropriate. When the writing is particularly small, a greater increase in size is required. The object of the choice of dimensions is to produce an illustration of that detail in the handwriting which is of importance in the examination; provided that this can be comfortably seen, the actual degree of enlargement is not very important.

Interfering coloured backgrounds which have no relation to the writing can be 'removed' from the photograph by the use of filters of the same colour. This may be impossible if the unwanted material is close in colour to the writing in question, but can be very successful if it is not. Other features such as dotted lines or writings on forms may be better left in to show how they relate to the writing.

Having obtained suitable photographs, the chart can be prepared in a number of ways. The simplest is to mount enlargements of complete documents on a piece of card so that they can be compared. This is satisfactory if the documents are similar in nature and if the wording is similar. In complete contrast it is possible to cut up the photographs so that each character is separate. They are then divided into the known and questioned writings, and each letter of the alphabet and each numeral is grouped together so that their general pattern and the variation between them can be seen. The more normal method to prepare charts is the middle way between these two. This is to cut individual words out of the photographs and to stick the known and questioned writings on to a card in separate but adjacent areas. The same word occurring in each, or words containing the same letters, are placed opposite each other, sufficiently close for a comparison to be made.

The choice of what to put on a chart is important. If it is possible to show all the writing, this should be done, but in many cases this is impracticable. What is needed is sufficient writing to demonstrate how each letter is made and how it compares with the known material. It may be best to use all the writings of one or two documents to represent the whole of those which have been compared, rather than to select small amounts from each. The writings chosen should be representative of the whole;

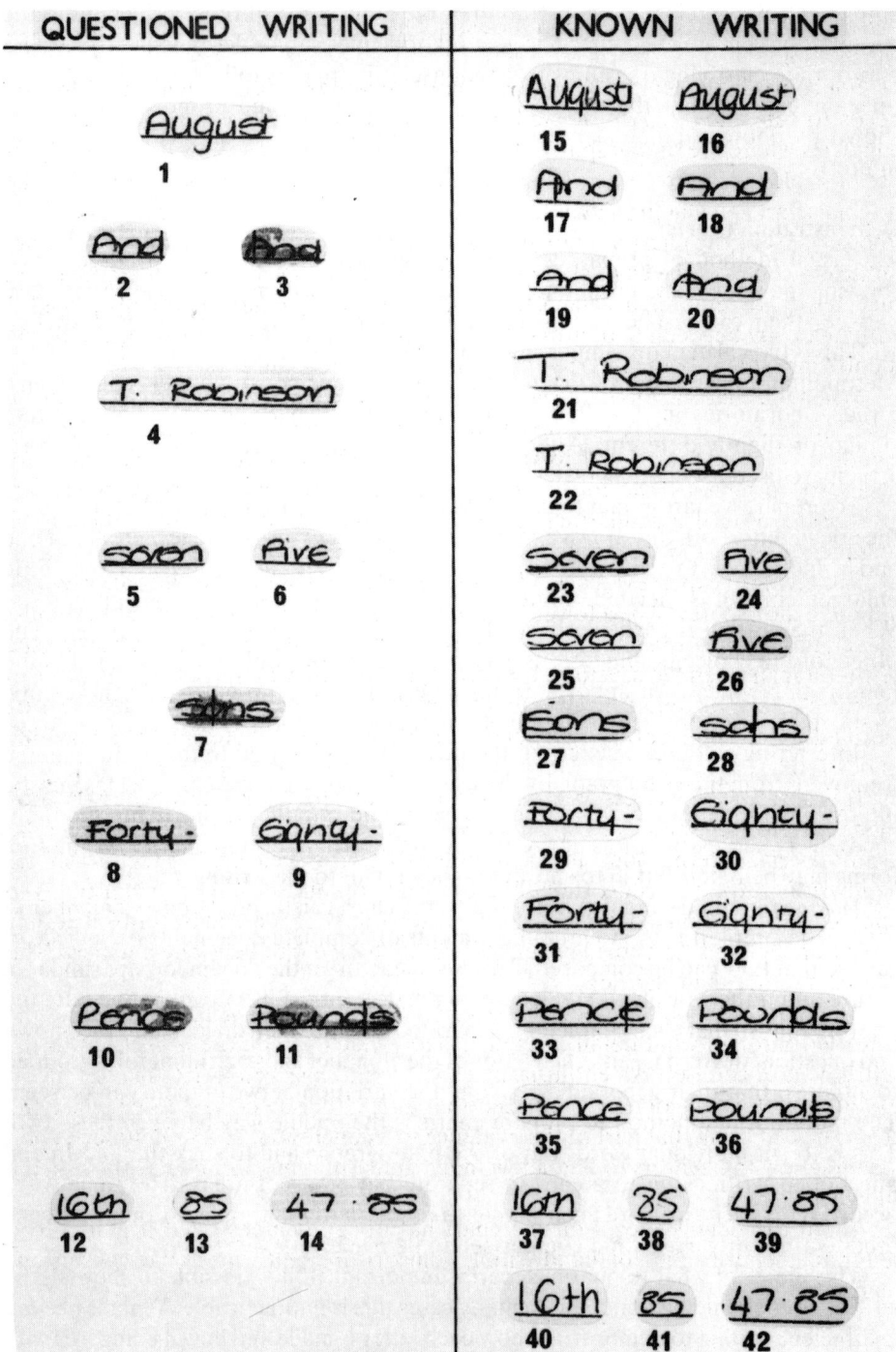

Fig. 16 — A photographic chart similar to those frequently used to demonstrate to a court conclusions drawn from handwriting comparisons. Each letter and figure of the entries on a cheque (the 'questioned' writing) can be easily compared with the same letter in the 'known' writing.

those which favour the conclusion should not be picked out to the exclusion of those which do not.

For courts in the United Kingdom a chart is copied so that everyone in court who needs to can study it. A projected image on a large screen can be used in those countries where the topography of the court and its practices allow it. Where this is not possible, as in the United Kingdom, copies can be made by photographing the original chart and making actual size prints. These will not lose any significant detail. Photocopies of the chart are not so satisfactory and should be avoided if possible. Sufficient copies of the chart should be made for the judge, counsel, defendant, and jury; fewer are required in a magistrates or civil court. The jury are usually provided with one copy between two jurors. In this way they are able to assist each other in identifying what is being referred to by the witness or counsel.

When the charts are used the witness should make clear, and should therefore be asked to point out, where each example appears on the document in question. He can then be asked to deal with as many letters or other features of the writing as are necessary to demonstrate to the court, referring to the chart to point them out. Differences as well as similarities should be noted; it is best not to allow these to be first mentioned in cross-examination.

The giving of expert evidence, like other evidence, is by question and answer, and although the expert will be allowed to expand for longer periods than would a witness of fact, there is clearly a need for counsel to ask the right questions. In some ways the testimony can resemble a lecture, but, properly handled with the right questions, can be more effective. What may be unintelligible to the hearers of a lecture can be clarified by an interruption by counsel when he realises that a point is not fully understood.

It is best for the witness to avoid jargon except where it is really necessary, and then the term used should be explained. Some people believe that the knowledge and use of specialist terms adds an air of authority to the speaker, but the aim of the handwriting expert in court should be to enable the judge, jury, or magistrates to appreciate the reasons for the conclusions, and not to be blinded by terms that they do not understand. Sensible laymen will not be fooled into believing a witness who confuses rather than clarifies.

The writing should therefore be referred to in plain and simple terms, and the court led through what detail is needed. How much is required is best left to the judgement of counsel. An enthusiastic expert left to his own devices may go on far too long, but when counsel is satisfied that enough has been said to convince the court, he can bring that part of the evidence to a conclusion. It is sometimes a good idea to allow the hearers to find a few more similarities on their own without being shown.

When the details shown on the chart have been demonstrated it is useful to reiterate the principles of handwriting comparisons and repeat the conclusions reached.

EVIDENCE OTHER THAN HANDWRITING

Presentation of the results of those areas of document examination which do not concern handwriting requires other consideration. While, despite its complexity, handwriting examination can be understood by the layman, techniques such as infrared luminescence, scanning electron microscopy, or electrostatic detection are outside the experience of most people. Some attempt must therefore be made to indicate to the court all the reasons for the conclusions arrived at by the use of these techniques, especially if the evidence is disputed.

Typewriting

One of the functions of the document examiner is to identify the make of the machine which produced a piece of typewriting of unknown origin, but this is rarely of interest to a court. The identification of a particular machine as that used to type a document is, however, of great interest. As with handwriting, the reasons for the conclusion can be explained, and the layman will understand. The concept of a mass-produced, and therefore very similar, population of machines is not difficult to describe, so the fact that typewriting may originate either from one particular machine or others like it will be accepted. Similarly, the layman will appreciate that faults in the typeface will be characteristic and will distinguish one machine and its products from that of most or all others.

It is possible to demonstrate the misaligned and damaged characters in a photographic chart. The simplest method is to prepare enlargements of about twice or three times the size of the original and mount these sufficiently close to each other so that the relevant features can be compared. If possible, the same words should be used so that the relative misalignments of various letters can be best compared; one letter misaligned in the same direction as its neighbours will appear to be in correct alignment, and it may therefore be misleading if it is compared with another word where it appears out of position.

Misalignments can be shown more clearly if a line is ruled under the word or if a grid is photographed over the typewriting, reproducing the method of the original examination. Often, however, it is not necessary for these aids to be employed because the relative position of the letters can be clearly seen in the enlarged photographs.

Special photography

Charred documents can be photographed in the most suitable conditions to enable a court to read what was written or printed on them before they were burned. Other forms of damage may make a document difficult to read, but a photograph can provide a record for the benefit of the court.

Micrographs — photographs made of a small part of a document greatly enlarged — are of particular value to show certain features, otherwise undiscernible by a court. Examples of these are the demonstration of guide lines in traced simulations and the illustration of how an underlying figure has been overwritten to alter it.

At greater magnification, photographs taken from the scanning electron microscope can be produced in court. These, however, present problems to the layman in that they show what is not within his experience. While a signature which is enlarged can be recognised as such, the high magnification of the scanning electron microscope produces a micrograph of a typewritten line crossing ball-point ink which is unrecognisable. Careful explanation of the picture is therefore needed if it is necessary to use such evidence.

Differences in inks

Whereas the evidential value of the similarity between handwriting or typewriting may be of great significance, it is normally the difference between two inks which is of great importance when it occurs on a document. Those methods that use infrared reflection or luminescence or similar techniques lend themselves readily to photographic illustration. Indeed, until the introduction of electronic methods of detection, photography was the only method by which such differences could be detected.

A photograph taken under those conditions which show that two inks are different or that an obliterated entry can be read, provides incontrovertible evidence in itself. Put side by side with a photograph of the same area taken in normal light, the contrast is there for any one to see, be he layman or document examiner. A fluorescing zero following two non-fluorescing digits may appear white, contrasting with the black of the figures before it, clearly demonstrating that two inks have been used.

The fact that the photograph shows an obvious difference may make unnecessary the technical explanation of why such effects occur. It is usually sufficient to point out that different inks can react differently in special conditions, and the court will require no more. However, it may be necessary to explain why there are such differences, and it is then up to the expert to put the reason into understandable terms. Any attempt to sound convincing by using as many technical terms as possible should be avoided, but over simplification to the point of inaccuracy is also undesirable. It must be borne in mind that what appears to be a difference between two inks when they are photographed in conditions showing the excitation of infrared luminescence may not be so, but merely a difference caused by the background paper. Such photographs can therefore be misleading, but it is extremely unlikely that a competent document examiner would not have already excluded this possibility before the picture was produced.

Indented impressions

In giving evidence about impressions the court must first be made aware of what they are and how they came to be there. Although it may seem obvious to those accustomed to their detection, it may not be clear to those who have never really thought about their existence. If no explanation is given, one or more jurors could be unaware of what was being discussed.

Oblique lighting photographs, showing the impressions which are readable under those conditions, will be helpful to the court, but it must be made clear in many cases that other impressions not visible in the photographs are also present. Similarly, any confusion about what may appear to be raised characters, the effects of optical illusion (see p. 140) must be cleared up. In those cases where the impressions which can be photographed do not include all that have been found, a second photograph can be made on which all the discovered impressions can be coloured in. This gives an indication of the position where those not clear on the first photograph have been found.

The transparencies produced by the electrostatic detection apparatus can be photographed or photocopied so that adequate copies are available for inspection by the court. Their origin can be described and the original transparency produced as an exhibit if required. The results obtained from this method are in themselves sufficiently clear to be read by the non-specialist.

Mechanical fits

Where an exact or close fit occurs between two documents, and the expression 'document' can be very wide in this context, such evidence can be sometimes demonstrated to the court by using the actual exhibits. In most cases, however, a more satisfactory illustration of the conclusion can be made by using photography.

Such fits occur in handwriting where tracing has been made from another piece of writing, in typewriting where gaps left in the carbon ribbon by the printing of characters can be shown to match those characters on a document, in the establishment of the source of indented impressions, and in the fit between two torn pieces of paper, as well as in many other areas.

In these cases, photographs of both documents or their relevant parts can be mounted side by side so that the close similarity can be seen. Alternatively, a transparency of one can be made together with a normal print of the other, and they can be hinged together with a staple so that the appropriate parts fit each other. The transparency can then be raised to reveal each document and lowered so that the fit is clearly apparent.

Transparencies can be produced more cheaply by using modern photocopiers, and they may be perfectly satisfactory for the purpose of demonstrating the fit between two documents. Similarly, the 'lift' from the electrostatic detection of indented impressions or a transparent photocopy of it can be used in court to show the origin of the impressions.

Not every technique in document examination can be demonstrated to a court. In some a description may be needed, but in others it may be impossible for the layman to appreciate how the test was applied. In some demonstrations, more harm can be done to the clarity of the conclusion if a picture is presented. What may be evident to the examiner, and to any other expert in the field, may be completely lost on the jury. If they feel that it is their duty to appreciate the reasons behind it, they may reject the conclusion because they cannot understand the reasons. On the other hand, without them they would have accepted the conclusion. It is important that the jury must not feel that they have to be experts themselves; the production of an illustration could have that effect. If it cannot be interpreted, the value of the evidence may be lost.

Index